VOYAGE OF MERCY

ALSO BY STEPHEN PULEO

American Treasures:
The Secret Efforts to Save the Declaration of Independence,
the Constitution, and the Gettysburg Address

The Caning:
The Assault That Drove America to Civil War

A City So Grand:
The Rise of an American Metropolis, Boston 1850–1900

The Boston Italians:
A Story of Pride, Perseverance, and Paesani, from the Years
of the Great Immigration to the Present Day

Due to Enemy Action:
The True World War II Story of the USS Eagle 56

Dark Tide:
The Great Boston Molasses Flood of 1919

VOYAGE OF
MERCY

THE USS *JAMESTOWN*,
THE IRISH FAMINE,
AND THE REMARKABLE
STORY OF AMERICA'S
FIRST HUMANITARIAN MISSION

STEPHEN PULEO

ST. MARTIN'S PRESS
NEW YORK

First published in the United States by St. Martin's Press, an imprint of St. Martin's Publishing Group

VOYAGE OF MERCY. Copyright © 2020 by Stephen Puleo. All rights reserved. Printed in the United States of America. For information, address St. Martin's Publishing Group, 120 Broadway, New York, NY 10271.

www.stmartins.com

Designed by Meryl Sussman Levavi

Library of Congress Cataloging-in-Publication Data

Names: Puleo, Stephen, author.
Title: Voyage of mercy : the USS Jamestown, the Irish famine, and the remarkable story of America's first humanitarian mission / Stephen Puleo.
Other titles: USS Jamestown, the Irish famine, and the remarkable story of America's first humanitarian mission
Identifiers: LCCN 2019043128 | ISBN 9781250200471 (hardcover) | ISBN 9781250200488 (ebook)
Subjects: LCSH: Ireland—History—Famine, 1845–1852. | Famines—Ireland— History—19th century. | Food relief—Ireland—History—19th century. | Jamestown (Sloop of war)—History. | Food relief, American—Ireland. | United States—Foreign economic relations—Ireland. | Ireland—Foreign economic relations—United States. | Forbes, R. B. (Robert Bennet), 1804–1889. | Mathew, Theobald, 1790–1856.
Classification: LCC DA950.7 .P85 2020 | DDC 363.8/830941509034—dc23
LC record available at https://lccn.loc.gov/2019043128

Our books may be purchased in bulk for promotional, educational, or business use. Please contact your local bookseller or the Macmillan Corporate and Premium Sales Department at 1-800-221-7945, extension 5442, or by email at MacmillanSpecialMarkets@macmillan.com.

First Edition: March 2020

10 9 8 7 6 5 4 3

To Kate:

The Irish joy in my heart

CONTENTS

PART III

IRELAND
"The whole country is one vast tomb"

PART IV

THE UNITED STATES
"The most prominent event of my life"

PART V

IRELAND
"The noblest offering that nation ever made to nation"

PART VI

THE UNITED STATES AND IRELAND
"America has been our truest friend"

PART VII

LEGACIES:
THE IRISH FAMINE
AND THE *JAMESTOWN* MISSION
"The links between our countries … have endured"

It is the noblest offering that nation ever made to nation.

—The Cork *Advertiser* on the USS *Jamestown* mission,
April 1847

What we are doing will be an example to be followed by some abroad who might shut their hearts to the calls of their neighbors—it will prove a seed sown in fruitful ground.

—*Jamestown* captain Robert Bennet Forbes,
writing in the *Boston Post*, March 17, 1847

AUTHOR'S NOTE

This is a story about hope, generosity, and soaring goodwill against a backdrop of nearly unfathomable despair; and like any story with such powerful themes, its lessons run deep and its ramifications are measured in decades rather than days.

Voyage of Mercy recounts for the first time the remarkable and unprecedented relief effort by the government and citizens of the United States to assist Ireland during the terrible famine year of 1847; remarkable because the mission undertaken by Captain Robert Bennet Forbes and the crew of the USS *Jamestown* to deliver tons of donated food to Ireland was the first step in a monumental effort that involved contributions from citizens of virtually every community in the United States and the official imprimatur of the U.S. government; unprecedented not only for the size and scope of American participation, but also because it was the first time the United States—or any nation, for that matter—extended its hand to a foreign neighbor in such a broad and all-encompassing way for purely humanitarian reasons. Prior to 1847, the bulk of interaction between nation-states consisted mainly of warfare and other hostilities, mixed with occasional trade; the entire concept of international charity existed neither in the moral consciousness nor as part of the political strategy of monarchs or elected leaders. If anything, such a gesture toward a foreign nation would likely have been viewed as a sign of weakness.

The *Jamestown* mission was, in modern parlance, the "tip of the spear," the most visible and most celebrated component of America's first full-blown charitable mission. The U.S. relief effort encompassed far more than the *Jamestown*, but it was the historic voyage of a retrofitted warship embarking on a mission of peace that most visibly symbolized the widespread willingness of the American people to offer up enormous stores of food and provisions to assist victims of the Irish famine.

The voyage itself and the subsequent outpouring of charitable relief captured hearts and minds on both sides of the Atlantic, of wealthy and poor, of royalty and commoners, of poets and politicians. In addition, the events of 1847 have served as the blueprint and inspiration for hundreds of American charitable relief efforts since, philanthropic endeavors that have established the United States as the leader in international aid in total dollars and enabled it to assist millions of people around the world victimized by famine, war, and catastrophic natural disasters.

Two compelling individuals occupy the center of this story.

Sea captain Robert Bennet Forbes of Boston was one of the most dynamic, determined, resilient, adventurous, well-traveled, generous, and interesting men of his age—or any age, for that matter—and until now, his story has never been fully told. I am grateful that he was also an excellent, frequent, and descriptive writer, able to relate both meaningful context and colorful details, understand the nuances of human nature as well as his own virtues and shortcomings, and express himself with passion, pathos, drama, and humor. In addition, he was the consummate collector and keeper of documents—a bit of a hoarder, actually—which has provided us with a rich trove of what others thought about him, his mission, and his world (see Bibliographic Essay).

The Reverend Theobald Mathew, known best as Ireland's "Temperance Priest," was the heroic and indomitable figure on the Irish side of the Atlantic, fighting—though mostly in vain—to save the lives of his starving countrymen and convince British authorities of the speed of the famine's onslaught, the extent of its horrors, and the desperate need for additional relief. In the decade before the famine, Father Mathew had achieved fame on both sides of the Atlantic for his efforts to convince hundreds of thousands of Irish to sign his temperance pledge; in fact, history records his crusade against drinking and alcoholism as his signature achievement. But his work in the trenches during the worst of the famine—offering food, shelter, medical care, and comfort to those suffering from near starvation and debilitating disease—would forever endear him to the Irish people, especially those from his home parish in Cork city. Still revered in his native country today, Father Mathew, like Forbes, is little known in the United States, despite a lengthy and controversial visit to America shortly after the famine. I'm grateful for the opportunity to tell his story.

What truly inspired me about this story were the actions of what I'll call thousands of other real-life characters, who together make up a single collective character of sorts: the American people. I had known something about the *Jamestown* voyage before researching this book, but I was completely unaware of the enormous scope of the U.S. relief effort to Ireland in 1847–48, the widespread generosity of Americans from all walks of life during a time when the very act of survival and supporting one's own family presented a grueling daily challenge and was far from guaranteed.

That Americans from across the United States contributed to Irish relief was extraordinary enough, but it was the *nature* of most of their donations that was most impressive. This was not a matter of entering credit card information or dropping off a bag of canned goods, though these are certainly generous acts in their own right. While many people sent small amounts of money, farmers often donated crops they had grown themselves to sustain their loved ones. They furrowed the ground, laid the seed, nurtured the plants, and harvested the crops—beans, corn, barley, wheat, and much more. Then those who chose to help the people of Ireland took a portion of those goods, packaged them in burlap sacks or wooden kegs, and delivered them by horse-drawn wagon to river ports, where rafts and small boats carried them to larger ships that navigated broader rivers and the Erie Canal. From there, the food made its way to major Atlantic ports like New York, Boston, Philadelphia, and Baltimore, where dockworkers loaded it upon ocean-sailing vessels bound for England and Ireland.

Farmers and planters in Ohio, Pennsylvania, Michigan, Tennessee, Maryland, Virginia, western New York, and western Massachusetts, in the mid-Atlantic states, across the South, and along the Mississippi—all of them literally took food out of the mouths of their own family members, or food they would normally sell at market to buy goods for their cabins and farms, and shipped it to strangers thousands of miles away.

It was as though Americans looked at their own children and felt the pain of Irish parents who were watching their youngsters starve. Or perhaps Americans appreciated the poetic, if mournful, symmetry of sharing the abundant bounty produced by their fertile fields with people whose land was blackened by blight and whose major crop rotted with disease.

Whatever the exact reason, such sacrifice and generosity were breathtaking to me, and I've thought about this often, especially when I walk into a supermarket and, almost without giving it a second thought, reach for virtually any food item I choose to buy. How much food would we give to strangers today if our survival, our families' survival, depended on planting, growing, cultivating, and harvesting everything we needed?

And maybe because Americans knew they were part of something much larger than themselves in 1847, the widespread desire to provide relief to Ireland also unified the United States—for a short time at least—in a way it hadn't been since the adoption of the Constitution sixty years earlier, and probably not again until the attack on Pearl Harbor nearly a century later drew the United States into World War II.

Charitable contributions of any kind at any time are worthy and noble; the American humanitarian mission to Ireland during the 1847 potato famine, while inexplicable in many ways, was something special altogether.

Any discussion of Irish history since 1847 begins with, and is driven by, the events of that year. It is the famine and its aftermath upon which much of Ireland's identity rested for as long as a century and a half: it was the famine that launched widespread Irish emigration, poisoned the Irish's relationship with England, and served as the underlying rallying cry for Irish independence. Irish musicians, poets, and novelists hearken back to the famine again and again; the events of 1846–47—but especially "Black '47"—are inculcated in and interwoven throughout Irish history and memory.

The genealogical and long-term demographic repercussions from the Great Hunger have long fascinated me, and my interest is not only historical, but personal; forty years ago, I married into a large Irish family whose U.S. lineage—like thousands of other Irish families in America, including in the Boston area, New York, Philadelphia, New Jersey, Baltimore, San Francisco, and many other locales—dates back to emigrants who left Ireland because of the famine. While the events of 1847 are not often the subject of discussion at our family gatherings, the famine story plays a part in the family history of my wife, Kate, as it does in the history of virtually every Irish family with multigenerational roots in the United States.

And it was America's response to the famine that established and then cemented the bonds between Ireland and the United States. I briefly wrote about the *Jamestown* story a decade ago when I published *A City So Grand*, which details the growth of Boston between 1850 and 1900 and includes the arrival of thousands of Irish immigrants to the city—most propelled by the famine's aftermath and the Irish's remembrance of the U.S. response in 1847. What I did not realize until I researched *Voyage of Mercy* was that the *Jamestown* voyage not only represented a spark of color across the bleak grayness of Ireland's landscape, but was part of a larger national charitable tapestry that would signal a seismic shift in international relations.

⌗

Voyage of Mercy is a work of narrative history that rests on a sturdy foundation of primary and secondary sources; in other words, layers of scholarship and research. My full Bibliographic Essay lists my sources and how I use them, and my Acknowledgments offer additional explanations of my research journey. Readers have appreciated this approach in my previous books, and I hope they will feel the same way about *Voyage of Mercy*.

With that as a backdrop, readers need to know that every word in the story is true. Everything that appears between quote marks is contained in a diary, letter, speech, government document, court transcript, piece of congressional testimony, newspaper, magazine article, journal, pamphlet, or book. My narrative and conclusions are based on an examination and interpretation of the sources and my knowledge of the characters and events; these also provide the underpinnings for any conjecture that I engage in. In those instances when I do speculate about people or events, I make it clear to the reader.

I have tried to tell this rich story with as much accuracy and narrative drama as the historical record allows.

VOYAGE OF MERCY

PROLOGUE

Sheets of cold rain lashed the decks of the USS *Jamestown* and gale-force winds battered the three-masted American sloop of war through the swells of the North Atlantic. Captain Robert Bennet Forbes barked orders as his energetic but inexperienced crew scrambled to haul up the mainsail, a daunting task on this moonless night of raging seas. Weak light leaked from deck lanterns, but beyond the ship's raised prow and forward riggings, the darkness was total— "black as Erebus," Forbes described it in the captain's log, referring to the mythological netherworld that serves as the passageway to Hades.

For the sixth straight day since leaving Boston, the ship and its crew were pounded by miserable weather as they fought their way toward Ireland—snow, sleet, hail, and cold that rendered all ropes "stiff as crowbars . . . and the men also," wind and waves that left the *Jamestown*, despite her solid oak frame, "bounding like an antelope" and unable to carry as much sail as Forbes wished. Dense wet fog rendered visibility to near zero. Snow slickened the ship's decks, crew members lurched with seasickness, ice floes hampered passage, and worst of all, the *Jamestown* leaked badly, at times taking on as much as ten inches of water an hour.

Most of the water poured through the rudder case in the wardroom when the sea rose aft or the ship settled, and crew members were forced to pump often and, finally, bore holes in the wardroom deck to allow water to run off into the hold.

As midnight approached, the wind howled and every *Jamestown* rope froze "as hard and stiff as January," but Forbes, who in his forty-two years had savored much joy and endured deep sorrow, remained unflappable in the captain's chair, determined to reach his destination ahead of schedule, and resolute in the moral certitude of his mission.

Years of experience had prepared Robert Bennet Forbes—his family called him "Bennet"—for the voyage and the task ahead. He had sailed the seas since his youth—first crossing the Atlantic and nearly drowning at age six; working as a cabin boy on a packet boat to China when he was thirteen; taking command of his first vessel at age twenty on the day after his father's funeral; earning his living through mercantile activities in Europe and the Far East; engaging in the often dangerous opium trade in China; building and owning dozens of vessels; piloting ships across stormy oceans and along jagged coastlines. His friends nicknamed him "Black Ben," in part because of the color of his curly, unkempt hair, but more for the manner in which his skin darkened after weeks on the open sea.

Undeterred by hard work and driven by an entrepreneur's spirit, Forbes's eclectic personality pulsed with energy, resilience, generosity, persistence, courage, restiveness, fierce independence, and, yes, sometimes, selfishness. Contradictions abounded: he possessed a spirit of derring-do tempered by a cautious streak that had emerged a decade earlier after a series of bad business decisions; he was compassionate but capable of holding grudges; optimistic but plagued by bouts of moodiness; garrulous but grateful for quiet; contemplative but thrumming with nervous energy; opinionated on domestic and maritime matters, but expert in the art of compromise in his commercial dealings. Duty-bound, reliable, and aware of his responsibilities from an early age, he nonetheless craved and relished swashbuckling escapades that sometimes bordered on the reckless. On the other hand, he also sought refuge in reading a good book, inking a few stanzas of poetry, or pouring out his feelings in long letters to his wife, Rose. And despite his devotion to Rose, he left her alone during some of her most fragile moments as he embarked on lengthy sea voyages.

Forbes had become wealthy in his late twenties through mercantile activities and the opium trade, lost everything in his early thirties through a series of risky investments in the midst of a poor economy, and recouped his fortune well before he turned forty—a century after his death, a historian would write that Forbes had "lived a life . . . that Hollywood would be likely to turn down as too improbable." He loved sailing but loved family more, and he experienced deep bouts of loneliness when thousands of miles separated him from Rose and their children. In his letters and in his heart he held them close, as if to guard against losing them, recalling, perhaps, that when he was a single young man, grief and loss had staggered him—and later had nearly broken him and Rose.

Nonetheless, Forbes contemplated the *Jamestown* voyage with "mingled emotions of satisfaction." His only "unhappy feeling" was the "momentary and easily forgiven weakness" of parting from his wife and children; still, he never thought twice about piloting the *Jamestown*. He had volunteered to do it—the conditions in Ireland left him no choice. Forbes understood his mission's importance and popularity; the voyage was a gesture of humanitarian beneficence that had captured the imagination of New Englanders and the nation.

Rose fretted about him leaving the family to command this mission. While she endorsed the humanitarian goals of the *Jamestown* voyage, she wondered whether Forbes was "undertaking too much" by leading an ocean journey that would be made more perilous by the need to reach Ireland as quickly as possible. Despite his piloting skills—or perhaps because of them—would Forbes tempt fate by carrying full sails, even in poor weather conditions, to increase his speed? Doing so ran the risk of the *Jamestown* being buffeted by wind and rough seas, perhaps tearing her sails or splintering her masts—or, worse, causing her to capsize. Rose knew he would never intentionally endanger his crew;

Bennet had spent a good portion of his adult life working to improve conditions for sailors.

But as she also knew, and Bennet himself conceded, her husband's proclivity for risk taking meant he did not always define danger in the same terms as other men. Prior to their marriage, Bennet's wanderlust had taken him on long and hazardous voyages to China multiple times, to the Philippines, Europe, the Mideast, and South America, and his confidence and capabilities saw him home safely each time. Transatlantic crossings were often hazardous—replete with crashing waves, freezing temperatures, fierce winds, torrential rains, and even icebergs—and Bennet knew well that these risks and his absences filled Rose with apprehension. While the allure of the high seas had become less tempting in the thirteen years since Rose and Bennet had wed, he nonetheless had been away for a cumulative total of three years since their marriage, nearly thirty months consecutively on one excruciating trip to China. The *Jamestown* trip would be of much shorter duration, but Rose dreaded the loneliness that engulfed her anytime her husband departed for sea.

A family friend tried to mollify her: "You must not only consent to Bennet's going away, but rejoice in it," adding that the voyage was "beautiful to think of," a "truly exhilarating" example of "warm benevolence running, like an electric shock, through the whole land." The friend implored Rose to feel "proud that you have such a husband and your children such a father."

PART I

IRELAND

"The food of a whole nation has perished"

Father Theobald Mathew comforts a poor Irish family during the famine. The image was published around 1900 in the Century Edition of Cassell's History of England.

CHAPTER I

⌐━━⌐

"The distress is universal"

When night finally came, a bone-weary Father Theobald Mathew dipped the nib of his pen into the ink and scratched the full measure of his despondency onto the page.

He aimed for precision with his writing, but he also needed to modulate his description of a truly appalling situation. Bold, direct words were necessary, but overly inflammatory language would raise skeptical eyebrows in London, damage his credibility, and, most importantly, put thousands of additional lives at risk. This was his fifth letter since August to Charles Trevelyan, assistant secretary at the British Treasury responsible for famine relief efforts, each more desperate than the last. Now, just days before Christmas, Mathew wrote with renewed urgency, hoping that his reputation for directness and honesty, and as a champion for the poor, would convince Trevelyan of his veracity.

"I am grieved to be obliged to tell you that the distress is universal," he lamented at the outset of his letter. "Men, women, and children are gradually wasting away." It was not the first time Father Mathew had underlined passages to emphasize the urgency of his message, and it would not be the last. Reviewing his opening words, he debated whether he had succumbed to the very temptation he sought to avoid—the use of sensational rhetoric. In the end he decided to let the letter stand: he knew of no more accurate way to describe the heartbreak he witnessed each day. These imperiled citizens were not anonymous "famine victims" but people he knew and loved—neighbors, parishioners, followers, friends.

He would speak for them.

In some ways, these were the most frustrating and dispiriting hours for the fifty-six-year-old priest, sitting quietly at his desk, fighting exhaustion, his eyes straining by his lantern's pallid light in the otherwise dark parlor, his desktop covered with ink-stained pages and the floor beneath him strewn with correspondence. Daytime hours were a blur, physically draining and mentally dispiriting—Mathew had just returned from several weeks' work in different parts of Ireland, assessing the potato blight, organizing relief efforts, comforting the sick, ladling soup to the hungry, kneeling at their deathbeds and praying for their souls, presiding over their burials. Upon his return to Cork he discovered that his city and county were among the hardest hit by the famine; again his daytime hours were consumed with tending to those burning with fever or filling their stomachs with "cabbage leaves and turnip tops . . . to appease the cravings of hunger." The night offered time to reflect, to be sure, but these were unwelcome and damnable hours, for it was while he sat alone in the darkness that the full tragedy of the widespread hunger, coupled with the futile sorrow that he could do little or nothing to stop it, pressed upon him like a great stone.

He had worked on behalf of Ireland's Catholic poor for years. Projecting humility, he was gratefully embraced by Irish peasants who were reminded daily of their subservient status by English landlords, church elders, even simple shopkeepers.

Born in 1790 to wealth and station in Thomastown House, a mansion in Tipperary, Father Mathew had nonetheless felt most at home among those who struggled daily to subsist. The fourth son in what would eventually become a family of twelve children born to James and Anne Mathew—James was the adopted son of a baron and Anne the daughter of a prominent attorney—Father Mathew knew his calling from the age of ten, when he delighted his mother by announcing at the family dinner table that he would become a priest. After he was ordained on Easter Sunday 1814 at the age of twenty-four, he joined the Capuchin Order in Kilkenny, which he would describe as "the lowliest and least influential" of the orders in Ireland. A year later, he was transferred to a small chapel in Cork.

Never enamored by the trappings of the priesthood, nor encumbered by what he saw as an imperious church hierarchy bound by restrictive canonical traditions, Father Mathew had, in the thirty years since his ordination, come to view himself as a people's priest, and comported himself accordingly. He was both respectful of and deferential to civil and ecclesiastic authority, but never cowed or affected by it; in the words of his closet friend and eventual biographer, Father Mathew was "thoroughly free from the vice of toadying to the great—whether the greatness was derived from power, position, wealth, or the accident of birth." Father Mathew's manner was "polished, but it was not artificial." He was "so full of fervor and zeal" in his efforts to help those in need, "so respectful to poverty," that the poor could not "think of him without love, or speak of him without enthusiasm." Father Mathew himself expressed his philosophy early in his career when he opined that it was "by the people alone [that] the churches are built, the educational and charitable institutions maintained, the bishops and parish priests and curates, the monks and friars of various orders, supported, sheltered, and clothed."

His selfless and indefatigable work over the last few months, heroic as it was, was simply an extension of the enduring work of his lifetime. Now, as then, the Irish poor trusted him, appreciated his generosity and magnanimity, came to him for advice and consolation, and flocked to his confessionals, some as early as 5:00 a.m., before beginning their workday in the fields, or as late as 11:00 p.m., when they had finished their drudging toil. He often spent as much as fifteen hours in the confessional box in the stifling heat of summer or the numbing cold of winter; he learned Gaelic to converse with parishioners from the countryside who struggled with or spoke no English. It was in the confessional that he laid the foundation for his future fame and widespread influence; his reputation as a spiritual leader spread from parish to parish in Cork city and then to the most remote sections of the county, and then beyond the borders of County Cork. One apocryphal story, narrated years later by his biographer, held that "if a carman from Kerry brought a firkin of butter into the Cork market, he would not return home until he had gone to confession to Father Mathew."

As a young priest, he established literacy schools for peasant children and provided charity to widows and orphans. He had ministered to the Cork peasantry during a dreadful cholera epidemic in 1832, risking infection and possible death within hours from the intestinal bacteria. "With the unselfish devotedness of a martyr and an apostle, he threw himself into the midst of the peril," wrote a fellow priest at the time—ministering to the afflicted in private homes and public hospitals. When local priests arranged schedules to sit vigil among cholera patients at one of Cork's largest hospitals, just a short distance from his home on Cove Street, Father Mathew insisted on taking the shift from midnight to 6:00 a.m., the least desirable and most difficult hours to cover. Several years later, he embarked on a nationwide and world-renowned crusade to combat the rampant alcoholism that brought "chronic misery" and threatened to paralyze his country. Distressed by the number of families shattered by excessive drinking—"children in rags and squalor, wives despairing and broken-hearted, husbands debauched or brutal"—he persuaded millions of people across Ireland to sign a temperance pledge, a feat that brought Father Mathew recognition across Ireland, Europe, and America.

His biographer noted that throughout his priesthood, Mathew encountered "misery and wretchedness in every imaginable form," yet he "never saw distress, in whatever shape, without attempting to relieve it." Perhaps this was because he had known distress himself; twice during his priesthood his faith had been tested, and because of these trials, he was prone to periods of gloom and despondency. When his pastor, mentor, and father figure died in 1820, thirty-year-old Father Mathew suffered a nervous breakdown that left him incapacitated for several months. He shuttered himself in his parish chamber, brooding alone, staring into the fire, fighting the temptation to imbibe on cognac stored in the cupboard. It had taken the friendship and assistance of a seventy-year-old priest from another parish to help nurture him back to active ministry.

But four years later, Father Mathew suffered his greatest loss when his youngest brother, Robert, died at the age of sixteen. The priest had brought his brother to Cork at a young age to live with him, so that he could supervise the boy's education, and Robert quickly became the joy of his life. When the high-spirited and adventuresome young man sought permission from Theobald to travel by ship to Africa with another brother, Charles, Theobald reluctantly agreed. Theobald soon received the crushing news that Robert had died from sunstroke on the voyage. "The mother that bore him could not have felt a keener anguish than did poor Father Mathew for the loss of that engaging youth," wrote one historian. "For some time he was inconsolable, plunged in an agony of grief." While Father Mathew eventually buried his grief under a mountain of work, he still—more than twenty years later—suffered from effects of the shock, his depression most profound after a scene of happiness or "gay conviviality."

Perhaps his parishioners sensed that Father Mathew's compassion was tinged with, even fueled by, such deep despondency; that in his devotion to duty he found solace, that in their desperate stories he saw some of himself. Father Mathew could recite the New Testament from Genesis to Revelations, but his simple expressions of kindness, his quiet dignity, and his willingness to share their burdens most endeared him to his impoverished parishioners. He won the hearts of thousands of poor Irish because he was always "respectful to poverty, in which . . . he ever saw the image of the Redeemer."

But what had occurred in Cork and across the country in the last four months, what he witnessed and what it foretold, shook his faith in man and left him fearful that God—finally, forever, and with swift cruelty—had visited His final judgment upon Ireland.

The destruction of the potato crop had occurred—or, rather, revealed itself—almost overnight. Mathew himself was one of the first to observe and report on the disaster. In late July, he was traveling from Cork to Dublin and saw fields of potato plants blooming "in all the luxuriance of an abundant harvest," a sight that heartened him after widespread potato-crop failure a year earlier had resulted in severe food shortages, but not full-scale famine. But six days later, August 3, during his return trip to Cork, Mathew's spirit was shattered when he "beheld, with sorrow, one wide waste of putrefying vegetation." The blight, caused by a fungus that thrived and multiplied in Ireland's damp climate, had reproduced with lightning speed. In many places along the road, "the wretched people were seated on the fences of their decaying gardens, wringing their hands and wailing bitterly against the destruction that had left them foodless."

Four days later Mathew expressed the worst in a letter to Trevelyan: "The food of a whole nation has perished." The *Times* of London concurred: "From the Giants Causeway to Cape Clear, from Limerick to Dublin, not a green field is to be seen." Indeed, on September 2, the *Times* declared that "total annihilation" had befallen the Irish potato crop. At this point, more than one-third of the entire Irish population depended exclusively on the potato for food and as a cash crop, but among poor tenant farmers, the proportion was even higher; a strong potato crop was their only hope for sustenance, for nourishment, for life itself.

Even pre-famine, survival had been precarious in Ireland, as tenant farmers and peasants scratched out a living raising and selling potatoes, or perhaps traded a pig or a cow for other goods. Food shortages were a near-constant peril, and temporary migration was a lifeline for many Irish families engaged in agricultural work, particularly those from western counties; seasonal trips to the grain-growing areas of the eastern counties, and to England, were commonplace. In the first half of the nineteenth century, seasonal migrants, often accompanied by their livestock, walked along Ireland's dusty roadways in search of work and food.

Now such searches proved more and more futile.

Since Mathew's August letter, the downward spiral had progressed with alarming speed. Now, he wrote to Trevelyan, more than 5,000 "half-starved wretched beings from the country" were begging on the streets of Cork city; "when utterly exhausted, they crawl to the work-houses to die." He estimated that more than a hundred people a week were dying in his parish. And because of the frightful calamity that had swept the countryside, where food was all but nonexistent, thousands of peasants straggled into the city in search of something to eat, further straining scarce resources. Ten to twelve people a day died from starvation in the village of Crookhaven, where the community organized a collection to purchase a public bier upon which to place the bodies of those whose families could not afford coffins. Mathew was filled with dread, not only for the current state of affairs, but for the unknown depth of the abyss that lurked ahead.

"This country is in an awful position," he stressed to Trevelyan, "and no one can tell what the result will be."

Father Mathew was hardly the only person alerting Secretary Trevelyan to the catastrophe as 1846 drew to a close; indeed, by late November and into December, eyewitness and news reports were as widespread as the famine itself. A coast guard officer employed in relief service, Captain Mann, wrote to Trevelyan in mid-November, still shaken by the swiftness of the famine's onslaught. Like Mathew, he had witnessed the potato crop's demise in a one-week period from late July to early August, from "thirty-two miles thickly studded with potato fields in full bloom" one day to a crop whose "leaves were all scorched black" the next. "The face of the whole country was changed," he said. "It was the work of a night." Another relief worker reported that in a tour of 800 miles, "all is lost and gone," that the stench from diseased potatoes was "perceptible as you travel along the road" in Cork. Colonel Knox Gore, lieutenant of County Sligo, found that "from Mullingar to Maynooth every field was black," and another report described "the fields in Kerry look[ing] as if fire had passed over them."

Disaster was universal. Irish peasants—impoverished, weak, emaciated, sick, clad only in tattered rags at the onset of one of the worst winters in Irish memory—limped, stumbled, fell, and died by the thousands on country roads and in rain-filled ditches, in town squares, in snow-covered bogs and on frozen hillsides, in dark windowless mud huts, in the slums and alleyways of cities, and often in holes they had scratched out in the ground in a vain search for grubs or to serve as protection against the elements. Snow had begun to fall in November, and for the most part it had not stopped. Desperate peasants in search of food now battled driving blizzards and deep drifts in the mountains, hail and sleet near the coasts, and raw winds and freezing temperatures across once-green meadows encrusted in ice and snow. One relief worker wrote of trudging through "wild mountain passes, rendered still wilder by the deep snow," a "constant succession of violent snowstorms," and peasants "crying with hunger and cold." In one small town, he reported, he had left a small amount of dried peat—"turf," the Irish called it—to enable several families to "keep up the smallest fire imaginable." Otherwise, he concluded, "in this severe weather, many would be frozen to death."

A British magistrate writing to the Duke of Wellington described walking into an Irish village that appeared deserted, only to find starving peasants shivering in corners of shacks, lean-tos, and cabins. "In the first, six famished and ghastly skeletons, to all appearances dead, were huddled in a corner on some filthy straw, their sole covering what seemed a ragged horsecloth," Nicholas Cummins wrote in a letter published in the *Times* of London on Christmas Eve 1846. "I approached with horror, and found by low moaning that they were still alive—they were in fever, four children, a woman, and what had once been a man. It is impossible to go through the detail." Other peasants doddered from their dark hiding places, and within minutes, Cummins reported,

> I was surrounded by at least 200 such phantoms, such frightful specters as no words can describe, [suffering] either from famine or from fever. Their demonic yells are still ringing in my ears and their horrible images are fixed upon my brain.

Nor were stories of hunger confined to official reports. Across the country, hundreds of fearful tenant farmers, laborers, even small shopkeepers and tavern workers, either put quill to paper themselves or—more likely, if they were among the nation's semi-literate or illiterate—scraped together meager funds to hire professional scriveners.

These letters were then posted, most often to addresses in the United States and Canada, to loved ones who had already fled their home country. The missives generally contained one central message—Ireland's situation was perilous—and one desperate plea: if at all possible, send money to bring some relief to family members left behind.

James and Elizabeth Prendergast of Milltown, County Kerry, parents of six, obtained the services of scriveners to whom they dictated letters to their three children—two sons and a daughter—and a son-in-law, each of whom had emigrated to Boston in search of employment.

Three of the Prendergast children were among the intrepid transatlantic travelers who'd left for North America between 1830 and 1845—sons Thomas and Jeffrey sailed for Boston in late summer 1839, a short time after daughter Julia Riordan and her husband, Cornelius.

At first, James harbored hopes that his family members were migrating temporarily—"I never will leave this life until I see you here," he wrote to his children in February 1841. But food shortages in 1844 and 1845 and the abysmal conditions spreading across the country now had dashed those hopes. Opportunities in Ireland were nonexistent; even the most devoted parents knew that any child who had escaped was far better off. Writing in November, just a month before Father Mathew pleaded with Sir Charles Trevelyan, James Prendergast thanked his children for the money they had sent in July, and then informed them of the worst: "The state of this country is almost beyond description. Nothing to be seen in all quarters but distress and destitution. Famine and starvation threatening everywhere unless God mercifully sends some foreign aid." He added that the last remittances from the United States were long gone "and we are considerably in debt. Therefore if ye can assist us as usual, do not delay your usual relief."

Also writing in November, from Belfast to his nephew in Philadelphia, stable groom William Dunne said: "A good job that your father, mother, and family went the time they did for there is nothing here but hardship and starvation."

As Christmas arrived, thousands of Irish peasants and farmers roamed the countryside and the city streets foraging for food of any kind. At the doorways of overcrowded poorhouses, mothers with six or seven children begged besieged workers to take in two or three—usually the youngest and weakest—for at least one night with hopes of securing them a hot meal and perhaps clean, dry straw upon which to sleep. In County Leitrim, a worker told the master of the poorhouse at which he worked that one sickly child "would trouble them but a very short time."

By late December, the sheep, cows, pigs, and poultry had long disappeared, and starving peasants turned for food to the ever-dwindling supply of dogs and horses. In cities, carpenters began to build coffins with bottoms and sides that dropped away, so that they could be reused. In many remote areas, corpses were left "uncoffined and unburied," Cove attorney Maurice Power reported, their bodies torn to pieces by vultures and "other evils no tongue could tell." Power was not alone in his reluctance to include excessive detail; in numerous contemporaneous accounts, writers explicitly noted their reticence to share their most gruesome observances of starvation's effects on the human body.

Coroners struggled to keep up with visits to homes of the deceased and soon ceased inquests to determine cause of death, too, knowing full well—as did mourning family members who gently closed the eyelids of their dead loved ones—that in almost every case, they would write "starvation" on the line designated for cause of death. Across Ireland, people who had yet to succumb stumbled toward death: in mid-December, 25,000 paupers were without food in County Wicklow; more than 400,000 were "totally destitute" in Mayo; and in Donegal, relief worker James H. Tuke reported that "fully half of the population subsisted wholly upon potatoes—a crop which is totally swept away from the face of the country as though it had never been."

And from County Sligo, one relief inspector wrote to Trevelyan in December with a warning and a plea not unlike the messages from Father Mathew: "I assure you that unless something is immediately done the people must die. Pray do something for them. Let me beg you to attend to this."

⟨—✦—⟩

CHAPTER 2

"Blest by God, and cursed by man"

Back in London, Mathew's pleas fell on Trevelyan's deaf ears. Like most of the city's bureaucrats, merchants, tradesmen, and well-to-do, the official responsible for providing Irish relief prepared for Christmas largely unaffected by the catastrophic conditions unfolding just a few hundred miles from his home. Londoners shopped for goose, bread pudding, and newly invented Christmas crackers; read aloud by the fireside Charles Dickens's *A Christmas Carol*, published just a few years earlier; and marveled at reprints of small, colorful illustrations produced for the chairman of the Society of the Arts—he described them as the first "Christmas cards" and had plans to distribute them to friends and business associates to celebrate the holiday. London residents were also entranced by a sketch published in the *Illustrated London News* of Queen Victoria, Prince Albert, and their children standing *inside* their quarters around what the royals and the press would soon call a Christmas tree; within fifteen years, most members of London's middle and upper classes would stand an evergreen tree in their homes and, on Christmas Eve, adorn it with lights and ornaments.

That Trevelyan appeared unmoved by the distressing reports from Ireland had less to do with the festiveness of the season than it did with his belief that everything that could be done for Ireland had been done, and that further steps—such as providing food—would disrupt corn and grain markets, damage the economy, and hurt the United Kingdom as a whole. "I deeply regret the primary and appalling evil of the insufficiency of the supplies of food [in Ireland]," he wrote on December 22 to a member of the Irish Relief Commission, "[but] if we were to purchase [corn and grain] for Irish use faster than we are now doing, we should commit a crying injustice to the rest of the country."

Even as he received pushback from British relief workers in Ireland who implored the British government to send food, even as the reports of starvation and suffering grew more descriptive, Trevelyan reminded his officials that there were "principles to be kept in view" to prevent a run on a limited supply of government foodstuffs to feed Ireland; exhausting those supplies would incur "reprehension" from the government and the public. Further, to protect private enterprise, Trevelyan concluded: "We attach the highest public importance to the strict observance of our pledge not to send orders abroad [Ireland], which would come into competition with our merchants and upset all their calculations."

No spirit of Christmas giving could offset Trevelyan's complex set of economic, religious, and political beliefs that influenced his decisions on Irish relief policy.

A thirty-nine-year-old civil servant with a first-rate mind, Trevelyan was the son of an archdeacon who'd hoped his son would follow him into the church. While Charles read the Bible and enjoyed quoting aloud from it in a "deep sonorous voice," he decided instead to pursue a position with the East India Company, which for 300 years had been a prominent pillar of London's financial, mercantile, and international trading community. At seventeen, Trevelyan became a student at the company training college in Herefordshire, where he won a prize in Greek, and formed a "lifelong attachment" to the laissez-faire economic and government views of Adam Smith and Edmund Burke.

His affection for conservative economic theories dovetailed with his religious upbringing and background. Trevelyan adhered ardently to Moralism, a near-evangelical sect that preached a "passionate gospel of self-help," in the words of one historian. Moralists objected to public assistance, arguing that public relief removed incentive for the poor to change destructive behaviors—including "alcoholism, sloth, indolence, sexual promiscuity." Offer relief to the poor man, warned Thomas Chalmers, the leading Moralist thinker of the Victorian age, "and you deprive him of the impetus to become self-reliant, self-disciplined, industrious, sober, and chaste." In fact, in one of his first recorded remarks about the relief policy, Trevelyan told a colleague that God had "sent the calamity to teach the Irish a lesson . . . [and it] must not be too much mitigated."

He began his career in India as a clerk, where his facile intellect and his economic and moral beliefs came together to produce a competent if soulless bureaucrat. One British political aide in India marveled that Trevelyan lacked a sense of humor and "has no small talk," conversing only about railway construction, roadway improvements, and, less directly, his own advancement. "His mind is full of schemes of moral and political improvement, and his zeal boils over," the official noted.

After leaving India, Trevelyan returned to England and joined the Treasury department, where he parlayed a penchant for hard work, moral rectitude, and ruthless political maneuvering into an ever-widening sphere of responsibility; one observer pointed out that Trevelyan would "use whatever tools came to hand" to succeed, including "debate, hyperbole, caricature, ridicule, intrigue, personal contacts, manipulation of the press."

But not all characterizations were negative. Even at the height of the famine, those who knew and worked with him noted that he was "immensely conscientious," had "absolute integrity and a strong sense of justice," acted from "a genuine conviction of doing right," and possessed a "powerful mind," a "praiseworthy devotion to duty," and an "obsession for work."

But most people came back to his lack of human warmth; as one colleague put it, he had a "remarkable insensitiveness" that made him impervious to emotional appeals. A picture emerges of a man with little sense of empathy or inclination for basic human connections, one with a rigid moral worldview that linked good character and good fortune on the one hand, and sloth and poverty on the other. At the same time, his Moralist views also drove him to become a hardworking, ambitious bureaucrat who possessed a strict integrity and righteousness when it came to following rules and procedures, a technocrat with a strong belief in the potential for human progress if only the right policies were implemented.

Further shaping Trevelyan's position on Irish relief was his Whig political affiliation—Whigs were more hostile to the Irish than Tories. The party reflected the views of most of the British public, which considered Ireland an international embarrassment, a backward nation tied to primitive forms of agriculture, overly dependent on a single crop, whose people eschewed any thoughts of industrialization and modernization, and instead clung to destructive expectations that priests and parishes would provide for them. Trevelyan and most residents of England would agree with an anti-Catholic American newspaper of the period whose editors wrote that an Irishman "would take the bread out of his living children's mouths to pay for Masses for the soul of a dead child." In short, the editorial concluded, "the curse of Ireland is her popish priesthood"—that is, Whigs argued, the Irish reliance on priests and prayers, rather than modernity and science, had doomed Ireland to a cycle of poverty that had repeated for decades.

This attitude further fueled the contention by Trevelyan and others that at least some of the blame for the famine must be laid at the feet of the Irish themselves, and perhaps God was punishing them for their own ennui and ignorance. The *Times* of London, the most influential newspaper in England, printed dozens of editorials on the perils of Irish dependency, reinforcing the Moralist view. "For our part, we regard the potato blight as a blessing," the editors declared in September 1846. "When the Celts once cease to be potato eaters, they must become carnivorous. With the taste of meats will grow the appetite for them; with the appetite, the readiness to earn them. With this will come steadiness, regularity, and perseverance." Two years after receiving his first letters from Father Mathew, by which time perhaps a million Irish people had died from starvation and attendant disease, Trevelyan declared that while the famine was "awfully serious," the country was "in the hands of Providence, without a possibility of averting the catastrophe, if it is to happen. We can only wait the result."

And a short time later he declared: "The great evil with which we have to contend is not the physical evil of the famine, but the moral evil of the selfish, perverse, and turbulent character of the people." In particular, Trevelyan feared further "breeding" among the Irish, which would result in more dangerous levels of overpopulation, which would aggravate the food shortage.

In short, Trevelyan and his peers had contempt for what they saw as the Irish's inability to care for themselves. He spoke for many in calling the Irish crisis a "thirteenth century famine affecting a nineteenth century population." In October 1846, by then well informed on the devastation wrought by the famine, he referred to it as a "cure . . . by the direct stroke of an all-wise and all-merciful Providence" for the overpopulation of Ireland, which was "altogether beyond the power of man" to remedy. And he saw the famine as the result of the Irish public's moral failings. By exposing the problem of excess Irish population, he held, the famine had laid bare "the deep and inveterate root of social evil."

Trevelyan's economic and social beliefs would be manifest in his response to the famine and result in the further misery of the Irish people.

After the widespread potato failure, the price of the limited supply that remained spiked well beyond what the Irish poor could afford—doubling in some cases—yet Trevelyan refused to institute price controls, which he viewed as overt and excessive government interference. To make things worse, much of the food beyond potatoes that Ireland was able to grow was actually *exported back* to England, demanded by English landowners of Irish property to sell on the open market.

A Limerick merchant and shipowner, Francis Spaight, recorded the exports flowing through the port of Limerick from June 1846 to May 1847; these included more than 387,000 barrels of oats and 46,000 barrels of wheat. Most of Ireland's cattle, butter, wheat, barley, and other vegetables went to markets in England, and from there around the world—some even finding its way back to Ireland at full market price. Trevelyan and the British government, wary of upsetting grain markets and affecting profits of traders and speculators, steadfastly refused to reduce or halt exports from Ireland in the first place, or to consider price controls, and the starving Irish could not afford market prices.

Lacking funds to buy "money crops," such as wheat, barley, and oats, and unable to eat their primary "food crop"—the blighted and ruined potato—the Irish had little choice but to starve. "Perhaps the most disgraceful aspect of the Famine was that in each of its six years there was probably enough food exported out of Ireland to sustain the nation, certainly enough to have saved the million who died," author Edward Laxton wrote.

During late 1846, and spilling into 1847, wagons full of produce and grains rolled along Irish roadways under the protection of armed guards, bound for the ports, as starving Irish peasants looked on. In fact, throughout the six-year period of the Great Famine, 1846–51, Ireland remained a net *exporter* of food. Years later, Dublin-born playwright George Bernard Shaw highlighted the perverseness of the situation, and summed up much of the hatred the Irish felt for the English, with this exchange in his play *Man and Superman:*

> MALONE: My father died of starvation in Ireland in the Black 47. Maybe you've heard of it?
> VIOLET: The Famine?
> MALONE: No, the starvation. When a country is full of food and exporting it, there can be no famine.

Irish famine historian and author Cecil Woodham-Smith concluded that "in the long and troubled history of England and Ireland, no issue has provoked so much anger or so embittered relations between the two countries as the indisputable fact that huge quantities of food were exported from Ireland to England [while] the people of Ireland were dying of starvation." Irish peasants seethed with resentment when food left small towns under the eyes of hungry men, women, and children, protected by military escorts. Such a sight, according to Woodham-Smith, the Irish people found "impossible to understand and impossible to forget."

It is no wonder that many Irish people repeated the slogan that "God created the blight, but the English created the famine." Others were more poetic, though just as mournful, insisting that Ireland was "blest by God, and cursed by man."

Trevelyan's reputation as a particularly effective bureaucrat—highly organized, self-assured, and unflappable—led the prime minister, Lord John Russell, to place him in charge of famine relief efforts shortly after Russell's ascendance to power in the summer of 1846, at about the time the blight destroyed most of the country's potato crop.

Russell's predecessor, Sir Robert Peel, had established a Relief Commission to provide direct government food assistance to the hungry Irish after the less widespread potato-crop failures of 1845. Peel also worked hard to repeal the Corn Laws, which mandated that large taxes be levied on any foreign crops brought into Britain. Such tariffs kept grain prices high, which satisfied British traders and speculators alike but made grain unaffordable for most of the destitute Irish. Peel, who pushed through the repeal in June 1846 to help the Irish, expended enormous political capital and paid a heavy price for his efforts when his Tory party split over the contentious Corn Law debate. On the same day he secured repeal of the Corn Laws, Peel was defeated on another, unrelated bill and resigned as prime minister.

In his final speech to Parliament, Peel spared no language as he castigated British lawmakers on their woeful response to the Irish famine: "Good God, are you to sit in cabinet and consider and calculate how much diarrhea . . . and dysentery a people can bear before it becomes necessary for you to provide them with food?"

And yet, Peel's emotional appeal had no lasting effect.

As the leaves of the potato plants curled and turned black, as blight destroyed the dietary mainstay for half the Irish population, as Father Mathew pleaded in letter after letter, Trevelyan's responses were inexcusably slow and inadequate. He seemed bound by the bureaucrat's desire for process even as the situation in Ireland descended into madness and headed toward the abyss. His penchant for tried-and-true management methods was inadequate for disaster on such an unprecedented scale. His commitment to order, paperwork, and details strangled any creativity he might have employed to provide food to the multitudes, left him powerless to hasten relief efforts that were put in place, and ultimately prevented him from giving appropriate consideration to the largest and most critical issues—such as how to transport goods to an agricultural nation with a woefully inadequate system of interior roadways.

In modern parlance, Trevelyan found himself rearranging deck chairs on the *Titanic*, clinging to London formality, and perhaps hampered by his lack of empathy, even despite the bleakest accounts of British officials dispatched to Ireland to assess conditions and report their findings. "I confess myself unmanned by the intensity and extent of the suffering," one shaken military inspector wrote, "women and little children, crowds of whom were scattered over the turnip fields like a flock of famishing crows, devouring the raw turnips, mothers half naked, shivering in the snow and sleet, uttering exclamations of despair while their children were screaming with hunger."

The inspector acknowledged the emotional toll the famine took on him: "I am a match for anything else I may meet . . . but this I cannot stand."

It didn't help that Trevelyan's boss, Prime Minister John Russell, held the same view: that only tough love would help the Irish. Russell's policies emphasized work rather than food for famine victims. Espousing the belief that the cost of Irish relief should be borne by the Irish people, he ordered Trevelyan to shut down Peel's direct Relief Commission, which his efficient bureaucrat did on July 21, 1846, just days before Father Mathew came upon the blackened potato crop.

In its place, Trevelyan established a vast, clumsy, and often cruel works program. Under the Board of Works, more than 12,000 civil servants organized a system of often meaningless public projects—building unneeded roads or bridges and breaking stone that would never be used—to provide employment for approximately 750,000 starving people, who were responsible for providing food for another 2.25 million family members and loved ones.

Each morning during the harsh winter of 1846–47, tens of thousands of Irish peasants, most of whom had not eaten a morsel in a full day or longer, would wake in dark unheated cabins, walk miles in wind, sleet, cold, and blowing snow—often barefoot and almost always coatless and half-dressed in tattered clothing—to engage in make-work projects to earn a pittance for food. The results were predictably horrific.

"Women with infant children could be seen breaking stone for bridges where there was no water, or for roads that led nowhere, and benefited no one," one Irish author noted. Many lacked resistance to stave off infections and they became feverish, which added to their weakened state and caused scores to drop from exhaustion and illness. The men and women most debilitated by disease and hunger often could not make it to work, and if they did, they could not work long enough to earn enough money. Perhaps cruelest of all, even if workers did perform backbreaking menial labor for an entire day, the wages the government paid were simply too low for them to buy sufficient food for their families, a reality that broke the spirits of even the strongest breadwinners.

Father Mathew was increasingly desperate. "No rate of wages will save the people from extreme distress unless the price of provisions be kept down," he wrote to Trevelyan in late September 1846, pleading with him to impose price controls on Indian corn or order the government to buy it outright to "protect the people against famine and pestilence." In late November, the priest tried again, contending, "If Indian meal can be had by the poor for a penny a pound all danger of famine would be at an end."

But it was to no avail. Sitting at his desk on the night of December 16, Mathew wrote that his parish was establishing soup kitchens in "all parts of the city, to supply the poor with nutritious and cheap cooked food," a desperate measure to compensate for the government's lack of action. He deeply regretted "the total abandonment of the people to the corn and flour dealers. They charge 50 to 100 percent profit."

The incontrovertible fact, Mathew warned Trevelyan, was that "the present exorbitant price of bread stuffs, particularly Indian corn, places sufficient food beyond the great bulk of the population."

Trevelyan largely shaped and resolutely enforced famine policies—one prominent historian referred to him as "dictator of relief"—but he took virtually no responsibility for their inexorable and disastrous results.

The Irish people's broad reliance on the potato—to eat, to trade, and to sell—meant that the crop's destruction created misery even beyond an insufficient food supply. After several years of at least partial potato-crop failure, the 1846 blight also made it nearly impossible for Irish peasants to barter for livestock, repay their debts, or pay the rent on the land they tilled. The feudal landlord-tenant system—in place since the 1800 Acts of Union made Ireland part of the Kingdom of Great Britain—drove wealthy and largely absentee British landowners to virtually enslave Irish peasants, who worked the land, grew the crops, and turned most food and any profits over to the landlords. When the Irish were unable to pay their rent, landlords evicted hundreds of thousands of them from their homes, forcing them to wander the countryside—now in hopeless search of food *and* shelter. "Ejectment is tantamount to a sentence of death by slow torture," stated a special report to the British House of Commons in the fall of 1846.

Throughout the famine, the word "eviction" seared its way into the Irish lexicon, evoking fear anytime it was spoken. Indeed, for Irish families the word would evoke the famine's misery for generations afterward, whether in the Old World or the New.

Turned off the land, evicted peasants wandered "begging, miserable, and turbulent," according to historian Woodham-Smith. Once landlords served eviction notices, they directed police and troops to remove tenants and their belongings from their homes and hired contractors to destroy the structures. Sometimes, evicted Irish peasants, desperate and with nowhere else to go, refused to leave, and their dwellings were torn down around them. Some died amid the debris; others collected scraps of wood and cloth, or clumps of straw, and attempted to fashion some semblance of shelter, often to die later along the roadside. One landlord in Mayo ordered more than a hundred families evicted in late December 1846, despite pleas from a clergyman to delay the action until after Christmas. On a night of "high wind and storm," a famine relief worker described the scene: "The people were all turned out of doors and the roofs of their houses pulled down. That night they made a tent or shelter, of wood and straw, but however the drivers [bailiffs] threw them down and drove them from the place . . . they had to go head first into the storm." He added: "Wailing could be heard at a great distance. They implored the drivers to allow them to remain a short time as it was so near the time of Festival, but they would not."

Writing to Trevelyan on that cold night in December 1846, the famine tightening its deadly grip on his county and his country, Father Mathew struggled for words to describe the horror he was witnessing.

"No understanding can conceive, no tongue express, the misery that prevails."

PART II

THE UNITED STATES

"A voice comes to us from across the ocean"

Boston ship captain Robert Bennet Forbes commanded the USS Jamestown on its humanitarian mission to deliver food to famine-stricken Ireland.

CHAPTER 3

⟨—✦—⟩

"THE YEAR OF DECISION"

As Father Mathew's pleas to Trevelyan went unheeded, as James Prendergast wrote to his children in Boston that "the [food] supply of the country . . . will soon be exhausted unless supplies are brought in from abroad," as starvation and deep despair enveloped Ireland, Americans in the fall of 1846 focused inward and remained largely indifferent to the crisis in Ireland.

What relief efforts there were came in the form of small remittances from Irish immigrants in the United States or charitable contributions from Catholics whose parishes organized collection efforts. In truth, the whole idea of an Irish famine had come under a kind of boy-who-cried-wolf suspicion. Ireland had suffered its first major potato failure and severe food shortage in 1845, and calls for assistance in Boston and other Irish Catholic strongholds raised modest amounts of money, mostly in small donations. But when the full-fledged famine predicted in American press accounts failed to materialize in the first half of 1846, people in the United States began to suspect—and their suspicions were proven correct—that reports of extensive starvation had been exaggerated. The cause lost much of its urgency by late winter, and by spring and into early summer, the Irish potato crop was in full bloom—the "abundant harvest" that Father Mathew reported on in late July 1846.

Further, fundraising in 1845 and 1846 took on a political tone in Boston that hurt the cause. Relief efforts were organized by the local Repeal Association, whose members demanded Irish independence from England (the name emanates from a desire to repeal the 1800 Act of Union to create the United Kingdom of England and Ireland); they were supporters of Irish nationalist Daniel O'Connell, who spearheaded the independence movement in Ireland. The committee cited food shortages in Ireland as yet another example of British incompetence, claiming at a December 1845 meeting that because of the "fatal connection of Ireland with England, the rich grain harvests of the former country are carried off to pay an absentee government and an absentee proprietor." True or not, most Irish believed the claim that mixing the repeal issue with charitable contributions soured many non-Irish Bostonians on the hunger relief effort.

Even after the terrifying overnight destruction of the crop that Father Mathew witnessed and reported on in early August 1846, Americans were slow to respond. Cities with large Irish populations, such as Boston, demonstrated their beneficence. Boston Catholics, most of them Irish, donated more than $150,000 (about $4.5 million today) to famine relief after recently installed Bishop John Bernard Fitzpatrick called upon his congregation to aid those who were suffering across the Atlantic.

But, unsurprisingly, non–Irish Catholics did not respond in great numbers. Certainly a sense of "disaster fatigue" had worked its way into the American mindset after overblown reports of famine earlier in the year; most U.S. residents, despite the fact that they were primarily farmers, did not make the conscious connection that a partially destroyed potato crop in 1845 left little or nothing in reserve after the nearly universal destruction in the summer of 1846.

But it was more than disaster fatigue that accounted for Americans' apathy in 1846—it was a focus on their own future, their own destiny.

The phrase "Manifest Destiny" had first worked its way into the national lexicon a year earlier, in the summer of 1845—New York editor

John L. O'Sullivan coined it to describe the vision of a vast and bountiful country stretching from the Atlantic to the Pacific, with harbors and naval fleets on both coasts, and a network of rivers and railroads throughout the interior that would enable commerce and growth, elevating the United States to a world power. Such expansion was the will of God, O'Sullivan opined, and the best way to ensure the country's continued prosperity, especially considering its population growth, its attractiveness to immigrants, and its promise to fulfill the dreams of natives and newcomers alike. A few years later, novelist Herman Melville reinforced the theme when he wrote: "We Americans are the peculiar chosen people—the Israel of our time."

In 1846, when they were not focused on the war with Mexico following the 1845 annexation of Texas and disputes over the border, many Americans looked toward Oregon and the Pacific Coast, distant destinations that people viewed with a sense of adventure, romance, and redemption. Eventually—either frightened by cholera outbreaks in the East, shaken by lingering effects of the 1837 financial depression, emboldened to seek their fortunes, or simply hoping for a fresh start—thousands succumbed to the westward tug and embarked on the long and sometimes torturous overland journey. Historian Bernard DeVoto later called 1846 "the year of decision" to describe the restlessness of Americans; and this was two years *before* the Gold Rush, which would soon make the decision to head west much easier and change the primary destination of most travelers from Oregon to California.

Technological and scientific progress also captured Americans' attention at home. The wonder of Samuel Morse's telegraph, invented two years earlier, still evoked near disbelief for its ability to transmit messages almost instantly; the power of railroads to open distant commercial and passenger markets produced a sense of restlessness and economic optimism; in Boston, the first use of anesthetic ether during surgery by doctors at Massachusetts General Hospital offered the possibility of pain-free surgical procedures. Americans marveled at the new technology and wondered how many more breakthroughs were forthcoming.

But in the midst of the optimism, hovering over the nation was a large cloud, dark and menacing and swollen with the intractable issues of slavery and sectionalism that divided North and South. To this point, a series of political compromises had staved off a deluge, but for how long? The annexation of Texas, which joined the Union as a slave state, outraged northern abolitionists and other progressives. Abiel Abbott, a prominent northern clergyman and writer, called the Texas annexation "a great offense against humanity and a monstrous transgression of the law of God." Now he and others feared that the war with Mexico, which many believed was President James K. Polk's perverse interpretation of Manifest Destiny, would allow the South to spread slavery over vast new areas if the United States acquired additional territory.

In 1846, North-South war winds were not yet blowing with sustained force, but in certain pockets—Boston, Charleston, Washington, D.C.—warning breezes rustled the trees and thunder rumbled in the distance. A storm was gathering. Americans wondered: Was it imminent, and, if so, how destructive would it be?

For all of these reasons, as late as the fall of 1846, neither the United States government nor most of its people had taken more than a cursory glance at the suffering and desperation that was consuming Ireland.

If Americans at home looked elsewhere, the country's diplomats abroad were indeed aware of the crisis, though they viewed it through the lens of economic opportunity rather than of human tragedy. George Bancroft, U.S. minister to London (he would later become the "father of American history" with his ten-volume work, *History of the United States from the Discovery of the Continent*), cabled President Polk and Secretary of State James Buchanan on November 3, 1846, noting that there was a large increase in British demand for American corn. He pointed to "the scarcity in Ireland and England consequent on the failure of the potato crop" and predicted that for at least two more years Britain would be "dependent on American exports." The English would have no choice due to "the appalling distress occasioned by the famine in Ireland."

Thomas Wilson, the American consular officer in Dublin, concurred, advising the president that the potato "will have to be replaced or supplied with that which can be procured in the cheapest terms." It was therefore highly probable "that Indian corn from the United States will have to be imported in very large quantities."

So as 1846 came to a close, the United States was focused on geographic expansion, economic growth, breakthroughs in communications and transportation, war with Mexico, the angst of slavery, and the path to its destiny.

The Irish crisis was but a footnote in the American story, except for its possible benefits to the U.S. economy.

⟨────⟩

CHAPTER 4

"I WAS BORN TO A HIGHER PURPOSE"

S hip captain Robert Bennet Forbes was among those Americans for whom the troubles in Ireland barely registered as 1846 drew to an end.

An avid consumer of news and current events, he certainly would have been aware of Ireland's food shortages, and of attempts by Boston's Catholic community to provide assistance to their Irish brethren overseas. He also was well aware of the thousands of Irish who had already arrived in Boston; many Irish laborers were digging the trenches for the fifteen-mile-long aqueduct that would bring Boston its first municipal supply of fresh water from a pond outside the city limits. But other news unrelated to Ireland would have interested him more—in particular the progress of the Mexican War, which could have a direct effect on his shipping interests.

For the most part, Forbes's focus in 1846—as it had been for several years—was on running his business and caring for his family.

He had turned forty-two in September, and by that time had likely logged more miles at sea than virtually any other man in American history. But in his view, seafaring adventures were a young man's game—a man was "unfit" to go to sea after age forty. His growing family occupied the bulk of his thoughts and labors, and he had assured his wife, Rose, that his domestic responsibilities had quelled some of his natural restiveness.

Life at home with Rose and their three children—Robert Bennet, who turned nine in October; three-and-a-half-year-old Edith; and one-year-old James Murray—seemed to suit him. At one point during a long voyage to China in 1838–40, Forbes had been reduced to a ropey 160 pounds. His 1846 portrait—after five years on land, relief from the physical demands of sailing, and regular home-cooked meals—shows a less wan and fuller-faced man. His eyes, once strained and weakened by the searing glare of the Pacific sun bouncing across the swells of a vast ocean, now reflected a gentle contentedness. As much as he loved the sea, he loved his family more, an affection that brought Rose both great joy and immense relief. Her husband's past journeys had left her alone and lonely, especially the excruciating thirty-month China voyage. And now that the couple had three children, the thought of any separation was even less bearable.

Still, he had to admit to himself, if not to Rose, that he was occasionally restless. He was a shipowner and a shipbuilder now, and while both were satisfying, neither filled him with the pure adrenaline rush of sailing on the open ocean, or the satisfaction of commanding a vessel and crew.

Family life in Boston had muffled the siren song of the sea, but the voice still whispered to him in soothing tones during quiet moments.

Beginning in 1817 at the age of thirteen, Robert Bennet Forbes embarked on a series of adventures the likes of which most people of the time only dared dream.

In a period when the vast majority of Americans never traveled more than a few miles from home—a scant handful left their states and fewer still traveled abroad—Forbes traversed oceans to ports of call around the globe, some exotic, some dangerous, all offering significant mercantile opportunities. Along the way, he climbed riggings, swabbed decks, piloted ships, battled storms, suffered seasickness, conducted trade, buried sailors at sea, and endured the death of his father and the tragic loss of his beloved brother, Tom, who was swept away in a typhoon a short distance off the coast of China when Robert Bennet was twenty-five. Tom was only twenty-seven, and his death severed a deep love and connection that the two brothers had shared since childhood; a decade later, Robert described Tom's death as "the greatest misfortune that ever happened to our family."

Forbes himself best summarized his life between the ages of thirteen and twenty-six: "For thirteen years I had been almost constantly afloat."

His first experience at sea actually took place when he was six, and it might well have deterred him from ever wanting to sail again. His father, Ralph Bennet Forbes, had been working in France as a merchant for more than a year, and in January 1811, Forbes's mother, Margaret, decided she could live without him no longer, and booked passage on a small schooner. A ne'er-do-well who struggled to make a living, Ralph Forbes lacked both skill and luck in business and invested repeatedly in schemes that ended badly. Concerned about their sister's well-being, Margaret's brothers, James and Thomas Perkins—prominent merchants of Boston who owned and operated a trading house, Perkins & Co., as well as a number of merchant ships engaged in business around the globe—had hired their brother-in-law to work for their company's branch in France.

Ralph Bennet Forbes left for overseas shortly after the death of his daughter Cornelia, Robert Bennet's younger sister. At the time of Ralph's departure, Mrs. Forbes was left with four children and grieving for her lost daughter. Her situation worsened when, in the fall of 1810, another daughter, Margaret, then four years old, was severely burned when the clothes she was wearing caught fire near a heating grate. By the time the child recovered, it was the dead of winter, and few ships were crossing the Atlantic, but Mrs. Forbes could wait no longer to join her husband. She turned her two daughters over to relatives for care, and she, Thomas, and Robert Bennet boarded the *Midas*, "laden with salt fish, quite deep in the water, and in every way uncomfortable," Bennet recounted later.

Sailors knocked the ice off the riggings, and the ship left Boston Harbor buffeted by howling January winds.

Margaret Forbes was miserable from the start of the voyage. "I am excluded from almost every object that is pleasant," she wrote. "My drawing room, which contains my sleeping place and that of the children, is about six feet square; a small glass in the deck admits the light which rests dimly on the paper I am scribbling." She could only pray that God would "shelter me as well on the wide waste of waters as in the full city."

But any prospects for a smooth voyage were dashed shortly after the ship cleared Cape Cod. A violent storm arose and raged uninterrupted for four days. Margaret and the boys huddled close, the wind a "complete hurricane, so that we could scarcely lie in our berths." The *Midas* lost its quarter boards, some of its rails, two casks of water, and one anchor; the relentless wind split the sails, stove the lifeboats, broke the tiller, and ripped the glass skylight off. "Torrents of water washed over us and came into the cabin," Margaret said; Robert Bennet was swamped and nearly drowned before Margaret and a crew member pulled him to safety. "All our fowls and two of our pigs were drowned," Margaret noted, "which I did not much lament as it put an end to their sufferings."

The weather improved, but the overall voyage did not. The *Midas* was captured by the British, who had established a blockade along the coast of France during the Napoleonic War, and Mrs. Forbes and her sons were held prisoner for three weeks on a British ship. They were eventually freed, but then quarantined by French authorities at Marseilles for three more weeks.

Eventually Margaret, Robert, and Thomas reunited with Ralph, and the parents deposited the boys at a French boarding school for nearly eighteen months while Mr. and Mrs. Forbes traveled to Italy, the Holy Land, and Egypt. No one at the school spoke English, so the two Forbes boys quickly became fluent in French. When the parents returned, they took the boys to Bordeaux, where they delayed sailing home until Mrs. Forbes gave birth to a baby, John Murray, in February 1813 (it was John who would proffer the idea of making a warship available for Irish relief in February 1847).

If possible, the return trip was more harrowing than the voyage to Europe. Britain and the United States were now engaged in the War of 1812, and the Forbeses' ship was captured twice by British cruisers. The second boarding was preceded by intense cannon fire that nearly swamped them. The battle went on in earnest for nearly two hours before the British came aboard and eventually towed the ship into the Tagus River on the Iberian Peninsula. Two days later, in a daring act, the Forbes family escaped in a small fishing boat and the group made its way to Lisbon, where they remained with a cousin for a month before finally boarding a ship bound for America.

After a thirty-six-day voyage, this time uneventful, they sailed into Newport, Rhode Island, before making their way by stagecoach to Boston. It was August 1813; Margaret and her two sons had been away for more than two and a half years and had packed a lifetime of peril and adventure into their transatlantic travels.

After all of it, Robert Bennet Forbes was one month shy of his ninth birthday.

After the year in France and about thirty months at Milton Academy—then a boys' prep school designed as a feeder institution for Harvard—circumstances required Forbes to end his education and enter the full-time workforce at the age of twelve. "My father had been unfortunate in business, and was much broken down in health," Bennet wrote, "and how to support a family now amounting to six or seven small ones became an anxious problem." Margaret's brothers had eased some of the financial pressure on the Forbes household by endowing Thomas with a financial gift, and one brother agreed to allow ten-year-old Margaret Forbes to live with his family, but the Forbeses still needed additional income to make ends meet.

Robert Bennet's uncle hired him to work at the Perkins firm at a building on Foster's Wharf doing whatever needed to be done. "My duties were to sweep out, make the fires, close and open the store, copy letters into a book, collect wharfage bills, run errands," he wrote. About a year into his employment, in October 1817, Robert Bennet was attending to his duties aboard the *Canton Packet*, a ship owned by Perkins, when his uncle came aboard and said, "Well, Ben, which of these ships do you intend to go in?" Bennet answered: "I am ready to go in this one." His uncle agreed and instructed Bennet to go home and tell his mother that he would soon join the ship's crew as a cabin boy; Bennet found his mother "much overcome" by the idea, "but when she saw that I had made up my mind to conform to the destiny imposed upon me by fate and my revered uncle, she gave her consent."

On October 19, 1817, the thirteen-year-old Forbes left home and sailed for China aboard the *Packet* as a cabin boy, "amidst the tears of the children" and his mother, who, despite having given her blessing, feared for her son's life. Initially, his second experience at sea was little better than the first; he became "deadly seasick" almost immediately and spent days in "tears and lamentations," crawling on deck in misery, "cold and exhausted." For days after that he lay in his bunk "ill and uncared for," while older, saltier crew members stole and ate his supply of apples. It would take nearly three weeks of "intense mental and bodily suffering" before he recovered.

One night, Forbes stood on deck transfixed by the enormous moon shining overhead, its golden glimmer playing upon the water. At this moment, he would later write, he found himself relishing the beauty of the open sea and the size of the world around him, and it awakened a sense that he was destined for bigger things. "I remembered that I was born to a higher purpose than merely keeping the bread from moulding," he wrote. He asked the captain for permission to go aloft and unfurl sails; when the captain assented, Forbes struggled up the riggings and performed the task, "I thought, very well."

After that success, the captain asked him to take a four-hour night watch and "ordered [him] to keep a good lookout for land." Forbes had "knowledge of geography, and knew there was no land near"—the captain was teasing and testing him.

Nonetheless, he was vigilant during the watch, keeping his eyes on the empty sea and the horizon beyond, and at midnight, when his watch tour finished, "went to my sweet sleep, feeling proudly conscious that I had actually begun my career as a sailor."

He was hooked.

The six-month voyage to Canton, China, began a seven-year odyssey as cabin boy and third mate that would take him to China several more times, as well as to the Philippines, Gibraltar, Rotterdam, Portugal, and London. He worked hard, performed his duties at a high level, turned over his meager wages to his parents, learned all he could about ships and the sea, earned the respect of his uncles—one of whom set aside $16,000 for Bennet when he came of age—and spent months and sometimes years away from home. His cousin John Cushing, who ran the Canton business operations of the family firm, recommended to Bennet's uncle that Bennet be promoted to an officer on the return voyage of the *Packet*. He wrote of the then fifteen-year-old Bennet: "He is, without exception, the finest lad I have ever known, and has already the stability of a man of thirty." Cushing also addressed a letter to Bennet's mother, in which he observed: "He already knows more than two-thirds of the ship masters . . . [he will be] at the head of his profession within a few years." He grew as a sailor and a businessman, but missed his mother and siblings dearly. He also lamented his poor relationship with his father.

Forbes's letters to his father are stilted, but between the lines it is clear that he longed for a more affectionate relationship. "My father's misfortunes in business, and constitution much broken by severe gout, had left him poor and dependent at a very early age," Forbes noted. "He had been so much away that we looked upon him as almost a stranger." In August 1822, not long before he turned eighteen, Forbes wrote his father from Rotterdam, saying he expected to be home within ten days. But plans changed overnight—Forbes's ship received orders to travel to London, load cargo, and proceed to China. "My disappointment is very great," he wrote. "I had fixed my mind on seeing home again this winter, but now I am in for another fourteen months' absence from all that is dear to me." Putting up a good front, Forbes recovered later in the note to his father: "Never mind. I can get over it as well as most people. I shall write again from London, but do not expect me for a year or two."

In the summer of 1824, Forbes had returned to Boston, where his uncle surprised him by saying that Forbes should command the *Levant*, a 264-ton schooner that was one of his uncle's favorites. Forbes, who would not turn twenty until September 18, questioned whether he was ready to captain a ship. His uncle replied: "If you are not fit . . . now, you never should be." During the next few months, Forbes assembled a crew and prepared the ship for its voyage, but was preoccupied with his father's poor health. "My father's health was entirely broken," he described. "He had fallen and fractured his arm, and it was evident to me that he could not long survive."

The *Levant* was scheduled to sail October 5 or 6, 1824, but Bennet's concerns about his father proved prophetic: Ralph Bennet Forbes died on October 5. Robert Bennet's last conversation with him was about his promotion to captain. "Go, my brave boy," Ralph said on his deathbed. "God will reward you. I die content in knowing that you and Tom are in a fair way of supporting your mother and the children."

Forbes's uncle agreed to delay the *Levant*'s departure until October 8, allowing Bennet to attend his father's funeral. Forbes recalled that he "slept but little that night, and rose early to take leave of the dear ones, and commence my responsibilities as captain at the early age of twenty."

The *Levant* shoved off that morning with cargo and several passengers aboard, one of whom, a Mr. Hopkins, became too ill to leave his berth. He deteriorated rapidly, and Forbes visited his cabin as Hopkins neared death. As his passenger struggled to draw his last breaths, Forbes showed him pictures of his two small daughters and tried to coax some last words from him—to no avail. "Placing my hand on his heart, I felt its last throb," Forbes recorded. "I could do no more."

It was the first death at sea that Forbes had witnessed, and he proceeded, in the midst of booming thunder and crackling lightning, to organize a hasty funeral for Hopkins. "A funeral at sea is a peculiarly solemn event," he wrote years later. The memory of his father's death fresh in his mind, Forbes tried to read a few words of prayer but was overcome.

His first mate took over, but he too could not continue; Forbes then resumed and finished the service. As the ship hove to, Hopkins's body, enclosed in a flag-draped coffin, was gently tossed overboard into the waiting sea. "All hands stood with bare heads and tearful eyes until the last plunge," Forbes noted. Hopkins's ordeal had a profound effect on Forbes. "The remembrance of my father's last days, and the new responsibilities connected with my early command, made this a hard trial for me," he said.

Forbes recalled that he had a "good crew" on his first voyage as captain. Never known for his modesty, he concluded that the crew "seemed to be favorably impressed with their young captain . . . who was known to them as 'the old man.'" One incident in particular convinced the crew that Forbes possessed the stuff of leadership. As the ship approached the coast of China, Forbes noticed several "suspicious-looking craft" disguised as junks closing in around his ship. "Not liking their movements, we made ready to repel them," Forbes reported. He ordered about twenty crew members to "lay low under the bulwarks, ready for action . . . with guns cast loose." One junk dispatched a skiff with two men and "a bunch of fish," ostensibly to trade, as the other junks drew closer to the *Levant*. But as the skiff operator came close, he saw Forbes's armed men ready to strike, and quickly turned his craft around, shouting to his junk and the others to flee. Forbes's crew members cheered. On his arrival in China, Forbes was "congratulated on our narrow escape, they being notorious pirates, who had captured several small vessels, and murdered their crews."

The *Levant* made it to China, and from there, Forbes sailed to Manila, where he connected with his brother Thomas, who ran the Perkins House business in the Philippines. Forbes was gratified to meet Thomas on "more equal terms." He shared the particulars of their father's death, and the brothers agreed that they owed much to their parents and realized "how much we must do for the education and maintenance of the younger members of the family." Their discussion was long and fulfilling for Robert. "We were drawn more intimately together than ever before," he wrote. Robert Bennet Forbes would meet Thomas once more, in April 1828 in China; his brother had taken over the Perkins business in Canton. "I parted from him with much regret," Robert Bennet recalled.

On August 9, 1829, a typhoon swamped and capsized the schooner Thomas was sailing from Canton to Macao. "A furious wave broke over her, and threw her sidelong among the roaring breakers," Robert Bennet wrote to his mother in an account he pieced together from eyewitnesses. He would feel the loss for years to come. "That he died when we were just *beginning* to feel like brothers has always been a source of great uneasiness to me," Bennet wrote on the tenth anniversary of Thomas's death.

Crushed by Thomas's death and now head of his family and its main breadwinner, Robert Bennet Forbes vowed always to care and provide for his mother and siblings. He pushed himself harder than ever as a ship's captain, embarking on lengthy voyages to China, Hawaii, the California coast, Mexico, Buenos Aires, Ecuador, Peru, the West Indies, Turkey, and the Greek archipelago. In the ten-year period between 1817 and 1827, Forbes estimated that he had "not been on shore more than six months," and much of that time had been spent in foreign ports, "very little at home." During a three-year absence from home he boasted of sailing "about 75,000 miles" but lamented that he had gone twenty-two months "without a letter from my family or my owners."

Forbes developed a reputation as a sailor's captain on the trip to China, and he never lost it. Because of his years of hard labor aboard ships, he always felt an affinity for his crews, and throughout his later years he worked to improve the lives of seamen. He would invent the famous "Forbes rig" for ships, which reduced the size of square sails and made them safer to handle, and he would one day author numerous papers and pamphlets on nautical safety.

By the time he returned home in 1832, Forbes was a wealthy man and ready to settle down. In 1833, in memory of Thomas and keeping his promise to care for the family, he built a house for his mother in Milton—complete with indoor plumbing. On January 20, 1834, he married Rose Greene Smith, and the couple settled into a house on Temple Place, a fashionable address in Boston. "At the age of 30, I had become gray, and imagined myself approaching old age," Forbes said. "I had retired from the sea professionally and had become a merchant," he said. "I began to think more of myself than I ever had done."

But for all of his accomplishments, Forbes was totally unprepared for the hardships he and Rose would face in the early days of their marriage. To help him deal with these, he was forced to un-retire and take to the sea again.

At the time, he was unsure their marriage—or Rose—would survive.

CHAPTER 5

"REMEMBER, DEAREST WIFE, THE TROUBLE AND MISERY OF THAT LAST YEAR"

Melancholy gripped Robert Bennet Forbes in a way he had never known on the evening of June 10, 1838, as the sails of the Perkins & Co. bark *Mary Chilton* caught the breeze and the ship skimmed over the soft swells of Boston Harbor toward the open sea. "I watched the sun set below the horizon and the eternal hills, too," he wrote to Rose, and felt the "fair wind that was wafting me away from all that I love."

The then thirty-three-year-old Forbes was embarking alone on a long trip to China, leaving behind Rose and their eight-month-old son, Robert, to whom they had affixed a trio of nicknames: "Bob," "Boy," and "Bennet." Forbes's younger brother, John Murray, had come to see him off, and when the two brothers said good-bye, Forbes wrote that the departure "seemed like the last link between life and death."

Separating from Rose and Bob at any time evoked anxiety in Forbes, but the forlorn familial and financial circumstances that forced this departure were especially painful. Since the joyful day of their marriage in 1834, Robert Bennet and Rose had battled bouts of fear and heartache, sandwiched around the glorious birth of Bob in October 1837, which seemed, at last, like a hopeful lifeline.

Bennet debated long and hard about leaving Rose to manage affairs at home—"if you were only here I should have nothing to ask for except *wind*," he wrote to her—but finally decided he had no choice. The financial fortunes of his family, and perhaps his own emotional health, depended on a successful voyage to the Far East.

"I am satisfied it is best," Forbes wrote to Rose. "Time will fly rapidly & we shall soon meet to part no more."

But neither sentiment would turn out to be true.

Rose and Robert Bennet Forbes were still consumed by the grief of having watched two of their previous children perish: a daughter, who was born and died on May 1, 1835, and a son, stillborn on October 1, 1836. The tragic deaths were one reason Rose and Robert Bennet considered Bob's arrival, one year after they lost a son, such a godsend. Forbes acknowledged the two deceased children in his letters during the long China voyages and wrote down their birth (and death) dates in his Bible, which was not discovered until 2019.

Other than these scant references, the two deceased children go unmentioned in the thousands of pages of Forbes journals, diaries, letters, and other correspondence; their communications during the China trip are the only time Bennet and Rose acknowledge the crippling sorrow brought on by the children's deaths. It's as though Bennet's 1838–40 trip to China served as a catharsis, allowing him and Rose, through the intimacy of heartfelt letters written across thousands of miles of separation, to invoke the memory of the children, share the pain of their deaths, and resolve to protect their sole remaining child with a steely fierceness.

In the hundreds of letters the two exchanged, one theme is irrefutable: vast distances and the rawness of great tragedy brought Robert Bennet and Rose Forbes closer together. The two agreed to pray at the same time on Sunday mornings, to write with as much detail and frequency as possible, and to leave out nothing in their correspondence. "I will write with tedious minuteness," Forbes acknowledged, adding that if Rose shared the letters with anyone, "be merciful—cut out any dull & trite sentiments." Forbes kept one of Bob's shoes hanging at the foot of his berth and tucked a lock of Rose's hair into the miniature framed portrait of her that stood atop his washstand. After Rose had sent a small portrait of Bob, delivered by another ship that rendezvoused with the *Mary Chilton*, Forbes wrote to thank her and informed her that "Bob is before me . . . I enjoy his society vastly more than that of the thousand cockroaches which infest my cabin." Writing to Rose, usually late in the evening after a busy day, assuaged his homesickness, and according to one family descendant, the habit "seems to be as essential to his well-being as eating and sleeping."

Throughout the voyage to China, Forbes's words reflected contradictory emotions. Some days he conveyed a palpable dread, fearing that in his absence tragedy would befall Rose or Bob; on others he dedicated paeans to Rose, laced with the poetry, romance, and playful flirtatiousness of Shakespearean sonnets. Some nights he expressed his hopefulness for the future; on others, with the ocean stretching black and endless before him, he was haunted by elegiac remembrances of the past. In some letters, he justified his long trip to China as the only way to reverse the family's disastrous financial fortunes of the past year; in others, he poured out his deep misgivings about his decision to leave his wife and son at a most fragile time.

"When I reflect that it costs us both such a pang to part for a few weeks, I can hardly believe that any circumstances would warrant this long a separation," he wrote to Rose on a late afternoon just twelve days into the journey. "Yet it is so, & we must make the best of it."

Forbes first broached the subject of the deceased children with Rose on Saturday, June 23, 1838, a fortnight into his journey. He mentioned that the previous evening he had recorded the birth dates of their children in his Bible and had reread a letter from Rose, the combination of which brought forth tears and difficult memories. "I must banish these intruders & seal them up," he wrote.

For both Bennet and Rose, this was easier said than done. She struggled with anxiety, depression, fear, and deep loneliness, especially in the first year of her husband's absence; Bennet knew of her struggles even as he set out on the voyage, but in many instances he lost patience with Rose in his letters. Five months into his journey, in November, he pleaded with Rose: "I hope you have followed up on your intention of bearing up—I am very anxious to hear of you." Later that same month, a dismayed Forbes received letters in Canton, China, from a Boston friend who reported: "I hear Rose is in great trouble, but I hope she may soon be more tranquil." In March 1839, Forbes received letters from Rose dated October 20–24 of the previous year in which she acknowledged contemplating suicide. In one, she confessed: "Were it not for you, I think I should long to sleep the sleep that knows no waking."

Unwilling or unable to fully grasp the severity of her condition— his insensitivity to her distress seems excessive even for an era in which the effects of psychological trauma were largely unknown—a distraught Forbes cautioned her that "if you get into a morbid state, it will be hard to get out of again, but I hope your depression was but momentary." He urged her to remember that *his* "happiness and success in my undertaking" depended on her state of mind: "If I have good accounts of you, I will be happy in spite of absence." In late May, he begged her to "take a great deal of exercise and keep up my old acquaintances" as a way to boost her spirits. "It is very important to me . . . that I find you younger on my return and not a moping desponding care worn body."

In the midst of endearments, he grew exasperated, almost scolding Rose with perhaps his most obtuse sentiment of the entire voyage: "I am convinced that you are reasonable and rationally happy & that you do not wish to fill me with pain & uneasiness by constantly introducing the subject of your lonely condition." After reading a letter from Rose dated December 27, 1839, in which she says she felt a little better "now that she has got through Christmas," Bennet replied, "I am glad you have had a good cry . . . remember, we are not the most unfortunate people in the world."

Even as Rose's physical health improved, she and Bennet regularly referenced and alluded to their lost children. Bennet mentioned a friend whose wife had given birth to twin daughters, referring to the event as "a catastrophe of twins." In another instance, Rose acknowledged her selfishness when a friend gave birth to a girl: "I can never hear of the birth of a daughter without a pang." Forbes desperately tried to shake her of such feelings from afar: "Cure yourself of such phantasies—why, there are born daily a million of daughters in the land & there is no reason you should have as many pangs."

Yet, 10,000 miles from Boston, Forbes was hardly immune to sadness and grief. He visited friends on Macao on Christmas Day and several children attended the gathering. This brought on thoughts of his own loss: "It made me feel strange to see the children and I have not called again," he confessed to Rose. On January 19, 1840, the day before his and Rose's sixth wedding anniversary, he wondered if he and Rose could take some positive life lessons from their financial woes and the deaths of their children. The fact that they had borne these together "showed how much we depended on each other" and "served to cement our affections." Such adversity, he tried to convince Rose, "has had a good effect on both of us. I have begun to read prayers every morning and think I feel the benefits already."

Nonetheless, despondent that he was thousands of miles from Rose, he promised: "I shall never be away from you another anniversary." Rose shared his sentiments and longed for his trip to come to an end. "When we meet again and my head rests on your shoulder," she wrote, "the flood gates will open."

The pain of losing two infants in the first thirty months of their marriage made life nearly unbearable for Bennet and Rose, but adding to their troubles—and the ultimate reason for Forbes's voyage to China and the couple's separation at the height of their grief—was the financial disaster they suffered during the depression of 1837. By the time he turned thirty in 1834, Forbes had amassed a fortune, built his mother a beautiful home in Milton, and all but retired from oceangoing mercantile activities. But he lost everything thanks to several poor investment decisions coupled with a financial downturn that, among other reasons, occurred in connection with President Andrew Jackson's decision not to renew the charter of the Bank of the United States.

"I had not acquired the art of saying 'no'" to requests for money, Forbes wrote. "I made several bad 'specs' in attempting to serve others."

In an episode that conjured up memories of his father's business misfortunes, Forbes lost more than $100,000 when he advanced money to a cousin for a risky nail-production factory in Pennsylvania after banks stopped lending funds during the financial crisis. The factory failed and the company's stock certificates "were not worth the paper on which they are printed," Forbes declared. He lost another $100,000 when he invested in silk from China, only to have potential buyers back out when the economy failed, unable to secure their own funding. Finally, Forbes dropped another $10,000 when he loaned his friend money to invest in a failed venture to transport sugar from Southeast Asia to the United States. "This was the last straw," Forbes wrote; he moved his family into a much smaller house on Mt. Vernon Street in Boston and decided to reclaim his fortune in the opium trade in China—then legal though controversial.

The Chinese government would eventually outlaw opium trafficking after addiction rates in the country skyrocketed—Forbes and other Western merchants were actually held as "house prisoners" at one point during his China visit. But because of his previous experience in China, and his overall merchant and shipping experience, Forbes believed a trip to China was the best and fastest way to "reclaim his competence" and stabilize his family's fiscal and emotional health, as well as quell his own anxiety. "Remember, dearest wife, the trouble and misery of that last year—be sure another like it would have killed me," he wrote. And while his departure for China while Rose was in such a "forlorn state" may have seemed cruel, "by coming here I have done all I could to retrieve my fortunes and procure an independence." Another day, after working on his account books for hours, Forbes admitted to Rose that "it makes me feel sick to remember those last days at home." Most of all, he felt it necessary to travel to China to ensure a healthy financial future for Bob. "When I get a competency again," he assured Rose, "I shall think little of style or location, but devote my means to the Boy if he is spared to us."

For certain he was conflicted about the voyage, especially considering Rose's fragile state of mind. He realized the risk of a lengthy sojourn. "Is it possible I am on a pilgrimage of years to the most distant land under the sun?" he asked Rose. "Is it I thats forsaken wife, child, home & all for filthy lucre? Why not have staid at home & got merely bread?"

But even as these thoughts crowded his mind, Forbes said, along came "my good (or evil) genius, which says: 'tis only for a short time, all will go well at home, & you will gain independence.' Hope I may—think I shall."

At sea he even imagined different visions of Rose, "recalling you not as we parted, nor as we *lived that last year*, but as you describe yourself now—playing with Bob or enjoying the society of our friends."

Forbes's trip to China was a rousing success. He earned close to $200,000 in the opium trade and other mercantile activities, and he implored Rose in a letter in April 1840 to be grateful for his decision to "forsake home & make one desperate effort at retrieving my losses." Moreover, he was coming home, deciding to cut his trip from a potential three-year journey to two and a half years. He would leave China in June or July and arrive in Boston in October or November. "I consider this decision as the most important of my exile & perhaps it may be the most important in my life (marriage excepted)," he wrote.

After an eventful five-month voyage aboard the *Niantic*—including a bout of brutal weather, a sick captain and crew, a need for Forbes to assume command at one point, and a gale storm off the coast of New Jersey as home beckoned—the ship sailed into New York Harbor, "the happiest hour of my life," he wrote to Rose in his final letter of the odyssey. From there, Forbes took a steamer to Boston, arriving home safely on December 11, 1840, well in time for Christmas, his finances and his family intact.

Years later he described his joy at reuniting with Rose and finding Bob "well grown & handsome." Since he had read Rose's bleakest letters early in his voyage, her condition had improved dramatically and Boy was the picture of health—he could not be more thankful.

"I had much, in thus rejoining my beloved family, to be grateful for," Forbes wrote. "And I was grateful."

Forbes's reunion with Rose and Boy was emotional but short-lived.

He had one more obligation to fulfill before he could settle down. In March 1841, after his return from China, he sailed to Europe for three months with his benefactor and uncle, Thomas H. Perkins, who was now an old man of seventy-six. Once again, he left Rose at home with Boy; perhaps even more concerning, Rose was three months pregnant. Forbes visited London, Paris, and the Netherlands to deal with business issues.

Little in the way of documentation exists about this European voyage, including Rose's reaction, but we can infer that she was not happy about it and said so—for after Forbes returned home in May 1841, he remained in Boston for the next five years. Tragedy also struck the couple again, which likely played a role in Forbes's decision to remain close and Rose's insistence that he do so: on September 27, 1841, Rose's pregnancy again ended in heartache when she delivered a stillborn baby boy, the third child the couple had lost in six years.

Forbes recorded the date and the sad event on the first page of his Bible, the only information that exists about the unnamed infant.

Life definitely improved for the Forbes family after the tragedy in the fall of 1841. Their son, Boy, continued to thrive, and Forbes, now fully restored financially, busied himself by buying and selling ships and becoming one of Boston's leading civic-minded citizens. Then, as though God were making up for the pain of the past, fortune smiled twice more when Edith Forbes was born in March 1843 and another son, James Murray, was born in July 1845.

At the end of 1846, with tragedy and uncertainty behind them, the Forbes family now seemed the picture of domestic bliss. Bennet had reclaimed his position as a Boston business leader and one of the country's foremost experts on ships; Rose's anxieties had diminished and her physical condition improved; the three Forbes children were happy and healthy.

After enduring years of extraordinary strife, it seemed Robert Bennet and Rose Forbes would now enjoy the contentment of daily ordinary life.

Then on January 20, 1847, when the weather cleared and the ice broke, the packet ship *Hibernia* arrived in Boston Harbor from England—the first vessel in more than a month bringing news and stories from Ireland, of unparalleled suffering, of disease and death, of hopelessness and utter despair among men, women, and, most gruesome of all, children.

And for the Forbes family, as well as the rest of America, everything changed.

CHAPTER 6

"THE CALAMITIES OF IRELAND . . .
HAVE TOUCHED
ALL AMERICAN HEARTS"

ODD FELLOWS HALL, WASHINGTON, D.C., FEBRUARY 9, 1847

D aniel Webster approached the stage as audience members shifted forward in their seats and murmured in anticipation. Even at the age of sixty-five, the legendary statesman—a U.S. senator from Massachusetts once again—could still command a room.

Intellectually, oratorically, and physically, he was one of the most imposing figures of his era, a period that spanned more than three decades of public service. Tall, broad-chested, with a massive forehead, jet-black hair, and deep-set black eyes that blazed with luminous intensity, his physical presence alone could transfix audiences and earned him the nickname "Godlike Daniel" among his admirers.

A graduate of Dartmouth College and a lawyer by training, Webster was first elected to Congress in 1813, and became a U.S. senator in 1827, before resigning in 1841 to serve as secretary of state under William Henry Harrison and John Tyler (an office he would hold again in 1850 until his death in 1852). He rejoined the Senate when the Massachusetts legislature elected him again in 1844. Throughout his time in the upper chamber of Congress, he was regarded as one of a triumvirate of giants, along with fellow Whig Henry Clay of Kentucky—who had since left the Senate—and the irrepressible John C. Calhoun of South Carolina.

As a master rhetorician, Webster blended a patrician's artistry of structure and linguistic elegance with burning passages and ringing crescendos that compelled workingmen to leap to their feet shaking their fists, waving their hats, and roaring their full-throated approval. He had argued cases before the Supreme Court, where his eloquence, command of facts, strength of logic, and thunderous voice won over justices. Those same qualities—though his voice had become less sonorous as he aged—electrified audiences; his speeches, thoughtful and persuasive and dramatic, were unpredictable, too, making them even more effective. Bankers and blacksmiths, friends and enemies, northerners and southerners traveled far afield to hear him speak.

One of his most famous oratorical feats had come during the so-called nullification debates of 1830, when South Carolina, declaring that federal tariffs were unconstitutional, had threatened to secede. His crowning reply to South Carolina senator Robert Hayne, which concluded with the words "Liberty and union, now and forever, one and inseparable!," would be memorized throughout the nineteenth century by American schoolboys of all stripes, whether clad in waistcoats at prestigious private institutions or seated in worn overalls at their desks in drafty one-room cabins, their cold bare feet resting on hard-packed dirt floors.

In a golden age of American oratory—Henry Clay excelled, as did statesman Edward Everett of Massachusetts, and abolitionists Charles Sumner, Theodore Parker, and a young, emerging Frederick Douglass— Webster sparkled brightest, a master mesmerizer, a force who moved hearts, opened minds, stirred souls.

Thus, expectations were high among members of the crowd that had gathered in the large second-floor meeting room of the Odd Fellows Hall in the nation's capital. He'd been invited by Vice President George M. Dallas, who hoped he would by force of argumentation win over the assembled cast of senators, congressmen, and other political heavyweights. Many of them had heard Webster speak before; the others knew of his legendary ability to move a room. All anticipated his evocative imagery and his formidable powers of persuasion.

The venue was a perfect setting for the virtuoso to work—a room that measured forty-two by seventy feet, with twenty-foot-high ceilings, no obstructions, and clear acoustics, symbolically fitting for the moral clarity Webster would bring to his topic.

President Polk opened the proceedings, telling the audience that he "rejoiced" to see so many respond to his call for a meeting to express national sympathy "for the suffering of a people upon whom a great calamity had fallen."

Now it was Webster's turn to impart the gravity of the moment. He walked to the rostrum, waited for the applause to dissipate, and leaned forward. The audience quieted in anticipation.

"A famine, bringing want and distress on a great portion of a whole people, is unprecedented in Christendom in this age," Webster began with characteristic boldness. "The calamities of Ireland have been heard and read throughout the country, and have touched all American hearts."

His purported role was to report the recommendations of the Committee for the Relief of the Suffering Poor of Ireland, a hastily conceived but bipartisan effort launched in mid-January once ships began arriving from Ireland with news of the famine. Established by President Polk, the committee was chaired by Vice President Dallas and consisted of national political luminaries including Webster and fellow senators Calhoun (South Carolina), John J. Crittenden (Kentucky), Lewis Cass (Michigan), and Simon Cameron (Pennsylvania), as well as three dozen more lawmakers, lawyers, and business leaders.

Webster would get to the committee's suggestions, but he appealed first to the crowd's humanitarian instincts. He pointed out that improvements in communication "have brought nations into nearer neighborhood with each other." Therefore, Americans could "hear the cries of suffering Ireland almost as fresh and as strong as if they had come from a part of our own country." Webster had devoted his life and his energy to keeping the Union intact; he vigorously opposed nullification early in his career, detested slavery, and objected to the Mexican

War as little more than an excuse by southern states to expand the institution. Within three years, he would craft the Compromise of 1850 with the singular goal of preserving the Union, though in his zeal to do so he would fail to foresee how the act's renewed enforcement of the Fugitive Slave Law—essentially requiring northern complicity in the capture of runaway slaves and their return to bondage—would outrage abolitionists, unsettle moderates, and drive the country closer to civil war, precisely the opposite of his intent. Second only to the law's passage, his declaration that "the union stands firm" would be his greatest and most sorrowful political miscalculation.

And yet, at his best, Webster imbued Americans with a deep sense of noble nationality, of *nationhood*, of pride in their country despite its regional and sectional differences and quarrels. He returned to those themes now.

Webster reminded his audience that America had bestowed many blessings upon its people, and he urged them to open their hearts to the plight of foreign neighbors. "In this land of abundance, we know nothing, by our own experiences, of famine," he said, "and can hardly conceive of people dying—in families and by groups—through want of food." He cited details, "apparently authentic"—by now, several ships had docked in Boston, New York, and elsewhere bringing news of conditions in Ireland—"of the shocking distress" the Irish people faced. America had a duty to help, and not just in piecemeal ways.

"It is a fit time for the activity and exertion of a national charity," Webster said, "and the flying moment should not be lost."

Webster's appeal was one of several that Americans had heard in the past week.

His former Senate colleague Henry Clay had accepted a speaking invitation in New Orleans on February 4 to address the Irish situation, where he urged New Orleans residents to engage in a "generous and magnanimous effort to contribute to the relief of sufferings" in Ireland. He reminded his audience of the "appalling and heart-rending" crisis, and of the indignity of starvation, so unlike a soldier dying "gloriously for [one's] country" on the battlefield; in the latter case, "poets, painters, sculptors, historians will record his deeds of valor and perpetuate his renown." Conversely, death by starvation "comes slow, lingering, and excruciating," and its victims often died alone in the dark corners of a mud hut or city alleyway.

Clay argued that the magnitude of Ireland's suffering mandated that New Orleans—"the world's storehouse of an exhaustless supply of all kinds of food" transported down the Mississippi—rise to the occasion and contribute "liberally" to Irish relief. "It is not fervid eloquence, nor gilded words, that Ireland needs—but substantial food," Clay concluded. An Irishman who heard the speech later wrote to Clay, thanking him for inspiring charitable giving that likely saved "thousands of our countrymen from a death of agony and horror."

Days later, on February 7, Boston's Roman Catholic bishop, John Bernard Fitzpatrick, who had heard harrowing tales of the famine carried by the recently arrived *Hibernia*, ascended the pulpit of the Holy Cross Cathedral and in a voice "saturated with emotion and sorrow" read his first pastoral letter, which described conditions in Ireland, focusing on the plight of children, and pleaded with the congregation, many of whom were Irish immigrants, to put aside political disputes—"it is vain and idle . . . to discuss the duties of Parliaments and landlords"—and focus instead on the humanitarian effort. Failure to do so would make "us faithless to our obligations as Christians." He called upon his congregation to share their "last loaf of bread" with those sad souls whose "wild shrieks of famine and despair" could be heard across the Atlantic.

According to one report, when Fitzpatrick finished, "a terrible silence filled the church" as the stunned congregation reflected on the bishop's message. While silent, these immigrant parishioners likely recollected their hard times in Ireland, "but here, in vivid terms [was] . . . a situation more serious than any they had imagined or experienced." Finally the silence was replaced by "weeping and anguished prayer."

Later, another priest, reading Fitzpatrick's letter, reportedly broke down under the emotional strain, "his cheeks wet with uncontrollable sorrow."

Now, five days after Clay had spoken at New Orleans, two days after Fitzpatrick's remarks, and at the conclusion of his own impassioned appeal, Daniel Webster told his Washington audience that speechmaking and sermonizing were insufficient—he urged that the nation swiftly act upon the committee's recommendations.

The suggestions were at once concise and comprehensive: that the mayor of New York establish a committee responsible for accepting charitable contributions from his city and from the nation's interior; that the mayor of New Orleans accept local donations and contributions from towns and outposts along the Mississippi that could ship their goods downriver; that the mayors of Boston, Baltimore, Philadelphia, and Washington, D.C., establish committees to accept donations in their cities, and that Boston's committee also handle contributions from across New England. And finally, "that it be recommended to the inhabitants of all [other] cities, towns, and villages in the United States" to appoint committees and receive contributions, and forward them to the "general committees" in New York and New Orleans.

Echoing Henry Clay's New Orleans message, Webster emphasized to his audience that the committee's goal was rapid emergency action, not political grandstanding. "Our object is not ostentation or parade," he made clear, "not to utter the sounds of empty brass or of tinkling cymbals, but to do a deed of effectual charity, and to do it promptly."

The next morning, the Washington committee dispatched a letter, signed by Webster and several others, to mayors in Boston, Baltimore, New York, Philadelphia, and New Orleans, officially requesting them to take on the responsibility of accepting and organizing donations on behalf of Irish relief. Citing "all the feelings of humanity" and "a deep sense of duty," the letter stressed that "no time is to be lost" and emphasized that "to give usefully and beneficially, we must give quickly. Every day's delay more and more embitters human suffering—and endangers human life."

No public funds would be involved and the letter was framed as a request, but the fact that the unprecedented appeal came from the nation's capital and the mass meeting was attended by the country's leading political luminaries had far-reaching and almost immediate impact. Relief committees were quickly established in key cities, and financial donations followed from Baltimore, Philadelphia, and Charleston; Baltimore's relief committee noted that the bulk of the contributions were made by "many hard-working Irishmen, who earn their bread by the sweat of their brow." New York quickly raised funds for Irish relief among both its Catholic and non-Catholic residents, with a promise for additional relief in succeeding weeks. Cincinnati was one of the first cities in the interior to form a relief committee, and by mid-March would raise more than $12,000. Committees in both New York City and Philadelphia expected additional donations—in money and possibly food—from the interior of their states and other places as soon as canals and rivers thawed and became navigable again.

Smaller cities followed; relief committees were organized quickly in Albany, Chicago, Rochester, Richmond, Louisville, Providence, Natchez, Alexandria, and many others. Hamlets and small towns also took heed of Webster's initial plea. The committee in Pottsville, Pennsylvania, near Philadelphia, raised money, and in Galena, Illinois, local women—who were praised as "Sisters of Charity" in one newspaper—led the donation effort on behalf of Ireland. In Cooperstown, New York, author James Fenimore Cooper, a celebrity since his publication of *The Last of the Mohicans* in 1826, presided over a fundraising meeting, while students at Georgetown University organized a school-wide collection for famine relief.

But nowhere was the response as multipronged and vociferous as in Boston, whose reach included efforts across Massachusetts and New England. This was partly because the region's already large Irish Catholic population increased its donations through parish fundraising efforts, encouraged by the sermons and pleadings of priests; partly because Massachusetts progressives felt that strong support for a humanitarian effort would serve as a salve for their anger about the Mexican War; and partly due to the guilt felt by Boston's literati and intellectual core about the mistreatment of Irish immigrants who had already arrived in Boston. In addition, that same group of educators, writers, religious leaders, and abolitionists prided itself on its support of progressive causes in general, including prison reform, mental health reform, and, of course, the growing anti-slavery movement. Writers in Boston, Concord, and across Massachusetts—Henry David Thoreau, Ralph Waldo Emerson, Nathaniel Hawthorne, Henry Wadsworth Longfellow, Herman Melville, John Greenleaf Whittier, Louisa May Alcott, and Emily Dickinson—all gave voice to Boston's Irish relief efforts, as did abolitionists Charles Sumner, Harriet Beecher Stowe, and William Lloyd Garrison.

So it was no surprise when the thirty-nine-year-old Whittier penned a letter immediately following the Washington, D.C., meeting that appeared in the February 11 *Boston Courier*. "The head is sick and the heart is faint in view of this dreadful apocalypse of woe," the poet wrote of the Irish crisis. "Wise legislation in the past might have prevented the great calamity . . . but our duty to relieve present suffering is none the less imperative."

Whittier called for an immediate public meeting to organize Boston's response and engage its leading citizens in Irish relief efforts; such a moral crisis demanded nothing less. Two days later, the *Boston Atlas* echoed Whittier's call for a meeting of "all classes of our fellow citizens at Faneuil Hall to take measures for instant and effective relief of Ireland." The paper reviewed the latest reports brought by the ship *Sarah Sands* from across the Atlantic and acknowledged the reality of the famine: "All suspicions that . . . the accounts . . . have been exaggerated must now be dispelled," the editor declared. "Something must be done—done promptly, substantially, and effectively."

Ordinary Boston citizens also picked up the cry for residents of all backgrounds and faiths to come together to address a crisis unlike any they had seen. A letter to the *Boston Post* urged the writer's fellow citizens to lay aside political differences and blame for the crisis, and to act upon the ages-old biblical precept that "from those to whom much is given, much shall be required."

These appeals and many others led to an extraordinary Boston mass meeting on February 18 that set the stage for America's first full-scale humanitarian mission.

CHAPTER 7

"I BESEECH YOU—
WHAT YOU DO, DO QUICKLY"

FEBRUARY 18, 1847, FANEUIL HALL, BOSTON

Some newspaper reports put the Faneuil Hall throng at 4,000, but Robert Bennet Forbes estimated that by 7:30 p.m. on this raw winter evening, nearly 5,000 prominent Bostonians had filled the historic room, the men standing shoulder to shoulder on the wooden floor of the great hall, the women crowded into the second-floor galleries. Hundreds of additional Boston citizens, unable to squeeze through the doors, went home disappointed, weaving their way in the darkness past tethered horses harnessed to private carriages outside of Boston's most prestigious meeting place.

Forbes, who arrived at the meeting with his younger brother, John, looked up at the portraits on the wall, later recounting how they stirred his patriotism. John Hancock, Samuel Adams, James Otis—all of them reminded Forbes that he was inside Boston's "Cradle of Liberty," a revered hall "where the voice of the oppressed, and the voice of the free, has always been heard since the days of the dawn of our independence." Here, mere yards from the ships and the docks and the ocean that Forbes loved, American colonists had first met to protest the Sugar Act and the Stamp Act; Boston's angry citizenry had come to protest the killing of five civilians by British soldiers in what would become known as the Boston Massacre; and the Sons of Liberty had first resolved "to do the utmost ... to prevent the landing of the tea," a decision that would provoke the Boston Tea Party. Within a few years, renowned abolitionists such as Frederick Douglass, Lucy Stone, Charles Sumner, and William Lloyd Garrison would bring their own calls for freedom to Faneuil Hall.

It was a venue of great causes, and tonight Boston's leading citizens and working people alike gathered at the behest of Mayor Josiah Quincy Jr. and other members of Boston's non-Irish elite to consider ways of sending aid to Ireland and bringing hope to the famine-stricken country's despondent people.

But the fact that the meeting was called at all, in Boston of all places, was astounding.

When Charles Dickens visited Boston in 1842 he might have had the Irish in mind when he told guests at a dinner in his honor: "Virtue shows quite well in rags and patches as she does in fine linen ... she goes barefoot as well as shod ... she dwells rather oftener in alleys and byways than she does in courts and palaces." He urged his audience to "lay [your] hands upon those rejected ones whom the world has too long forgotten," and to understand that "these creatures have the same elements and capacities of goodness as yourselves."

But when it came to Irish immigrants in Boston, Dickens's message went unheeded.

Thousands of poor Irish immigrants had already arrived in Boston by February 1847 (the remainder of 1847 through 1849 would bring thousands more), and they met a nativist reaction born of fear, suspicion, ignorance, and prejudice. Boston's closed Protestant, Yankee society, its deep anti-Catholicism, its educated literati—all of these were completely foreign to, and conspired against, the bedraggled Irish who stepped weakly off lice-ridden famine ships and sought refuge among Boston's narrow streets.

Beginning in earnest years earlier with the ransacking and torching destruction of the Ursuline Convent in nearby Charlestown in 1834,

Boston—the Athens of America, one of the most progressive and educated locales in the New World (or the Old World, for that matter)—rejected the Irish with an unprecedented, unrelenting, white-hot vitriol that left the newcomers dispirited and disillusioned. The Irish battled poverty, illness, ridicule, humiliation, and religious and ethnic hatred in Boston. Men encountered "Positively No Irish Need Apply" signs at warehouses, workshops, hotels, factory gates, fishing boats, and restaurants; women saw the same restriction in classified ads seeking domestic help to care for children.

Irish Catholicism also frightened Puritan Boston. Newspapers warned of undue international influence, particularly from the papacy, and a sinister surge of popery and "Romanism" in Boston. The *Boston Courier* warned its readers that politically active Catholics of foreign birth would vote "precisely as their spiritual guides shall dictate." The paper had blamed the 1844 election of James K. Polk on the influence of Catholic priests who were part of a "well-connected scheme" among the Catholic powers in Europe to bring the United States "under subjection to the Holy See."

In short, the new Irish arrivals were aliens in every sense. The thousands of poor, unskilled, famine-weary immigrants threatened the very social structure and rigidly defined hierarchy of Boston, cocooned in its snug parochialism, lorded over by the people who organized the February 18 Faneuil Hall meeting—wealthy urban aristocrats whom Oliver Wendell Holmes labeled "Brahmins."

Historian Thomas O'Connor pointed out that this made life for the Boston Irish uniquely difficult. Irish immigrants who traveled to Chicago, St. Louis, and other new cities of what was then called the American West had the advantage of growing up with their cities. Those who settled in New York and Philadelphia lived among populations that were socially, economically, and ethnically more diverse in their origins and more receptive in their attitudes. Further, those cities' larger geographic footprint provided the Irish newcomers with more space to settle without infringing on either nativist neighborhoods or downtown commercial centers; this relieved tensions and provided the Irish additional time to become accustomed to urban American culture.

In Boston, however, a destitute and downtrodden Irish underclass confronted homogenous and wealthy Brahmin elites who dominated political and civic life, and because of the city's relatively small size, the two cultures abutted each other and clashed almost immediately. Dealing harshly with an Irish underclass was a way for Boston's old guard to fiercely cling to power (it is also worth noting, perhaps, that Boston's liberality and abolitionist reputation notwithstanding, its 1847–48 city directory of residents still listed "People of Color" under a separate heading that began on page 230). Purported progressives such as Thoreau initially believed the Irish were foolish, superstitious, and shiftless; the Reverend Theodore Parker, so compassionate and tolerant in his abolitionist beliefs, found the Irish to be "idle, thriftless, poor, intemperate, and barbarian," more like a group of "wild bison" than human beings.

And yet despite all of this, once news of the full extent of Ireland's suffering reached America's shores in early 1847, something remarkable happened: Bostonians of all stripes responded with outsized, unbridled, and nearly unanimous warmth and generosity.

Whether frustrated by war and slavery, inspired to work together in a common purpose, persuaded by Daniel Webster's appeal at the Washington, D.C., meeting, or moved by the appeal of a humanitarianism that sought to cure social and economic ills—or maybe a combination of all—the city's most prominent residents found the famine news heartbreaking and the desire to help a compelling sacred duty.

"Cities, towns, villages—whether near or remote—have been deeply stirred and are coming to the rescue in the spirit of universal brotherhood," William Lloyd Garrison wrote in February.

Whittier, too, was impressed with the widespread support for Irish relief: "Surely there is good in all; the hardest heart is not wholly stone."

Mayor Josiah Quincy, who hosted and chaired the February 18 meeting, provided another reason for embarking on a full-blown effort to assist Ireland in his opening remarks. He suggested to the packed room that assisting England "in feeding her starving children" would be a step toward lasting peace with America's former enemy.

Not only had America battled England during the revolution and the War of 1812, but the two countries were squabbling over the Oregon Territory, and the United States had bristled over British meddling during the annexation of Texas and the war with Mexico. Perhaps assisting the Irish people with their most basic needs would be a "harbinger of that day foretold in prophecy—'when nation shall no longer lift up the sword against nation.'" Quincy urged the crowd to extend its charity to relieve Irish suffering and offer hope to a people mired in despair.

Others followed Quincy to the platform with similar messages; each called upon those in the crowd to draw upon Boston's philanthropic sensibilities and business acumen to devise practical and rapid plans for Irish relief. Forbes later described how inspired he was to hear the "bursts of eloquence from experienced orators and full hearts."

Most experienced and inspirational of all was the final speaker of this memorable night, the man who, like Daniel Webster, had elevated oratory to an art form during his years of service in Boston as a university teacher, a congressman, a governor of Massachusetts, an envoy to Great Britain, and currently president of Harvard University. One day he would become a senator and then secretary of state, and be renowned for his two-hour oration at the dedication of the Union cemetery at Gettysburg. For now, Edward Everett—whose greatest strength, according to Oliver Wendell Holmes, was the "full-blown, high-colored . . . rich, resonant, grave, far-reaching music of his voice"—stepped before the thousands assembled at Faneuil Hall and began to speak.

Forbes would later say that Everett's appeal served as the "key by which the hearts of the citizens of Boston were in some degree unlocked." What Webster had accomplished in Washington, D.C., the estimable Everett achieved to an even greater extent in Boston.

Described by one historian as "the imposing Ciceronian figure of his day," Edward Everett possessed an accumulation of rich and eclectic talents that added up to oratorical gold: an actor's stage presence, a philosopher's wisdom, a politician's canniness, a nobleman's gravitas, a poet's gift for imagery, a bookkeeper's attention to detail, and a preacher's ability to summon fire and brimstone at the opportune moment.

These attributes, along with the richness of his superior voice that so impressed Holmes, were his greatest strengths; he also displayed brimming confidence tempered with enough humility to suggest a whiff of vulnerability, which endeared him and his message to his listeners. The underlying theme of much of his discourse was that he had answers, but not *all* the answers. Could his audience fill in the gaps?

Unlike Webster's, Everett's oratory was typically florid and lengthy— two hours was not unusual—and he often delivered his words with a fiery animation that left him exhausted at the conclusion of his speeches. Tonight, though, his remarks would be short and somber, the gloomy subject matter itself making overt showmanship inappropriate.

He began by identifying not just the scope of the Irish problem, but the dilemma in trying to define its magnitude. Speaking about the hunger in general terms "fail[s] to bring the dreadful reality of things with sufficient vividness to our minds." On the other hand, any attempt to repeat "horrid details" of starvation posed the danger of "plunging into scenes too dreadful" to recount in public. So he began with a recitation of facts. More than 2 million people in Ireland subsisted almost exclusively on potatoes, and under the most prosperous circumstances, these people "live on the borders of starvation." The failure of the potato crop for two "disastrous seasons" had left "nothing to fall back on." Every wretched substitute for wholesome food—"bark, roots, apple parings, turnip skins—have been exhausted, and now famine in all its horrors stalks through the land," he said. And so the alarming questions: "How is want to be supplied? How are the horrors of general starvation to be staved off?"

To which Everett supplied his own answer: "Heaven knows."

It was not for the assembly before him to answer the larger question of how to end starvation in Ireland; Everett pointed out that the "wisest heads in England and Ireland seem confounded at the extent of the evil." History had shown that widespread famine often produced irrational behavior, he pointed out. Seeds for corn and potatoes, meant to be planted, were instead consumed as food, thereby threatening the next harvest and extending the disaster. With food so scarce, "those who have little will hoard; those who have nothing will plunder." Perhaps these actions were inevitable—and perhaps it was true that "no individual, no community can do much to relieve the sum total of this mighty calamity."

But, Everett added quickly, "every community, every individual can do *something*," and the aggregate of these "somethings" could provide "the only stay of famishing millions."

Indeed, he implored the crowd, "don't tell me we can do but little, when the *little* that we and others can do is the *all* of a starving country."

Next, Everett echoed Webster, emphasizing the comparative abundance and prosperity of the United States, and in particular of Bostonians, a theme that would be repeated at similar meetings around the country. Everett said he would be "deeply grieved" if anyplace in America would "stand higher than Boston" in contributing to Irish relief. Everett regarded providing assistance to Ireland as a "high and sacred" duty, one that, if neglected, would bring "the walls of our warehouses, filled almost to bursting with every article of food," tumbling down, "crush[ing] us as we passed."

He implored them to remember what should be considered unthinkable: that Ireland's starvation was taking place *not* in the Dark Ages, not in the Middle Ages, not in an era of knights and castles and dungeons and plagues, but "in the nineteenth century; in this all-daring, all-achieving, all-boasting nineteenth century—an astonished Europe and astonished America stand looking on, paralyzed by the extent of the calamity."

America could change that.

Boston could change that.

In the last two weeks, he declared, "a spirit of Christian charity has been awakened," first in Washington, then in cities and towns north and south and west, and now Faneuil Hall was the place it would "burn with fervor."

Everett ended not with a soaring crescendo but with a plea for urgency: "I beseech you—what you do, do quickly," pointing out that even if Boston acted immediately, "not a barrel of flour . . . can be laid down within the Cove of Cork [in] under six weeks at the very soonest," due to uncertain winter sailing conditions and a paucity of privately owned ships whose owners would be willing to undertake charitable missions. Most shipowners were engaged in commercial activities, including—ironically—transporting corn and other goods to Europe and the British Isles, an arrangement profitable to merchants on both sides of the Atlantic, but of little help to starving Irish without means to purchase food or anything else.

In addition, the increase in mercantile shipping and commerce between the United States and Europe had added to the scarcity of private vessels. Searching for an appropriate vessel would be time-consuming; Everett entreated the audience to make haste in securing any available ships, else the very families that charity was designed to save "will have perished before it gets there."

His somber conclusion rang out through Faneuil Hall and drove home the perils of inaction or delay: "While I fill your ears with these empty words, some of our poor fellow-Christians in Ireland have starved to death."

Virtually overnight, two significant actions occurred as a result of the Faneuil Hall meeting.

First, the assembly established a Boston-based relief committee, formally called the New England Committee for the Relief of Ireland and Scotland (NECRIS)—Scotland was also suffering from the potato blight—whose responsibilities included organizing relief efforts and accepting contributions from across the city and across New England.

Second, the Forbes brothers took Everett's words to heart—Robert Bennet would later say that Everett's speech provided "much of the inspiration" for all that followed. Moments after the great orator finished, Robert Bennet and John huddled to hatch the outline of a bold and unorthodox plan intended to bring assistance to Ireland as swiftly as possible. They shared their thoughts with Mayor Quincy and Abbott Lawrence, textile magnate and prominent Whig, who had been named vice president of the relief committee.

On Sunday, February 21, three days after the Faneuil Hall gathering, Forbes shared the plan formally in a letter to Lawrence: "We think that if your Committee would petition Congress at once" to make a warship available for the Irish relief effort, "the subscriptions in flour, grain, and provisions would be sent to them as they could be stowed away." For speed's sake, due to the shortage of merchant vessels, it was preferable to retrofit a warship that currently sat idle in the Navy Yard awaiting upgrades and improvements to become seaworthy.

To this point, virtually all aid to Ireland had been in the form of money—the notion of loading a ship with direct aid was something new. But the timing was right. Food was more expensive in England and Ireland, meaning dollar contributions did not go as far; it would take precious time for British authorities to purchase food and deliver it to the people who needed it; and even when it was purchased, bureaucratic delays and perhaps fraud could delay or sabotage shipments or derail the purchase of food.

And each day's delay could mean the deaths of hundreds of people.

In fact, Father Mathew had already expressed these thoughts in a letter thanking an American businessman for monetary contributions to Ireland. "Tenfold more effectual would American aid be if, out of your abundance, bread-stuffs were shipped for Ireland instead of money," he wrote. "We are in the deadly grasp of corn monopolists, who compel starving creatures to pay . . . for what could be purchased in your country for little more than one-third of the famine price."

Forbes also believed that New Englanders would be more generous with food than dollars. "Many a man who would not subscribe his ten or twenty dollars would send his barrel or two, or his few bushels of grain," he wrote in a letter to the editor on February 22, "and in a few days [the] stevedore would have to cry, 'hold, enough.'"

Further, the race to fill the ship's holds with food would bring enthusiasm and a healthy competitive spirit to the Irish relief effort as contributors saw tangible evidence of their donations delivered to the docks. "I am confident that all sorts of supplies would be sent to [the ship] in sufficient quantities to load her speedily."

He also surmised that volunteers would flock to man a warship that would be used for charitable purposes, especially with Boston's general opposition to the Mexican War. "Many a hardy web-footed citizen, who would flee from the drum and fife of the recruiting sergeant, would enroll himself under the flag of suffering humanity," Forbes contended. With trained and experienced navy personnel already engaged on warships off the coast of Mexico, civilian volunteers would relish the chance to "stow the cargo, bring it to the ship, caulk down her hatchways, pilot her to sea on her mission of merciful duty—and few . . . would demand or expect money for these services."

Moreover, if Congress approved the loan of one or more naval vessels to the merchants of Boston, "I should be glad to command one," Forbes offered to Abbott.

Forbes even assured Lawrence that he would "freely trust myself and our donations" aboard the historic USS *Constitution*—Old Ironsides—which had just returned from a long voyage. He also noted that the "*Jamestown* sloop is almost ready for sea."

Lawrence quickly forwarded Forbes's letter to Mayor Quincy, who gathered signatures of Boston's principal merchants. On February 22— George Washington's birthday—Lawrence petitioned Boston's U.S. representative, Robert C. Winthrop, requesting the loan of the *Jamestown* for the Irish relief voyage. Winthrop filed the unprecedented petition in Congress the same day. There is no documentation indicating why Mayor Quincy shied away from requesting the *Constitution*, but it is likely that he wished to avoid the potential political backlash the Boston committee might face in Washington if it recommended that a civilian captain pilot the navy's best-known and oldest commissioned warship, whose performance during the War of 1812 was already ensconced in American military lore.

Forbes was more than content with the *Jamestown* recommendation. "She is the very thing we want for this purpose," he wrote in a separate letter to Congressman Winthrop, "perhaps better adapted to carrying out the donations of Boston than any other vessel in the Navy. She can carry about the bulk of 8,000 barrels, without her armament, and this is the amount we expect to raise for her."

With war against Mexico raging, with ships gathering for a battle off Veracruz, Forbes knew that Winthrop might have hesitations about loaning the *Jamestown* for a mission of charity. He sought to assure the congressman that his constituents in Boston supported the measure. "I dare say the idea may be considered *absurd* in Washington," Forbes wrote, "but it is here a very *popular* idea." With enthusiasm that would have made Rose blanch, he added: "Nothing would give me more pleasure than to volunteer in the business, and go to Ireland."

Again, Forbes stressed the need for urgency, though he admitted he was skeptical of Congress's ability to move fast: "I *hope* you will be able to get a bill through by acclamation," he wrote to Winthrop, "but I *fear* the pressing business before Congress will exclude any action on this subject."

CHAPTER 8

⌒━✦━⌒

"Europe stretches her hand to America for aid"

LATE FEBRUARY 1847, WASHINGTON, D.C.

Congress surprised Forbes, Mayor Quincy, and the entire Boston committee when it took up the Irish question just two days later, February 24. It was not just Winthrop's petition to loan the *Jamestown* that prompted the swift action, but two additional near-simultaneous actions.

First, the mayor of New York City and New York ship captain George C. DeKay, a former officer in the Argentine navy, requested Congress to grant the use of the war frigate *Macedonian* for an Irish relief voyage. The petition, nearly identical to the Boston committee's request, stressed that a direct food aid mission was a matter "not only of mercy but of DUTY to our starving brethren and sisters of Ireland." Whether the New York request was coincidental or officials had received word of the Boston activity (Forbes visited New York City on either February 22 or 23, according to his letter to Abbott Lawrence), the petition achieved additional visibility when DeKay traveled to Washington, D.C., to press for its adoption.

Second, on February 24, U.S. senator John Crittenden, a Whig from Kentucky, proposed that the United States government appropriate

$500,000—just under 1 percent of the federal budget—to purchase food and provisions for Ireland and Scotland to alleviate "suffering from the great calamity of scarcity and famine." It was an enormous amount of money—America had never before expended such funds for aid to a foreign people—and Crittenden, recognizing the lateness of the hour, suggested the Senate debate the measure within a day or two. Crittenden's proposal appeared to catch both John C. Calhoun and Daniel Webster by surprise, but they offered their support for a full Senate debate.

After a flurry of activity on behalf of Ireland, Congress now had three bills to consider related to Irish relief: Boston's request for the *Jamestown*, to be commanded by Forbes; New York's petition for the *Macedonian*, to be piloted by DeKay; and Crittenden's resolution calling for a half million dollars in government funds with which to purchase food.

On February 26, just eight days after the Faneuil Hall meeting, the Senate gathered to debate the measures. Before the dust settled, the discussions would involve the president and his cabinet, invoke the United States Constitution, and, for the first time in the country's history, raise serious questions about the benefits to, and moral obligation of, the United States to authorize public funds and resources to assist a foreign nation in need.

Born one week before the adoption of the United States Constitution, Kentucky's John J. Crittenden grew up with the country, and, when it became clear that the nation was marching inexorably toward civil war, he expended enormous political capital working to keep the Union together and keeping his border state part of it. He followed the estimable Henry Clay as the senator from Kentucky, and while he lacked Clay's passion and gift for speechmaking, he possessed a sharp intellect, a love of country, and—like Clay—the ability to find middle ground between competing factions.

A talented lawyer who would serve his country in various capacities for more than four decades, he would, alas, be best remembered for a proposal he offered in December 1860, after southern states had begun to secede; it would become known as the Crittenden Compromise, a series of measures unfortunately designed to maintain slavery in some areas—and extend it in others—as a way of avoiding civil war and keeping the Union intact. "History is to record us," he warned his colleagues at the time. "Is it to record that when the destruction of the Union was imminent . . . we stood quarreling?"

For Crittenden, as with Daniel Webster, the Union came before all else. He vehemently opposed secession and concurred with Abraham Lincoln that it was the government's right and duty to maintain the Union by force. But President Lincoln's strong stance against any extension of slavery scuttled Crittenden's peace compromise proposal, put the two at odds, and placed the Kentucky lawmaker in the crossfire of history, where his unforgivable position on slavery doomed his reputation in the annals of American politics.

In the late 1840s, however, John Crittenden was still one of the most powerful, respected, and influential men in Congress. While his views did not always win the day, his colleagues listened when he spoke. He had opposed the annexation of Texas as unconstitutional, had reservations about the Mexican War, and, in keeping with his desire to maintain the peace, discouraged American animosity toward Great Britain in debates about the Oregon boundary. He was dignified, cordial, and an able debater with a voice that was "musical in conversation," and his words carried impact beyond the halls of Congress with his many friends in legal and business circles.

Describing his bigheartedness, Crittenden's daughter called him a man of "grand, simple, and loving nature." Normally undemonstrative in public, in December 1846, while attempting to deliver a eulogy on the Senate floor for his dear friend Louisiana senator Alexander Barrow, Crittenden "uttered three or four almost inarticulate words," and then, "convulsed with grief and both eyes and voice filled with tears," took his seat, bowed his head, and wept uncontrollably.

Crittenden's response was so uncharacteristic that "sobs were heard from every part" of the Senate chamber. The next day, North Carolina senator Willie Mangum wrote to Crittenden to inform him that the emotional scene has "dwelt upon my mind, my heart, and my memory . . . burned in *all* with a brand at white heat." Mangum added: "I would not exchange such a heart as yours . . . the more I know of you, the more I respect and love you."

Now, rising from his seat in late February 1847, Crittenden would express equally heartfelt emotions about America's obligation to assist Ireland.

This time, with the entire Senate once again assembled before him, words did not fail him.

Crittenden began with a simple but powerful plea, avoiding a sensationalistic accounting of events in Ireland. His colleagues knew what the whole world knew—a calamity had befallen Ireland that was unprecedented in the nineteenth century and perhaps for many centuries before that. "I do not come here with an empty parade of words to impress the picture of a famishing people upon [you]," he began. "I come to discharge only what I consider a solemn duty." The disaster in Ireland was far beyond the ordinary; moreover, it did not occur because of "idleness or folly" on the part of Irish citizens. Instead, the famine was "one of those inscrutable dispensations of Providence . . . and the whole world must feel for the sufferers."

Next, the Kentucky senator made what he believed was a preemptive argument against questions about the constitutionality of providing public funds to assist a foreign nation. While the Constitution did not explicitly prohibit such foreign aid, neither did it include language that allowed Congress to transfer public funds outside the boundaries of the United States. Once before in its history, thirty-five years earlier in May 1812, the United States government had appropriated federal funds to assist another country. Congress had approved $50,000 to charter two ships to provide bread and grain to victims of a Venezuelan earthquake, something much less dire than the "great national calamity" the Irish were facing, and President James Madison had signed the bill. Was that not precedent enough?

In fact, the Venezuela example was a shaky foundation upon which to base his argument. At the time, the constitutional question about the legality of the United States government appropriating funds for foreign assistance had been debated at length, with opponents arguing that such an expenditure exceeded congressional authority. President Madison had reluctantly signed the bill into law, and it became clear— both from contemporaneous debate and from future congressional response—that virtually no one viewed the Venezuela bill as precedent-setting from a legal, moral, or philosophical viewpoint. To make matters worse, the whole thing seemed to have been a debacle: there was a question of how much of the supplies reached Venezuelans in need—the owner of the ships later sued the federal government for recompense after his ships were looted by Spanish royalists in La Guara, heavily damaged, and rendered unserviceable. Some lawmakers actually viewed these results as a warning *against* America providing assistance beyond her own borders. For example, Congress voted down federal aid to the Canary Islands and Greece in the 1820s, with the majority arguing that such contributions were unconstitutional.

But in 1847, with the entire Irish nation imperiled, Crittenden was having none of it: "As far as the constitutional argument is concerned, with the voice of suffering ringing in my ears . . . I lay down all objections at the feet of charity."

After reiterating the theme of American abundance echoed by numerous leaders during the Irish crisis, Crittenden moved to an argument that would have profound implications for his own country and the world. He contended that by offering charity to a foreign country the United States could usher in an entirely new era of enlightenment and cooperation among nations. For the first time, America could look to Europe without fearing war, but with an eye toward assisting the continent's impoverished people. "Can you imagine any spectacle more sublime than that of one nation holding out the hand which is full of plenty to the suffering people of another nation?" Crittenden asked. Such generosity would encourage a "common brotherhood that would bind nations together," meaning wars would become less frequent except for reasons of "overwhelming necessity."

Delaware senator John M. Clayton jumped to his feet and seized on this theme, agreeing that providing aid to Ireland would establish the

United States as a leader in a world that was becoming more interconnected and in which the power structure was changing. "The day has arrived when Europe stretches her hand to America for aid in an hour of distress which has scarcely a parallel in modern history," he told his colleagues.

Moreover, Clayton said, extending a generous hand to Ireland would atone for the U.S. government's actions in the war with Mexico, which he opposed. "Let us now show the world that the . . . government is not powerless for other purposes than those of war and desolation," he said. The United States had the opportunity to demonstrate that the "genius and essential character of our institutions, lead us . . . as a nation [to] the best feelings of the human heart, and the noblest of impulses." Lewis Cass of Michigan agreed that the United States could make an important statement with aid to Ireland: "It is a case beyond the reach of private charity," he said. "[The Irish crisis] is a *national* calamity, and calls for *national* contributions." John C. Calhoun acknowledged that "this appropriation was a very heavy one to make when the country was in a state of war," but said he had no constitutional objections and would support the bill.

The push against Crittenden's bill was strong. In addition to the argument that the Constitution did not provide any language that permitted foreign aid, some contended that the United States had no moral obligation—indeed, no *place*—assisting foreigners with money from U.S. citizens.

Even granting that the Irish were suffering, said Connecticut's John Niles—and even granting that Ireland's national crisis was beyond the reach of private aid—the question was, did it demand "the pouring out of the national purse"? And if the famine required public funds to alleviate, "if it demands national interference," didn't that obligation "belong to the government to which the Irish people belonged"? It was extraordinary, unnecessary, even disrespectful to Great Britain, a presumption on America's part "that the most powerful and wealthy nation on earth . . . was not able to provide for its people's wants." It might lead to a slippery slope "to which there was no end." If the United States provided funds to Ireland, then what of France and Prussia, "where the people are suffering from scarcity"? Niles concluded that Crittenden was "forgetting the great maxim: charity begins at home."

Back and forth the debate went, spilling into a second day. Alabama's Arthur Bagby opposed the bill on constitutional and precedent-setting grounds, as did South Carolina's Andrew Butler. Virginia's James Murray Mason announced he would be voting against, viewing the proposal as a "perversion of the trust reposed in [me] under the Constitution of the United States."

On the other hand, Daniel Webster of Massachusetts was inclined to support the bill, as was Edward Hannegan of Indiana, who found nothing in the Constitution that prohibited America from "carrying out the great and eternal principle of charity."

The first extended debate in American history on the country's obligation to provide humanitarian foreign aid ended when Crittenden's bill passed the Senate, 27–13 (there were twenty-nine states in the Union, meaning that several of the fifty-eight senators were absent or did not vote). Calhoun, Cass, Clayton, Hannegan, Webster, and of course Crittenden were resolute in their support. Bagby, Butler, Mason, and Niles held firm among the nays.

But proponents' jubilation was short-lived—perhaps a day or two—as the bill died quickly in the House, where many members vociferously questioned the constitutionality of using public funds for foreign aid. Other House Democrats opposed it because they believed Crittenden's proposal was an attempt by Whigs to secure Irish votes.

And even had the House passed the bill by a narrow margin, President Polk, who ironically probably owed his election to Irish voters, signaled during the debate that he would veto the relief measure on constitutional grounds. A few days after the debate he wrote in his diary that he would not sign such an Irish relief bill due mainly to the "want of Constitutional power to appropriate the money of the public to charities either at home or abroad." Polk shared his views with his cabinet, who offered "no dissent . . . to the opinion which I had given."

Polk also shared in his diary that he had "all the sympathy for the oppressed Irish and Scots which any citizen can have," and that he had contributed $50 of his own money toward famine relief.

"But my solemn conviction is that Congress possesses no power to use the public money for any such purpose," he wrote.

As March 3 approached, the last day of the session, Congress was now left to consider the petitions from Boston and New York, requesting that the navy make the warships *Jamestown* and *Macedonian* available to transport direct food aid to Ireland and Scotland, and place both ships under the command of civilian captains.

Lawmakers had pondered a similar measure during debate on the Crittenden bill, when Senator Mason of Virginia, an opponent, had proposed an amendment that eliminated the $500,000 financial provision, and instead authorized the president to employ navy ships and personnel to transport food to Ireland. Supporters of Crittenden, hoping to pass his full funding bill, voted the amendment down, but Mason's amendment did offer some hope to Irish-aid supporters that the use of ships, rather than funds, could pass constitutional muster—or at least would mute any vehement objections on constitutional grounds.

Rather than resurrecting Mason's specific measure, Congress agreed to debate in joint session the petitions from Massachusetts and New York; with the exception of the states' desire to place the ships under civilian command, their requests closely mirrored Mason's amendment. To avoid delays and committee debates, Massachusetts lawmakers, led by Representative Robert Winthrop and Senator John Davis, attached the Boston proposal to that of New York.

Davis offered an amendment authorizing the secretary of the navy to place the *Jamestown* "at the disposal of Robert B. Forbes of Boston." He made his Senate colleagues aware that the New England committee had as much as $60,000 available with which to purchase food, and that Captain Forbes "was a gentleman whose character and ability for the purpose contemplated were well known."

CHAPTER 9

⚬——❦——⚬

"WE CAN MAKE THE BOUNTY NATIONAL"

I n case his colleagues needed reminding, John Davis on March 3 laid out the credentials of the man to whom the United States Congress considered turning over the USS *Jamestown* for a humanitarian mission to Ireland. Robert Bennet Forbes was a tough, experienced, smart, responsible, ambitious, duty-bound captain and leader with thousands of miles of seagoing experience in all kinds of weather; a self-made entrepreneur and independent decision-maker who recognized the trust the country was placing in him, grasped both the altruistic and symbolic natures of his mission, and understood the importance of piloting the American warship to and from Ireland safely.

In the debate that followed, lawmakers leaned toward approving the warships for aid to Ireland, but even on the final day of the session, several congressmen voiced strong dissent.

Senator William Archer of Virginia was apprehensive that warships, "which cost a great deal of money," could be committed to "private hands without incurring great risk of loss to the country." Who would be responsible if the ship was damaged or destroyed? What would be the government's remedy? He was fine with using a vessel owned by the United States government, but it should be "manned by officers and men belonging to the United States." Daniel Webster said he was inclined to vote in favor, but also questioned the odd arrangement. Wouldn't the ship be an "anomaly on the water"? Was she a public ship or a private one? If she was a public vessel, a "national ship," how could she sail across the Atlantic "under private command"?

But those who supported the idea of placing the warships under civilian command cited one major practical reason for it: virtually all competent navy personnel were otherwise engaged in the war with Mexico, or if they weren't, they wanted to be. Officers, especially, would be "unwilling to turn their backs on the war," said Maine's John Fairfield. "They would be reluctant to go on a voyage in any other direction than that which conducted to hazardous enterprise, and the prospect for glory."

In addition, Fairfield pointed out that DeKay and Forbes had impeccable reputations and were recommended by their states' "highest citizens." New Jersey's Jacob Miller agreed, calling both captains "of high character, trustworthy," and looking for "no recompense." What was there to debate? It was a "matter of little consequence whether [the mission] was carried out by a private individual of known character or a public officer."

Crittenden urged lawmakers not to get sidetracked with *who* would command the vessels, but to keep the importance of the mission top of mind. Approving one or more American warships for a humanitarian voyage would epitomize a brotherhood between nations and send a message that mere private donations could not send. "We can do what individual charity cannot do," he declared. "We can make the bounty *national*." Imagine the message the United States could send to the world, he added; imagine the "great and glorious spectacle" to see an American warship stripped of its deck guns, carrying food and provisions, "a present from the government of one people rejoicing in plenty, to another government, to be distributed among its people, suffering from a great national calamity."

As the day grew late, with the end of the session looming, debate ended and Congress finally voted. Members passed a joint resolution authorizing the secretary of the navy to grant the use of the *Macedonian* to Captain George C. DeKay of New Jersey, and the *Jamestown* to Captain Robert Bennet Forbes of Boston, "for the purpose of transporting to the famished poor of Ireland and Scotland such contributions as may be made for their relief."

For the first time in the sixty years since the United States had adopted its Constitution, Congress had agreed to use American warships on a humanitarian mission, and to place government-owned ships in private hands to transport private contributions to a foreign country.

Congress agreed to one amendment as a caveat: if Secretary of the Navy John Y. Mason was unalterably opposed to DeKay and Forbes taking command of the warships, he was required to find qualified naval officers capable of piloting the ships in their stead.

At Mason's request, President Polk called a cabinet meeting at 1:00 p.m. on March 5 to discuss the congressional action and seek direction from cabinet secretaries. The senior leaders of the United States decided unanimously that the "vessels of war should be turned over to the persons named in the Resolution of Congress, instead of being commanded by officers of the Navy."

Mason himself later acknowledged that the navy "could not procure the crews necessary for the public service in giving protection to our commerce and in the prosecution of the war."

DeKay's proposed *Macedonian* voyage encountered bureaucratic entanglements as well as resistance from the New York relief committee, and was delayed for several months.

Not so in Boston. Even before official notification from Washington, Forbes had presumed congressional approval and was moving fast—and people were noticing. "Relief for Ireland," wrote Boston Bishop Fitzpatrick to Bishop Murphy of Cork, "seemed to engross all his thoughts, to be his only business." Forbes wrote to Joshua Bates in Liverpool, a lawyer and former Bostonian who was a partner in the influential London banking firm Baring Brothers, asking Bates to use his influence to obtain an order from the Lords Commissioners of the Treasury allowing the *Jamestown* to discharge its cargo into government warehouses at Cork, and to receive help ballasting the ship for its return voyage. "I take it for granted that the usual government dues [port charges] will not be exacted," he added. He corresponded with Liverpool's William Rathbone, also a lawyer, a former mayor, a philanthropist, and a well-known supporter of Irish nationalism, asking him to prepare officials of the Society of Friends of Cork for the *Jamestown's* delivery.

A day after Polk's cabinet meeting, Forbes wrote to Secretary Mason asking whether he would feel more comfortable if a naval officer sailed with him, and to say that he had visited the Navy Yard again the previous day to inspect the *Jamestown*. "The ship can be made ready for sea in a week's time," he wrote. "We take it for granted that she will be rigged and equipped in all important particulars, except armament, [and] ready for sea by the United States." Forbes said he expected to complete the entire voyage in no more than sixty days, and he would make every effort to shorten the trip by ten days or more.

Mason did not require a naval officer to accompany the *Jamestown*, but he did remind Forbes that "Congress has reposed in you a large confidence" by placing the ship at his disposal, and he urged the Boston captain to "use all practicable care and dispatch in accomplishing the voyage contemplated." He also issued a warning to Forbes: "Any disaster to the ship while in your hands would be a source of regret to you."

With no further elaboration, but having spoken his piece, Mason then ordered the Charlestown Navy Yard commodore to furnish the *Jamestown* to Forbes with its "tanks, and with the ballast, spars, cables, anchors, sails, and riggings, which in your judgment will be necessary for her safety in a voyage to Great Britain and back to Boston." Further, Mason added: "You will have her caulked if necessary," and "furnish her with the necessary charts and compasses."

And most symbolically: "You will cause her guns to be taken from on board, with the exception of not exceeding four, if any should be desired by Captain Forbes."

Mason's letter to Forbes and order to the Navy Yard's commodore were dated March 8, 1847; one day later, General Winfield Scott, with assistance from an armada of navy ships, landed an army of 10,000 men on a beach south of Veracruz, Mexico. Covered by guns from those ships, Scott's troops came ashore without a single loss of life in the largest amphibious landing in U.S. history until World War II.

After receiving Mason's approval and instructions, Forbes wrote to Boston mayor Josiah Quincy, chairman of the New England relief committee, tendering the *Jamestown* to the committee and formally asking the committee to place him in charge of "manning and victualling the ship" on its behalf. The committee agreed unanimously, authorized the use of funds to procure food for the *Jamestown*'s voyage, and voted to urge pastors across the city to collect donations to defray any expenses and "contribute towards sending out a ship of war on a mission of mercy."

Forbes assured the committee of his commitment to the mission: "I shall do everything in my power to carry out the humane views of the citizens of the State and City, entrusted to your care, as cheaply as possible." The *Jamestown* would operate on a shoestring, and his efforts to prepare her for the transatlantic voyage would begin forthwith.

"Our bill of fare *shall* and *must* exclude all luxuries," Forbes assured Quincy. "We will neither eat the bread of the starving Irish, nor the bread of idleness."

PART III

IRELAND

"The whole country is one vast tomb"

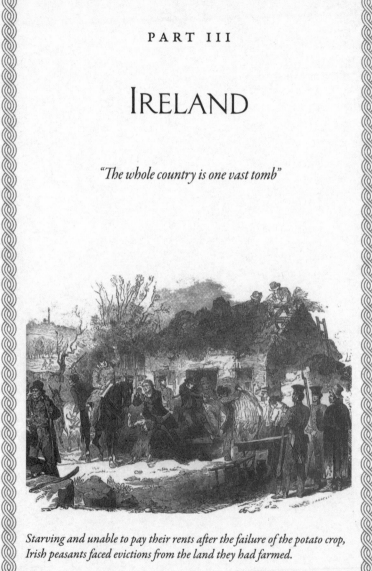

Starving and unable to pay their rents after the failure of the potato crop,
Irish peasants faced evictions from the land they had farmed.

Illustrated London News, December 16, 1848

CHAPTER 10

◦──✦──◦

"THE LIVING ENVY THE DEAD"

FEBRUARY–MARCH 1847, COUNTY CORK

One month before the United States Congress approved the use of the *Jamestown* for the relief mission to Ireland, an exhausted Father Theobald Mathew sat hunched at his desk and outlined the extent of Irish misery, six months into the famine, in his latest letter to Sir Charles Trevelyan.

Conditions in Cork city were now in a "deplorable state," worse than ever, as more than "10,000 foodless, homeless people, young and old, from several counties around us" roamed the urban area seeking scraps of food and any semblance of shelter—twice as many as just two months earlier. The priest would later describe this inundation from the counties as a "living tide of misery" flowing into the city from the western regions of the county, rendering the streets "impassable with crowds of country persons."

The human suffering was taking its toll on Mathew, who had witnessed hardship among the poor many times, but nothing like this. "I am in horror whilst I walk the streets," he wrote on February 4, "and I return to my besieged dwelling in sadness and hopelessness."

As the calendar turned from 1846 to 1847, conditions in Cork and elsewhere in Ireland had gone from intolerable to unspeakable.

The brutal winter, which had throttled Ireland in November and December, now pounded it with unrelenting fury. Heavy snow, icy gales, and bitter cold swept across the country. If possible, food became scarcer and the hunt for food more desperate. Irish peasants—bewildered, fearful, starving—struggled through deep snowdrifts and impassable roads searching for food. Carts could not navigate paths buried by blizzards, and the few horses still alive sank in drifts and met their demise soon after, their weakened owners, themselves incapacitated by cold and overcome with lethargy, unable or unwilling to dig out their animals with crude implements or bare hands. Starving Irish men, women, and children shivered in their cabins and mud huts, gathered scraps and sticks and turf to light fires for warmth, and then froze to death, as wood and peat ran out, flames flickered and died, and embers grew cold. Often, families without food or fuel simply lay down on the floors of their cabins and "very many perished unknown."

Relief worker Edward Forster wrote some of the most vivid accounts of the desperate conditions during his tour of much of the Irish countryside and seacoast in the winter of 1847: "When we entered a village, our first question was, 'how many deaths?' 'The hunger is upon us' was everywhere the cry. . . . As we went along, our wonder was not that the people had *died*, but that they [still] *lived*." What is clear about Forster's reports is that the famine had now gripped the entire country, "rapidly levelling all localities to an equality of destitution." In the small town of Clifden, deaths outstripped the supply of coffins and victims were simply wrapped in blankets before burial. In Galway, police found dead bodies in almost every cabin they visited. Fishermen pawned nets and tackle for tiny amounts of cash, and those who once harvested potatoes were forced to pawn their clothing for "trifling sums" to buy a small amount of overpriced food. In Dublin, Forster was shocked at the deprivation—"bad as were my expectations, the reality far exceeded them." In his view, "the blackness of the truth" was clear: "Like a scourge of locusts, '*the hunger*' daily sweeps over fresh districts, eating up all before it. One class after another is falling into the same abyss of ruin."

William Bennett, a London resident who spent six weeks in Ireland and recorded his observations in a collection of letters to his sister, noted that he kept the worst images to himself. Suffice it to say, Bennett wrote, that his hand "trembles while I write" and that afterward, "the scenes of human misery and degradation we witnessed still haunt my imagination."

Perhaps more chilling, even relief workers, once focused on offering comfort and hope, now viewed the hunger as unstoppable, as something living and contagious and all-consuming. "Involuntarily, we found ourselves regarding this hunger as we would an epidemic," Bennett wrote, "looking upon starvation as a disease."

American schoolteacher and writer Asenath Nicholson, who traveled throughout Ireland ministering to the suffering throngs and encouraging relief workers, recorded her activities in one of the most compelling first-person accounts of Ireland during the famine. She was part of an eclectic group of people—English Quakers, American philanthropists, British aristocrats, even a Polish count—who visited Ireland, traversed much of the country, and distributed small but life-saving amounts of relief. The fifty-five-year-old widow, who had visited Ireland once before in 1844–45, was shocked upon her return in 1847 by the widespread destitution, the grinding, relentless, twenty-four-hour omnipresence of the famine. "The hunger never sleeps," she wrote, "never neglects its watch. If you have never seen a starving person, *may you never!*" she wrote in her *Annals of the Famine in Ireland*, informing her readers that "the specters that had been before my eyes constantly haunted me. I could scarcely believe that these creatures were my fellow beings."

Active in both the U.S. temperance and abolitionist movements, Nicholson was openly critical of both the British government and individuals who profited from or neglected the sufferings of the poor. She compared the poor Irish to slaves, writing that "these poor creatures are in as virtual bondage to their landlords and superiors as it is possible for mind or body to be." One account noted that her writing was "infused with compassion," a stark contrast to the impersonal reports written by government officials, which were "so frequently cold, clinical, and condemnatory."

Stephen Moore, the third Earl of Mountcashell, a prominent and generous Irish landlord who provided for his tenants, wrote to Robert Bennet Forbes just as the *Jamestown* sailed that of the "9,800 souls living in Kilworth, County Cork, more than 7,000 were in the greatest state of misery and distress." He added that 5,000 of those "have not . . . a single meal to provide for their wants tomorrow." He had offered food and shelter for as many as possible, but now his resources were at an end. "I can do little more for them," he lamented.

To make matters worse, the British government passed the Poor Law Extension Act of 1847, which heaped upon Irish landlords the entire burden of paying for what little relief there was forthcoming from England. In turn, many landlords, faced with financial ruin, evicted their tenants, exacerbating and accelerating the evictions that had begun in late 1846. Poor Irish farmers now faced eviction from two fronts: their own inability to pay rent and their landlords' inability to pay heavy relief taxes imposed by the new Poor Law.

This combination proved disastrous for the poverty-stricken Irish. They had no land to work, no firewood to burn, no food to eat, and, for thousands, no shelter to protect them from winter's savagery.

The twin evils of starvation and evictions touched Father Mathew directly. In the Cork workhouse alone, where he tended to the sick and the hungry, nearly 2,000 people died in the first three months of 1847, frightful carnage that was "increasing at a prodigious pace." For months, Father Mathew had distributed food in the workhouse kitchens, and he begged Trevelyan to instruct his "soup committees" in the workhouses to "introduce flesh-meat, fish, or milk into the soup—otherwise it will not be fit food." In Mathew's opinion, and to his ongoing horror, he attributed the astronomical number of deaths in the workhouses, "especially amongst children . . . to the want of animal food." If workhouse kitchens could add "beans, peas, and biscuits" to a little meat, perhaps twice a week, he predicted it could save thousands from destruction.

And those seeking shelter in Cork city—the homeless and the

evicted—often were left with only one refuge. Many, on reaching the urban center, went directly to Father Mathew's house. "They knew he would never turn a deaf ear to them," Father Mathew's grandnephew Frank wrote years later. "Every penny he possessed, the very food bought for his own plain meals, went to them." Father Mathew's biographer asserted that the priest "expended his last shilling and involved himself in new [financial] difficulties" to relieve the starving.

But often, heartbreakingly, even he had to turn away the most desperate of people—either he had no food left or every room in his home was filled at night with "peasants he had brought in from the streets and sheltered." The shelter demands from wandering famine sufferers were unceasing at his modest Cove Street house. A traveler who visited Mathew in 1844 wrote in his diary that the priest's home was "inside as plain and unpretending as the outside. Small room, no carpet." Frederick Douglass, African American abolitionist and former slave, met with Father Mathew in 1845, and considered the sparseness of the priest's home unbefitting the "Apostle of Temperance," especially considering his widespread popularity in Ireland. "Welcome, my dear sir, to my humble abode," Mathew greeted Douglass, at which point the former slave stepped inside and was struck by the simple, unprepossessing living area. "The breakfast table was set when I went in," he recalled. "A large urn stood in the middle, surrounded by cups, saucers, plates, knives, and forks . . . all of a very plain order . . . too plain, I thought, for so great a man."

Standing in awe of Mathew's dedication to the temperance cause at the time, Douglass's words could easily be applied to the priest's work during the famine: "His whole soul appeared to be wrapped up in the cause . . . his time, strength, and money are all freely given to the cause, and his success is truly wonderful." British author William Makepeace Thackeray, who visited Cork, marveled at Mathew's knowledge of the people ("prodigious") and their confidence in him ("great"). "No man seems more eager than he for the practical improvement of this country," Thackeray wrote.

Mathew's dedication to famine victims was unquestioned, but his efforts, notwithstanding Douglass's characterization of his temperance work, produced little real "success," and, despite the eagerness Thackeray observed, his impact was limited. The fact was, conditions were gruesome in Cork—epitomized by the wretched state of the poor who stumbled into Cork city from the countryside, the deep fear of city residents that the incoming hordes carried deadly diseases, and the terrible overcrowding and lack of food and shelter. At first, city dwellers expressed sympathy, "but when fever began to spread in Cork [city], they became alarmed for themselves, and they were anxious . . . to get rid of those wretched creatures." Cork lacked "fever hospitals," workhouses were overflowing, and lodging houses that may have had room "always turned them out when they got sick." As a result, "those poor creatures perished miserably in the streets and alleys—every morning a number were found dead in the streets . . . many perished in rooms and cellars without it being known."

Officials might surmise that all this misery painted the citizens of Cork city in a bad light or that they had "neglected their duty" to care for their brethren, but that presumption would be incorrect and unfair, Mathew instructed. The situation was simply "so great and so overwhelming that it was impossible to prevent those calamities." Mathew's grandnephew recounted the attitude among Cork residents that had been passed down in family lore: "By this time, the peasants had passed from frenzied despair to heartbroken resignation."

It is no wonder that the Reverend Leslie Badham, an Anglican clergyman of Irish origin, resorted to startling language from the pulpit to describe the destructive effect of the famine in his home country.

In Ireland, he said, "the living envy the dead."

CHAPTER II

⚬—✕—⚬

"THOUSANDS HAVE DISAPPEARED"

M ore deadly even than starvation was the disease—the pestilence—
that accompanied the famine.

　　Most Irish called it "the fever," and in thousands of cases
it was; typhus and "relapsing fever" stampeded across the country, the
latter so named because it would return to its victim with renewed ven-
geance about a week after its initial departure. But often the sick and
their loved ones used the word "fever" to describe the vast array of ill-
nesses caused by lack of nutrition, a poor diet, and outright starvation:
cholera, smallpox, dysentery, pulmonary disease, kidney failure, tuber-
culosis, xerophthalmia—an eye disease brought on by the absence of
vitamin A—and scurvy, caused by a lack of vitamin C, a disease that was
virtually unknown in the country prior to the famine due to high levels
of the vitamin contained in the potato. Pellagra, triggered by a lack of
niacin, was commonplace and, in the words of a twenty-first-century
author, was characterized by the "four Ds"—dementia, diarrhea, der-
matitis, and death.

　　The fearful epidemic that ravaged Ireland in the winter and spring
of 1847 had two main causes: bodies weakened by hunger and lack of
nutrition simply were incapable of staving off general disease and

infection, and the rampant multiplication of the human body louse, an incubator and transmitter of both typhus and relapsing fever. By February, deadly lice had bred and spread like wildfire, whether teeming in filthy, overcrowded workhouses, nestling in the unwashed clothing of peasants, burrowing into the skin folds and hair of those laid prostrate by hunger, or carried along the roads of Ireland by orphans, laborers, evicted farmers, delirious peasants, and would-be emigrants making their way to ports and ships.

In early February, relief workers reported alarming news to the Central Board of Health: fever was rapidly on the rise in Kerry, was prevalent "to a fearful extent" in Leitrim, was "making havoc" in Kenmare, had a "firm hold" in Cork, and was spreading rapidly in Mayo. Even in King's County, once one of the country's prosperous districts, people were "dying fast . . . if something is not done, the summer will be awful."

Overcrowded workhouses, now often serving as makeshift hospitals as well as lodgings for laborers, were not equipped to handle the volume of sick residents, could not effectively separate the fever-stricken from the healthy, and had no means to adequately examine and diagnose patients. The Central Board of Health established fever "sheds" and "tents" to care for the sickest; these provided some initial relief and care, but soon contagion roared through these facilities. The Irish poor came to hate and dread both the workhouses and the fever hospitals because so many had died in each. In Ennis, deaths were far fewer among those *not* hospitalized, while in Tralee, "persons who would go to hospital *contrary to all advice* were quickly attacked by fever," one clergyman reported to Charles Trevelyan.

If disease was going to claim them, they'd prefer to die at home.

Caregivers perished in great numbers, too.

Priests, nuns, doctors, orderlies, workhouse officers—any person who came into repeated contact with those suffering with fever was threatened by and susceptible to contagion. More than a hundred workhouse officers died from fever in 1847, and Trevelyan reported that thirty English and Scottish priests perished from attending to emigrating Irish "who carried the pestilence with them in their flight to other portions of the United Kingdom." Another thirty-six Catholic priests died in Ireland during 1847 from famine-related diseases. The *Tralee Chronicle* in Kerry reported the death of Father John O'Donoghue and added that "at the present moment, in this diocese, there are no less than eight Roman Catholic Clergymen on the bed of fever contracted during their ministrations." The paper also paid tribute to Catholic nuns who "caught fever . . . and paid the supreme sacrifice."

Doctors, too, fell victim—one report revealed that of the 473 government medical officers assigned to "famine duty," thirty-six died. Historian and author John Kelly reported that in one Connemara district, two of three physicians died; in County Cavan, seven doctors perished, as did four more in the region between Clifden and Galway city. Mortality among caregivers was especially cruel, since it deprived the ill of treatment and worsened sanitary conditions in the workhouses and hospitals. Thus, like a raging forest fire gobbling oxygen to increase its heat and fury, the pestilence fed itself and roared on unabated.

As conditions deteriorated, the fever found other ways to spread. The growing number of unburied or improperly buried corpses created a sanitary nightmare, heightening and accelerating the spread of germs, which in turn caused more deaths. Perhaps worse were the random manner and locations in which the dead *were* buried. In Lurgan in County Armagh in the north, for example, the fever hospital doctor reported that bodies were buried four yards from the hospital building—and in the center of the burial ground was the well from which the hospital drew its water.

Though not a young man—he was fifty-seven in 1847—Father Mathew waded unhesitatingly into the workhouses and fever sheds and alleyways at all hours, comforting victims and performing last rites. So respected and loved by the poor was he that, frequently, dying fever sufferers called for him by name and sought his absolution before they passed, and he made an effort to oblige each one. This commitment further enhanced Father Mathew's reputation and demand, and increased the frenetic pace of his famine work. He had performed similar heroic acts of mercy during the great Irish cholera epidemic in 1832;

whether that dreadful experience had fortified his immune system or offered him guidance on reducing the chances of infection, he remained healthy, if fatigued, during the worst of the famine.

The contagious diseases spawned by the hunger and weakness accounted for perhaps 70 percent of the famine's total deaths in Ireland, though it's difficult to say with certainty. Often corpses would be buried, or even burned, before they could be counted. "There are no records, even round figures," one inspector wrote to Charles Trevelyan, adding simply: "Thousands have disappeared."

Nor did the fever's deadliness stop at Ireland's borders. Thousands of emigrating Irish took it with them; many stopped in Liverpool for several days before embarking, bunking in temporary, filthy, overcrowded quarters. They carried and transmitted lice and disease onto departing ships and brought "the fever" to England, Canada, the United States, and other destinations. Outbreaks on small Liverpool packet ships were especially lethal; by the time vessels had cleared British waters, as many as 15 percent of passengers would be dead and another 15 percent delirious with fever.

So powerful was the lingering fear of fever and epidemic from Ireland in the years following the famine that up until around 1940—nearly a century after the Great Hunger—emigrants from Ireland were deloused when they arrived in Liverpool during their stopover on the way to North America.

—◆—

CHAPTER 12

"THE GREATER PART OF THEM ARE *ANXIOUS* TO GO"

Robbed of hope, thousands who were still able fled Ireland in the winter, spring, and summer of 1847, some bound for England, but most for North America.

In many parts of Ireland, small towns virtually disappeared, while some Galway villages lost a third of their population to emigration in the spring of 1847. Another son of James and Elizabeth Prendergast, Michael, departed for the United States the day after Easter. "We pressed him to go," his father wrote to his other children in Boston, "as we knew that if he remained, he would spend the rest of his days in misery." Writing to her brother John, Hannah Curtis proclaimed: "Every one who can go to America is going this year, as there is no prospect of any thing here but poverty and distress." In one Cork village, a writer described: "Every house on . . . the street has been long since torn down, most of the people having died and a few managing in some way to go to America," and a Wicklow woman observed: "There are very few boys left on our side of the county."

One famine chronicler noted that only one in three Irishmen born in Ireland around 1831—making them sixteen at the time of the famine—would die in Ireland of old age. The rest would perish or emigrate.

He added: "The desire to go was so powerful, people left without luggage, without money, without forethought, without shoes."

For the Irish who hoped to escape the famine through emigration, their problems began at home and grew exponentially worse along each step of the process. Many were undernourished or on the verge of starvation when they left their homes and villages. Only about 120 miles of railway operated in Ireland in 1847, which meant that even if peasants could afford rail travel, the trains could handle only a tiny percentage of those eager to leave. The same issue presented itself for boats operating in canals around Dublin and other port cities—they were too few and too expensive, and emigrants needed to save what little money they had for their fares across the ocean. For most, the only solution was to walk to the nearest port to reach those ships, usually hauling their few possessions on their backs or in rickety carts.

People who did manage to make it to port cities such as Cork and Liverpool were often crowded into filthy, unventilated cellars and lodging houses for days or longer as they tried to arrange passage; the vast majority of Irish who died on ships en route to Canada or the United States did so from fever.

Unscrupulous "brokers" also preyed on unsuspecting or sick emigrants, most of whom had not traveled beyond their village or county line. Working with other dishonest merchants, brokers took a cut of almost everything emigrants spent: rent for lodging houses, purchases for items they would need at sea, and passenger tickets for travel to the New World. More than 17,000 emigrants sailed from Cork alone in 1847, and one local official claimed that they "were defrauded from the day they start from their homes until they were at sea." Father Mathew decried the "rogues called brokers" who were adding two shillings to the cost of sea provisions sold to emigrants during the spring of 1847. Brokers, lodging house owners, and tavern and restaurant proprietors also welcomed delays in sailing—due to weather, a mix-up in plans, or an insufficient number of ships—since it gave them the opportunity to extort more money from the poorest of souls. Plus, as demand for transatlantic passage soared, so did prices, almost doubling in most Irish ports. In many cases, emigrants could not afford the increases and were required to languish much longer in the port city as they attempted to scrape together additional funds. Others would never be able to secure the extra money. One historian said that at Cork a full 50 percent of the emigrants who were waiting to emigrate were being turned away; demand was so great that some emigrants with sufficient funds were buying passenger berths and then selling them at higher prices.

For those emigrants whose money ran out—and it happened by the hundreds—they were turned out of lodging houses and taverns and forced to sleep on the streets; if they had contracted fever, they often died in alleyways.

More than 90,000 Irish poor fled to Liverpool alone between February and April 1847; by the end of June, more than 300,000 Irish had landed in Liverpool. Many could afford to go no further, but for the Irish who were able to scrape up fare, conditions were as hideous aboard ship as they were in the sorrowful hamlets of Ireland; for Irish emigrants, their method of famine-flight was nearly as painful as the life they fled. The vessels that carried these lost, desperate emigrants were labeled "famine ships" by some observers. But others who knew of the brutal conditions on board whispered a name far more accurate and far more chilling: the coffin ships.

If the Irish needed another reason to despise the British, it was the government's inability or unwillingness to properly supervise emigration and weed out unscrupulous and dishonest sea captains, shipowners, agents, and other middlemen. Conditions aboard most emigrant ships were unspeakable. People were regularly denied the food and water promised with the price of their ticket. Ships often exceeded the legally allowed number of passengers and provided less than the eighteen inches of sleeping space required for adults.

The cramped living conditions, coupled with the fact that people had no means of changing their clothing or bedding, provided the ideal breeding conditions for the spread of body lice, fever, and disease. Typhus and other afflictions spread quickly as the ships became fever and disease factories. "If one passenger had contracted the disease before he came on board, others soon caught it," author John Percival pointed out. "Typhus was often called 'ship fever' precisely because it was so common in these overcrowded and dirty conditions." On some ships the first deaths occurred within a few days at sea and multiplied as the voyage continued. Percival detailed the sorrowful journey of the *Virginia* from Liverpool, on which a staggering 158 passengers died from typhus.

Shipboard dysentery also claimed many lives. Bad or undercooked food and contaminated water caused outbreaks of dysentery on almost every ship. Most passengers, many belowdecks with hatches closed during poor weather, had access to little more than a bucket for their waste. "Conditions do not bear thinking about," one author wrote. While making the five-week journey to America aboard the *Washington*, with more than 900 passengers, mostly Irish, on board, Vere Foster, a wealthy philanthropist who took a special interest in the plight of Irish emigrants, wrote the following: "Another child, making about 12 in all, died of dysentery for want of proper nourishing food and was thrown into the sea, sewn up, along with a great stone, in cloth." With no clergy on board to perform a funeral service, crew members sang a sailor's song and threw the child overboard "at the sound of the last word of the song, making use of it as a funeral dirge." In its own right, the story is heartbreaking; what makes it unimaginable is its commonplace occurrence.

While disease, exposure, and lack of food and water were the biggest threats, emigrants faced other deadly perils. Insensitive crew members—many of whom hated the Irish—treated men, women, and children with callous indifference at best and, far more often, with shocking cruelty. Further, when ships began leaving year-round during peak famine years, passengers faced even more terrifying weather-related hazards: deck fires, often started by emigrants to stay warm, created conflagrations that crews and passengers battled just to keep their ships afloat; vicious North Atlantic gale-force winds, sweeping storms, hurricanes, and dangerous ice fields all conspired against emigrants as they attempted to flee the famine.

Wrote one commissioner of emigration in the United States: "If crosses and tombs could be erected on the water, the whole route of the emigrant vessels from Ireland to America would long since have assumed the appearance of a crowded cemetery."

Father Mathew testified on these hardships in June 1847 to the House of Lords Select Committee on Colonization from Ireland; he was one of more than forty witnesses who would offer expert advice to the lords on the wisdom of encouraging emigration from famine-ravaged Ireland—or even forcing thousands of Irish residents to leave their homeland through compulsory emigration—as a way to alleviate over-crowding and reduce starvation.

Father Mathew believed that any plan for compulsory emigration would be "utterly destructive." The Irish simply would not be forced out. Rather than mandated emigration, government officials should actively prevent desperate peasants from leaving the country unless they had "sufficient food and clothes, and the vessels were properly pre-pared"; perhaps most important, "they should have agents on the other side to send them to those places where there was preparation made for their getting labour." If all that could be ensured, Father Mathew testi-fied, "there is an inclination" among the poor to emigrate; actually, the priest restated, "inclination" was not a strong enough word. "The whole of the poor population seems to be in motion. . . . The greater part of them are *anxious* to go."

Like a good ship captain, Father Mathew was navigating his way through testimony before the House of Lords committee, officially formed to consider two seemingly contradictory ends: the "means by which colonization may be made *subsidiary* to other measures for the improvement of the social condition of Ireland," but, if all else failed, "furnishing the means of emigrating to America" for those "praying" to leave, while "promoting their comfort and prosperity" after they de-parted from Ireland.

By the summer of 1847, the British government paid great lip ser-vice to sanctioning widespread Irish emigration only as a last resort; but in reality, after the catastrophe that had engulfed the country and the hardships looming ahead, no one in authority was quite sure what to do about Ireland or how to save its people. The British government, purveyor of a vast empire that blanketed much of the globe—from Canada to Australia, from Singapore to Africa, from Bermuda to India—continued its ineffectiveness, incompetence, indifference, and impotence in dealing with an ongoing human catastrophe on its own doorstep. House of Lords members sought information on the potential for Irish emigration to the United States, over whose borders the British government had no control, and to every corner of the British Empire, all of which fell under the lords' purview: Scotland, Wales, British North America—Nova Scotia, New Brunswick, Newfoundland, Prince Edward Island, and "East" (lower) and "West" (upper) Canada—the West Indies, the Bahamas, Australia and New Zealand, the Falkland Islands, Hong Kong, Singapore, Ceylon (now Sri Lanka), British India (Bengal, Bombay, Madras), and British possessions in the southern region of Africa (South Africa, Cape of Good Hope).

Mathew wanted the government's assurance that emigrants would be safe and cared for, but he did not want undue interference from London in the emigration process. Emigrants should be free to leave when they wanted and should be free to travel and live where they chose. Excessive government involvement and rulemaking would likely do more harm than good to any aggressive emigration program; after the horrors of the past year, Irish distrust of the British government had reached a peak and was nearly universal across the country.

The lords heeded Mathew's advice. In its summary report, the committee stressed its strenuous opposition to "any scheme of emigration which is not perfectly voluntary on the part of the emigrant." Compulsory emigration would be not only "repulsive to the spirit of our free Constitution" but "fatal to the success of emigration itself."

Perhaps so, but in Black '47, not a single high-ranking government official in London would regret seeing thousands of additional Irish leave the country—without delay and permanently.

For Father Mathew, what made the odious conditions aboard the emigrant ships so maddening was the British government's refusal to tackle major problems—corruption, disease, unsafe conditions, lack of food, overcrowding—even while it issued scores of guidelines dictating how the ships should be run.

Irish peasants who foraged for food scraps aboard ship and whose clothing was often teeming with swarming lice must have found great irony in official instructions dictating that "children should be washed and dressed" each morning and "the decks swept before breakfast and after every meal." Or that fires on deck were not permitted prior to 7:00 a.m. and needed to be snuffed out by 7:00 p.m. Or that bedtime was 10:00 p.m. Each day, after the morning meal, bedding should be rolled up, taken on deck, and aired out. Mondays and Fridays were designated as "washing days," when passengers could attempt to launder clothing, and on Sundays, at half past ten, they were to assemble on deck for Lord's Day services, where "it is expected that every person will then appear clean, and put on clean linen and decent apparel." Not only did the guidelines offer no warning that typhus-infected lice thrived in the folds of clothing, they also neglected to mention that during torrential rains, turbulent seas, and ferocious winds, clothes could be swept overboard in an instant.

Passengers heading to Australia were informed that the voyage could take up to four months, and that they should prepare for a range of weather when assembling clothes for the journey. Men should consider packing a lined "beaverteen" jacket, lined trousers, "one waistcoat with sleeves, 6 striped cotton shirts," boots, shoes, towels, razors, and a shaving box. Women should bring on board a warm cloak with cape, two bonnets, a small shawl, and "2 flannel petticoats," as well as "4 nightcaps, 4 sleeping jackets, and 4 pocket handkerchiefs." The instructions pointed out that "as a general rule . . . the more abundant the stock of clothing each person can afford to take, the better for health and comfort during the passage."

During a discussion of ship safety, the House of Lords subcommittee chairman asked Father Mathew if the emigration agent at Cork "is now adequate for the protection of the poor emigrants." Unwilling to blame a low-level functionary for a broken and neglected system, the priest answered diplomatically but with little doubt of his between-the-lines meaning: "The present agent is certainly very active, and does what he can, but sometimes the numbers are so great that he is not able to inspect and superintend every individual case."

In the succeeding years of the famine, much as the Irish mass exodus itself, the seagoing disasters would continue unabated. For every death on board an American ship during the period, there were three on board a British ship. One famine historian estimated that of the more than 100,000 emigrants traveling on British ships to Canada alone in 1847, more than 25,000—or one in every four—died while crossing the Atlantic or within six months after arrival.

Many deaths were due to disease or accidents; others were caused by outright criminal behavior. In one of the era's most flagrant examples of criminal negligence, seventy-two Irish emigrants were killed—one Boston newspaper said "murdered"—on the night of December 1, 1848, on board the steamer *Londonderry*, transporting passengers from Sligo, Ireland, to Liverpool, for eventual passage to America. A violent storm rocked the ship, driving the 150 passengers below into the small forward cabin for protection; only one ventilation aperture provided air for the congested room. In a disastrous decision, one mate—in an attempt to protect the compartment from water rushing over the sides of the ship—closed the ventilation door and nailed a piece of tarpaulin over it. The violence of the storm masked the screams of the passengers below as they suffocated.

When the storm finally passed, one mate went below and witnessed the "full nature of the catastrophe," according to one steerage passenger who had forced his way out of the fetid cabin. "There lay, in heaps, the living, the dying, and the dead, one frightful mass of mingled agony and death, a spectacle enough to appall the stoutest heart," he wrote. Nearly half of the ship's passengers had perished in the most gruesome and terrifying way, frantically clawing for air, climbing over each other as they tried to reach the aperture, tearing at the nailed door in vain as they attempted desperately to escape. "It was evident," the eyewitness reported, "that in the struggle, the poor creatures had torn the clothes from each other's backs, and even the flesh from each other's limbs."

A coroner's jury found *Londonderry*'s captain, Alexander Johnstone; first mate, Richard Hughes; and second mate, Ninian Crawford, guilty of manslaughter, and, according to one newspaper report, "expressed in the strongest terms, their [the jury's] abhorrence of the inhuman conduct of the other seamen on board."

In other cases, ship captains and crews had great compassion for their passengers, but shipboard conditions could not prevent tragedy. In sharp contrast to the actions of the *Londonderry*'s crew, Captain James Murdoch and the crew of the *Ocean Monarch* tried heroically, but in vain, to prevent a disaster after his ship left Mersey in September 1848. The tragic event proved that despite even the best intentions, unsafe and crowded conditions aboard the famine ships could invite death and destruction at a moment's notice.

A few hours outside of port, a fire broke out in a belowdecks cabin of the *Ocean Monarch*; in less than five minutes flames had enveloped the stern. Murdoch pleaded for calm, but his orders could not be heard in the noise and confusion. Passengers fled from the stern and crowded in the forepart of the vessel, their "piercing, heart-rending shrieks for aid carried by the breeze across the dark blue waves," Murdoch's official statement read. Then the unthinkable occurred: passengers, many of them women with small children in their arms, began jumping overboard to escape the flames. "They sunk to rise no more," Murdoch said. "Men followed their wives in a frenzy, and were lost." Murdoch said. "I pointed out to them that there were several vessels around us, and that if they preserved order, they would all be saved—it was of no avail." Later, after Murdoch finished tallying the lost souls against his passenger list, he learned the heart-wrenching news that 173 *Ocean Monarch* passengers had perished in the disaster.

In an act of compassion, and influenced by Murdoch, the Liverpool mayor quickly put together a committee to raise funds for the emigrants who had lost everything when the vessel went down. And, Murdoch pointed out, "the agents of the ship will provide a free passage for those steerage passengers wishing to proceed to America."

Fire was one hazard; ice another. Four ships carrying Irish emigrants went down after colliding with ice in 1849, and hundreds were killed, either drowned or crushed between ice floes. One of the most tragic of these was the sinking of the *Maria*, sailing from Limerick to Quebec in May 1849, which hit an iceberg at night just fifty miles from the Canadian coast. She sank rapidly. Nine passengers jumped onto the ice as the ship went down and three crew members grabbed a lifeboat, but the remaining 109 passengers died. The daily shipping newspaper *Lloyd's List* reported in July 1849: "The immense field of ice that has been encountered in and near the Gulf of St. Lawrence this season has not been equaled for many years." The paper noted that "scarcely five minutes" elapses from the moment a ship strikes ice to its foundering.

And if ice didn't get one of the emigrant ships, gale-force winds or hurricanes often did. On October 7, 1849, Massachusetts Bay recorded one of the period's greatest disasters when the brig *St. John*, traveling from Galway, Ireland, encountered a vicious storm just as it approached Boston Harbor. The captain dropped anchor and attempted to ride the storm out. But its anchors failed to hold, and the ship was smashed on the rocks off the coast of Cohasset. The crew abandoned ship and left behind 120 passengers to fight for their lives, perhaps no more than a mile from land. Only ten were able to survive by clinging to debris from the disintegrated ship.

Most of the bodies washed ashore at Cohasset Harbor, including those of Patrick Sweeney of Galway, his wife, and their nine children. Forty-five bodies were never identified and were buried in a mass grave in the Cohasset Central Cemetery.

Writer Henry David Thoreau visited the scene and was struck by the number of spectators searching for relatives, looking through bodies, examining the fragments of the wreck. "Some were lifting the lids of coffins and peeping under the cloths—for each body, with such rags as still adhered to it, was covered loosely with a white sheet," he wrote. Sometimes, Thoreau noted, there were two or more children or a parent and child in the same box. "On the lid would perhaps be written with red chalk, 'Bridget such-a-one and sister's child.'" Thoreau also commented on the irony of these emigrants, who had suffered so much already, losing their lives so close to their goal. "All their plans and hopes burst like a bubble! Infants by the score dashed on the rocks by the en-raged Atlantic Ocean!" he wailed.

How could fate be so cruel?

Yet Thoreau also captured the courage of the many Irish emigrants who survived the horror of the famine and the frightening conditions aboard the coffin ships to reach the New World. "The strongest wind cannot stagger a Spirit," he wrote after witnessing the aftermath of the *St. John* tragedy. "It is a Spirit's breath. A just man's purpose cannot be split on any material rock, but itself will split rocks till it succeeds."

Despite the dangers to emigrants, in 1847 the famine ships departed without interruption for the United States, Canada, and other British possessions. The Irish saw little hope at home and, after a year of suffer-ing, were encouraged by letters from those who had already emigrated.

Father Mathew told the House of Lords subcommittee that hun-dreds of letters from Canada and the United States had been delivered to him, posted by relatives who had addressed letters improperly or incorrectly—to "John Ryan or William So-and-So, in such a place, as if those persons were all well known." He was forced to read the letters to ascertain their final destination, and almost all of them "describe it [their adopted country] as one of comparative comfort, much better than it was at home; and they tell their friends to be of good cheer, for they will soon send them money to come out [emigrate]." Father Mathew assured the committee: "A great part of those letters last year [1846] contained money to enable the friends of the emigrants to come out."

Father Mathew viewed emigration as the ultimate steam valve to alleviate the pressure Ireland would continue to face as summer 1847 progressed and the fall approached. Irish residents knew what was com-ing, too. Their country, frightfully weakened by famine and disease, was clawing for its very survival, and unprepared for the summer harvest. For that reason, Father Mathew told the lords: "I think that there is a great anxiety all over Ireland among the lower classes to emigrate."

The British government initially tried to encourage emigration to its North American colonies by significantly reducing the price of a ticket to Canada in comparison to passage to the United States. But while thousands of Irish emigrants did settle in Canada, the majority had no desire to do so—their hatred of the British made settling in British North America repugnant to them. "The native Irishman had become convinced that no justice or opportunity could exist for him under the Union Jack," famine scholar Cecil Woodham-Smith wrote. Or as one Irishman wrote from Boston, Canada represented little more than "a second edition of Ireland, with more room."

Most Irish either boarded another ship from Canada to Boston or New York—they were often referred to as "two-boaters"—or simply entered the United States by way of an overland route from Canada. Most had a burning desire to escape any vestige of English supervision. "With an almost frantic longing, they wished to go to the United States," Woodham-Smith wrote.

CHAPTER 13

"WHAT HOPE IS THERE FOR A NATION WHICH LIVES ON POTATOES?"

All of it—the hunger, the disease, the evictions, the impoverishment, the dismantlement of families, the hopelessness, the suffering, the tsunami of emigration, and the terrible deaths—swept across a defenseless Ireland after the widespread destruction of a crop the Irish people had depended on for decades.

The humble, lowly potato, mocked by the wealthy as the manna of peasants, provided the Irish with a nutritious food and irreplaceable revenue source. On the other hand, overreliance on the potato often proved fatal to the Irish when the crop failed, as it did to some extent numerous times in the nineteenth century prior to the outright disaster of 1846–47.

The Irish people's almost universal dependence on the potato had as much to do with anti-Catholic bigotry as it did with the vegetable's high yield per acre, its rich supply of vitamins and other nutrients, the minimal care it required during planting and growing, and the numerous ways it could be cooked and eaten.

Historically, the potato's ascendance in the Irish diet and peasant economy coincided with the brutal oppression of Roman Catholics by

English leaders, dating back to Oliver Cromwell and later William of Orange, the intensely anti-Catholic Dutch ruler invited by the English to assume the throne when King James was exiled. Crowned as William III, the new king introduced in 1695 the Penal Laws, which banned all public practices of the Roman Catholic religion, stripped the huge Catholic majority in Ireland of their wealth, position, homes, and estates, and rendered most Catholics penniless. Catholics were barred from purchasing land, Catholic schools were closed, churches were shuttered, and no Catholic could vote, hold office, practice law, serve in the army, or carry a sword or gun.

The Penal Law provisions, which were not repealed until 1829, produced hundreds of thousands of Catholic paupers, and over time, barely 5 percent of Irish land remained owned by Catholics. Any land Catholics did own had to be distributed upon their death equally among all the sons in the family, unless the eldest son converted to a Protestant sect, in which case he could retain the entire estate. This resulted in smaller and smaller slices of land owned by Catholics—historian Edward Laxton points out that one estate in County Clare was farmed by a single owner in 1793 and by ninety-six tenants in 1847.

Hundreds of years of grinding persecution took its toll on Ireland's impoverished Catholics. During a six-week tour of Ireland in 1835, French diplomat and historian Alexis de Tocqueville, who would become best known for his observations of democracy in the United States, wrote to his father: "You cannot imagine what a complexity of miseries five centuries of oppression, civil disorders, and religious hostility have piled upon this poor people." He described Ireland as a "ghastly labyrinth, in which it would be difficult to try to find one's way."

Coincident with their economic degradation well into the nineteenth century was the increase in the Irish birth rate. The population of Ireland tripled between 1741 and 1845; the latter was the year the partial famine struck the country and weakened the Irish population prior to the total potato failure of 1846–47.

To stay alive, maintain any semblance of a healthy existence, and perhaps even occasionally achieve contentment—for outright happiness was exceedingly rare—the Irish needed a nutritious crop that would yield enough food even when planted on tiny strips of tenanted land.

The potato filled the bill.

First, the vegetable's yield per acre was unparalleled, and to the Irish almost heaven-sent; even Trevelyan pointed out that potatoes planted on a piece of land would support three times the number of people as corn planted on the same parcel. The potato's high yield, Trevelyan acknowledged, was the main reason "this root" exercises "important influence . . . over the destinies of the human race." An acre and a half of healthy potato plants would provide a family of five or six with food for a year, whereas to grow equivalent grain required acreage four to six times as large, plus more advanced tilling knowledge. Further, the potato required only a spade to plant and little skill to nurture, and it thrived in Ireland's often damp climate.

The potato's nutritional value also surpassed that of corn and grains. Food science in the 1840s had not progressed to the point where the potato's full and specific benefits were known—but it was indeed a potent source of calories, was rich in vitamins, especially vitamin C, and also contained healthy levels of protein, iron, calcium, potassium, and magnesium. It was easily digestible; rare were gastrointestinal problems among the Irish peasantry.

The potato was also easy to cook, and it could be prepared in numerous ways—steamed, boiled, or roasted over an open flame. On larger farms with more resources, potatoes could be boiled, crushed, mixed with butter and milk and mustard seed, stirred vigorously until the combination was lumpless and resembled the appearance of thick cream, and served as what would become the commonplace dish called "mashed potatoes."

In short, a tenant farmer harvesting a successful crop could first meet his family's food needs, his rent responsibility, and his landlord's quota (to ship to English markets), and then sell or trade excess potatoes for clothing, a farming implement, or perhaps a chicken or pig or horse. And potatoes considered too small for people to eat were fed to pigs and other animals.

By 1840, as the famine years approached, more than one-third of the entire Irish population depended exclusively on the potato. Contrary to the question Sir Charles Trevelyan posed in his report of the Irish famine—"What hope is there for a nation which lives on potatoes?"—Ireland's poor tenant farmers knew that, more often than not, a strong potato crop was their only hope for sustenance, for nourishment, for life itself.

But what the potato giveth it also taketh away.

The potato's most dangerous drawback was that, unlike foodstuffs that could be cured, canned, or salted, it did not keep for long and could not be used from one season to another, which created enormous pressure on poor tenant farmers. Between the time the old crop became inedible and the new crop was harvested, "two-and-a-half million labourers who had no regular employment more or less starved," in the words of one British historian. The only upside to this three-month dearth of food was that it occurred in the summer months; June, July, and August were often called the "meal months," because if potatoes ran out, laborers had to eat meal instead, which they bought on credit at exorbitant prices, or else families lived in a state of continuous hunger until the next harvest. Worse, if the next potato crop failed, the Irish poor had nothing to replace it on a widespread scale—and worse still, if two consecutive annual harvests were subpar, vast food shortages and cases of starvation were inevitable.

Worst of all, a partially blighted crop—as occurred in 1845—followed the next year by plants almost totally putrefied by blight, led almost inevitably to famine. Prior to the outbreak of An Gorta Mor—the Great Hunger—in 1846–47, Ireland experienced localized famines during the nineteenth century in 1800, 1818, 1821, 1822, 1830, 1833, 1835, 1839, and 1842. "The unreliability of the potato was an accepted fact in Ireland, ranking with the vagaries of the weather," one writer noted, which is one reason the partial failure of the crop in 1845 "caused no particular alarm."

The same unreliability meant, in the words of one author, that "famine hung over the mud cabins of Ireland like the sword of Damocles."

The fact that potatoes failed so frequently was due to their suscep-
tibility to blight, caused by a fungus called *Phytophthora infestans*, a
microscopic organism that thrived and multiplied in Ireland's damp climate, and reproduced with lightning speed. The fungus first attacked
the leaves of the plant and then penetrated the soil to the potato's un-
derground tubers, essentially both devouring and choking the potato
plant. Moisture helped the spores germinate, one reason the potato
plant is not out of danger even after digging. "Countless thousands of
live spores are on the leaves of surrounding plants, and as the potatoes
are dug they are showered with spores," one historian explained. If the
weather is dry, no harm will occur, but if the spores receive the drop of
water they need to germinate, "in a few weeks the potatoes which were
sound when dug are a mass of rottenness."

The potato betrayed the Irish in gastric and culinary ways also. Because
the vegetable was so easy to digest, the Irish had great difficulty breaking
down other food such as the rough Indian corn that Sir Robert Peel
imported for relief in 1846, or other meal, which families learned they
had to grind once or twice more before ingesting. Out of necessity, Irish
peasants eventually grew accustomed to potato substitutes, but they initially suffered from diarrhea, dysentery, and gangrene—and some even
died—when they were forced to vary their diets.

Nor did the Irish adapt well to preparing other foods even when
forced. Their dependence on the potato for so many decades had
blunted both their knowledge of cooking and their inclination to try.
Trevelyan and Father Mathew, who agreed on virtually nothing else
during the famine, concurred with this point as the Irish struggled to
survive. In a letter to Trevelyan on March 4, 1847, Father Mathew said
his "great anxiety is to teach our unhappy simple people to manage to
advantage their scanty means." This would be difficult because of their
reliance on the potato in previous decades, "which swept away all other
food . . . and sank in oblivion their knowledge of cookery." Trevelyan
was blunter in his account of the famine: "The habit of exclusively living
on this root produced an entire ignorance of every other food and the
means of preparing it." Unwilling and unable to hide his contempt for

the Irish, he added, "There is scarcely a woman of the peasant class in the West of Ireland whose culinary art exceeds the boiling of a potato."

Father Mathew was convinced that the potato was much more than a suitable food source for the Irish; the overall value and life-sustaining importance of the vegetable were ingrained in his countrymen's psyches, the potato plant's care and feeding almost a second religion. It would be an exaggeration to say the Irish worshipped the potato, but inarguable to conclude that they viewed it with reverence; they celebrated an abundant harvest with a joy far beyond any relief that their families would avoid starvation, whereas anything less than a bumper crop sent their spirits plummeting. The fates and the lives of the peasant and the potato were intertwined because the planting, cultivation, harvesting, preparation, and cooking of the vegetable consumed so much of the family's daily existence.

In his testimony to the House of Lords in 1847, Father Mathew attempted to capture the all-encompassing nature of this relationship: "Whenever you go into a poor man's cabin, and inquire for him, the answer always is that he is digging the potatoes, or doing something connected with the potatoes. If you ask where his wife is, she is always washing the potatoes, or boiling the potatoes . . . almost the whole time of those poor people is taken up in the cultivation and dressing of those potatoes. There is a constant drudgery going on."

But, he added, the brutal famine and the unspeakable conditions it had wrought were likely to produce profound and irreversible changes in his country.

"I do not think," he testified to the panel, "that the people of Ireland will ever again depend upon the potato crop."

CHAPTER 14

"ARE YOU GOING TO ABANDON US?"

I f one ranked the egregiousness of the British government's orgy of
bureaucratic and moral missteps in its handling of the Irish famine—
its obscene exportation of food from a starving country, its demean-
ing and ineffective public works program, its statutory enablement of
inhuman levels of evictions, its reluctance to disrupt British markets
with desperately needed grain imports—high on the list was its administering of government-operated soup kitchens beginning in the late
winter and early spring of 1847.

In this case, London's *intent*, though much too late, was noble and
necessary; the execution, however, was a demonstration of management
ineptitude and excessive paper shuffling that led to the deaths of additional thousands of Irish people.

The good idea—replacing the failed works program with direct
food assistance—went badly almost from the start. Lord John Russell
introduced the Temporary Relief Act on January 25, 1847, announcing the closing of the works program, and, determined not to repeat
mismanagement errors, appointed the highly respected General John
Burgoyne to head the soup operations, under Trevelyan's watchful eye.
The sixty-year-old Burgoyne, a veteran of both the French Wars and

the Battle of New Orleans and one of England's most admired soldiers, sailed for Dublin in February. Despite his orders to have the first group of soup kitchens running in six weeks, around mid-March, and to have 2,000 in place by June, Burgoyne focused the bulk of his efforts on establishing a sound administrative infrastructure before serving a bowl of soup to the Irish people.

But a nightmare ensued—or rather intensified—when the government began shutting down public works before most soup kitchens were operative. This "hiatus in the provision of government relief," in the words of one historian, proved disastrous. Officials in County Kerry described the Treasury's decision as equivalent to signing a "death warrant" against the poor of Ireland.

Unmoved by pleas from Irish officials to reconsider dismissing workers from government projects until soup kitchens were functioning, Burgoyne, who shared Trevelyan's bureaucratic mindset, plowed ahead with his administrative plan. As hunger deepened and pestilence spread, the soup kitchen program churned out paper: it generated "fourteen tons of documents, ten thousand record books, eighty thousand sheets of paper, and three million food cards that would wrest order out of chaos," according to one account. "Instructions were issued on who qualified for relief, how to color-code index cards, who should stand where in the soup line, and what to do when a relief recipient failed to respond when his name was called." Burgoyne and Trevelyan alike were concerned about fraud and thus insisted that only cooked food would be distributed to the hungry, lest, in Trevelyan's words, "undressed meal might be converted into cash by those who did not require it as food."

Trevelyan made a point of stressing the importance of fraud prevention, pointing out that "even the most destitute often disposed of it [uncooked food] for tea, tobacco, or spirits," which was why the "cooked food test was . . . particularly efficacious in preventing abuse."

For weeks, British bureaucrats hammered out soup kitchen rules and regulations. And while they did, no food was served.

Meanwhile, the public works system laid off more Irish peasants, causing the *Nation* newspaper to predict that the outcome would be "even more death from starvation." The paper vilified the British government for its "utter apathy to the tremendous responsibility with which they are trifling."

Sir Lucius O'Brien, a County Clare official, begged London not to close down the works in Clare, or else provide funding to bridge the gap, until the soup kitchens were operating. Otherwise, "I am going out to meet hungry and excited mobs [and] what am I to say to them? Is the population to be left to starve? Are you going to abandon us?"

Eventually, the soup kitchens would provide relief; by July, more than 1,800 divisions would be feeding 3 million people daily, an unprecedented feat in a country with a limited network of interior road access.

But in March 1847, the answer to O'Brien's question about abandonment—unspoken, unwritten, but for all intents and purposes—was yes.

In the absence of government relief, and until the soup kitchens were operational, Father Mathew and other volunteer relief workers toiled desperately to save the people of Cork. Mathew almost single-handedly operated a parish soup kitchen near his house that fed between 5,000 and 6,000 people each week; he paid about half the expenses from his own savings and received "contributions from the benevolent" for the remainder. When the soup kitchen was closed, Mathew distributed food from his Cove Street home at any hour of the day, fighting exhaustion and depression; visitors noticed the sadness in his soft blue eyes and the wrinkles in his "straight, high" forehead.

He also spent hours at the Catholic cemetery he had established, presiding over funerals or assisting with the digging of makeshift graves. For him it was a place that evoked both solace and sadness. Here, he had erected a monument to his youngest brother, Robert, who had died at age sixteen, and for more than thirty years afterward Theobald placed flowers on the grave on the anniversary of the boy's death.

Now thousands of famine victims were buried near and around Robert's stone monument; during March and April 1847, as many as thirty-six bodies were interred each day. Father Mathew would estimate later that between November 1846 and June 1847, between 6,000 and

10,000 bodies were buried in the Cork Catholic cemetery, victims of starvation or famine-related disease.

It was no wonder that a chronicler of the famine noted that the Cork Patent Saw Mill was the one business in the region that thrived in the first six months of 1847, "with twenty pairs of saws constantly going, from morning till night, cutting planks for coffins, planks for fever sheds, and planks for the framework of berths for emigrant ships."

The rest of Ireland was no different from Cork in the wake of the public works closings. Across the entire country, March 1847 was the worst month thus far.

From Galway, the secretary of the Industrial Society wrote in late March that "thousands of our fellow creatures are now dying—thousands are already dead." From Limerick came reports that peasants were clawing the bark from tree trunks and eating it raw. In small fishing towns that dotted the Irish coast, residents nearly mad with hunger collected and boiled seaweed, which served as their only source of food.

Relief worker William Bennett, who had previously reported to London that his hand trembled while he wrote of famine horrors, was brokenhearted that what he witnessed in Donegal in late March could actually take place under English rule. He watched people "dying like cattle" and was haunted by the most basic questions that served as indictments of his home country's government: "How could such a thing happen? Is there any possibility of a change for the better? Are there any remedies that can be applied to prevent the recurrence of the same evils?"

From the coastal village of Ballydehob in southwest County Cork, one volunteer at a private soup kitchen had similar concerns. He helped feed nearly 300 people on March 28 (the day the *Jamestown* sailed) and another 300 a day later, yet he wondered whether it was too little, too late. Every person who queued up for food had "the smell of the grave" about them.

Dispirited, he feared for Ireland's very existence.

"The whole country," he wrote, "is one vast tomb."

PART IV

THE UNITED STATES

"The most prominent event of my life"

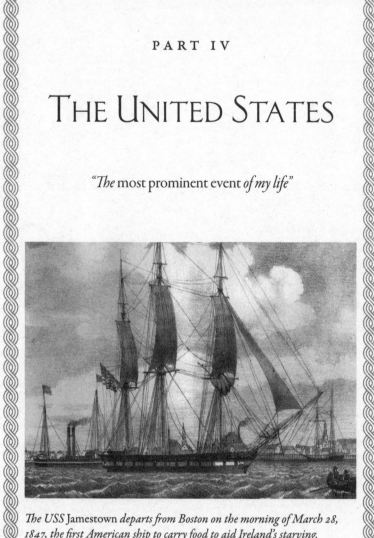

The USS Jamestown *departs from Boston on the morning of March 28, 1847, the first American ship to carry food to aid Ireland's starving.*

CHAPTER 15

"IT IS NOT AN EVERYDAY MATTER · TO SEE A NATION STARVING"

MARCH 17, 1847, CHARLESTOWN NAVY YARD,
JUST OUTSIDE OF BOSTON

As dusk crept across the piers and a chill wind blew from the harbor, Robert Bennet Forbes marveled at the first-day progress of the longshoremen who had spent hours bowing their backs and loading food and provisions aboard the *Jamestown*. It was a "happy coincidence," Forbes noted, that the men—members of the Boston Laborers' Aid Society—were almost entirely of Irish descent and that their work commenced on St. Patrick's Day. In a letter of thanks to the society for offering its workers' services free of charge, Forbes had wished "that all good saints may bless the enterprise and quicken your exertions," and on this day the saints had obliged.

The crews had stowed more than 1,000 barrels of food, one-eighth of *Jamestown*'s full load, as well as more than twenty barrels of clothing. Working for no wages, the men nonetheless were toiling without delay, knowing full well that speed and efficiency in Charlestown could save lives in their beloved Ireland.

While Forbes admired the first-day progress, he was not surprised by it. This whole endeavor had occurred with whirlwind speed: securing congressional and White House approval for an unprecedented mission; his agreeing to lead it; notifying Irish and British government officials and receiving their endorsement; finding and retrofitting a ship and enlisting a crew; obtaining contributions and now loading cargo aboard a warship about to embark on a mission of peace. For the past eight weeks, since the first ships of 1847 had arrived in the United States from Great Britain and passengers and crews revealed the full horror of the hunger besetting Ireland, Boston and America could not have moved with greater swiftness and urgency if their own country had been imperiled.

Forbes, whose life credo was defined by doing his duty, often in the toughest of circumstances, summed up the gravity of the emergency that had prompted such a rapid response: "It is not an everyday matter," he wrote, "to see a nation starving."

Surveying activity around the Navy Yard, Forbes again was reminded of the improbability of assuming command of an American warship for humanitarian purposes while his country was at war. Every place he looked reminded him that the navy was on a war footing; sailors, stevedores, dockworkers, and tradesmen were busy improving and enlarging the Navy Yard or ensuring the seaworthiness of the warships moored there. Workers had completed a new wharf and pier on the west side of the yard, and crews were readying the grounds for construction of another wharf, a brick barn, a plumbers' shop, and a carpentry shop, and were planning to reconstruct a third wharf in need of repairs—all authorized by a recent Naval Appropriations Act and overseen by Commodore Foxhall A. Parker, who had become the Navy Yard's commandant just two years earlier. The warship USS *Vermont*, still in dry dock, finally was nearing completion thirty years after it had been laid down, and the USS *Constitution*—"Old Ironsides"—was undergoing minor repairs after a long stint at sea; Forbes had actually inspected the *Constitution* for the mission to Ireland but found she could not be "made ready to sail" within the quick time frame he envisioned.

The Charlestown yard, more than forty years old, was now a jewel in the navy's crown—President James K. Polk was scheduled to visit in June to inspect the progress and improvements—and its strategic importance as a wartime base had grown after Congress declared war on Mexico on April 23, 1846.

And yet it was the *Jamestown*—carrying "corn not cannon," in the words of one Irish newspaper after twenty of her twenty-two deck guns were removed to make room for food—that was the talk of the Navy Yard, New England, and much of the United States. The enthusiasm among Americans for her peaceful mission was the capstone of nearly two months of national support for Ireland that was nothing short of extraordinary; it seemed people were anxious to rally around a cause that transcended both politics and U.S. borders. Many Americans were frustrated by the polarizing Mexican War and the ongoing acerbic North-South debates about slavery, and perhaps found in Ireland's woes both a cause for unity and a release of tensions. Some said assistance to Ireland would improve long-strained Anglo-American relations, easing acrimony left over from both the American Revolution and the War of 1812.

Others—and Forbes was among these—expressed the belief that God had bestowed great abundance and blessings upon the United States that should be shared with the less fortunate.

On March 28, from the top floor of his house in Boston's Pemberton Square, Robert Bennet Forbes gazed upon a morning that had broken bright and clear. A cold, steady wind from the northwest had blown a stubborn three-day storm out to sea; the late March day was ideal for the *Jamestown* to embark.

Since St. Patrick's Day, when workers began loading provisions onto the ship, Forbes had engaged in a flurry of last-minute preparations. He wrote to Joshua Bates again on March 23 repeating his request that Bates exert his influence to expedite the unloading of the *Jamestown* once it reached Cork. In a letter to William Rathbone, also dated the twenty-third, Forbes stressed his hope that upon his arrival in Cork he would find "*everybody*—Treasury, Admiralty, and private citizens— prepared to discharge the cargo with the utmost expedition and the least expense." He also needed help ballasting the ship for her return voyage; the *Jamestown* would need 250 tons of dead weight as return cargo. Could Rathbone procure "salt or iron . . . preferable to coal or stone . . . at a low rate, or free of freight?" And could he do so "*without* delay to the ship"? Forbes was unsure whether the Boston relief committee would permit him to accept remuneration from the British government for expenses—"this would, I confess, take away much of the poetry of the voyage," he wrote to Rathbone—but some members believed that this was preferable to taking expense money from relief funds, which would only serve to subtract from the amount that could be used to purchase additional food. In virtually every letter he wrote after loading began, Forbes indicated his desire to complete the mission quickly; it was his goal to return to Boston and his family as soon as possible, and to return the *Jamestown* safely back into the navy's hands.

Others penned important letters of introduction on his behalf. Boston Bishop Fitzpatrick provided one to Bishop John Murphy of Cork, marveling at Forbes's "generous heart and noble spirit [that] leaped at once into action" when he became aware of the Irish crisis, "and never since has tired." Two letters came from Edward Everett—Forbes described them as "warm and flattering"—one addressed to Lord Bessborough, lord lieutenant of Ireland, and one to Henry Labouchere, the British government's chief secretary for Ireland. In his letter to Bessborough, Everett described Forbes as a "merchant of great public spirit and worth—a gentleman of high standing . . . who has volunteered his services for this occasion." Attorney John Tappan wrote to his good friend Father Mathew, referring to Forbes as one of "nature's nobles, who [was] leaving the endearment of home . . . to cross the ocean . . . to feed the hungry and raise the desponding."

All of these valuable introductory letters would open doors for Forbes when he arrived in Ireland, and for him, they represented the last "link in the chain of sympathy afforded me at all hands."

Assembling the final crew had also consumed many hours.

Forbes was delighted to accept commitments from four officers who volunteered their time, among the most trusted captains in the region, all experienced and professional seamen, all of whom had served in China on Russell & Co. ships. Frederick W. Macondray, who had retired after making a fortune as a long-distance captain, wrote to Forbes, exclaiming, "I *must* go!" Forbes immediately installed him as first mate and assured Macondray that "the pleasure of this cruise is much enhanced by the prospect of your going as chief officer." Forbes said it was imperative that he and Macondray convey to any other volunteer crew members that the voyage ahead would not be easy. "We must not . . . allow the idea to go forth that we are going on a summer's day frolic—it will be all hard work," he wrote. In addition to Macondray, shipmaster James Dumaresq Farwell volunteered his services as second officer, while captains James H. Foote and John B. White offered their services as third and fourth officers, respectively.

To serve as surgeon, Forbes selected Dr. Luther Park, recommended by, among others, Boston physician Oliver Wendell Holmes. In keeping with the austere nature of the voyage, Forbes stipulated that Dr. Park must "find his own tools & medicine, not exceeding sixty dollars in value for the latter."

As for the remainder of the crew, a flood of young Boston men sent letters to Forbes responding to his advertisement for volunteers, though he could only promise "a room to swing a hammock on the gun deck, plenty of bread and small stores, plenty of hard work under strict discipline, and a return to Boston in about two months." Thousands of experienced seamen—ropemakers, sailmakers, mechanics, and others—had enlisted in the navy at the start of the Mexican War, and captains of merchant ships up and down the East Coast had trouble assembling crews. Thus, Forbes expected responses from the inexperienced and the idealistic, from those who were attracted to the idea of participating in a celebrated humanitarian mission even if they had no idea how to tie a double half-hitch. Most hard-bitten sailors were either on military duty or otherwise in demand on merchant ships; Forbes would likely attract a few veteran seamen, but he had no doubt the *Jamestown* crew would also be manned by well-intentioned but inexperienced landlubbers.

Forbes's offer was alluring enough for a lawyer from Lowell, who was "no sailor" and "should make very poor work at cooking," to offer his services as a clerk; he could report for duty in twenty-four hours.

Two Boston men offered their services as "surgeon and physician." L. W. Hart informed Forbes that he had "never been in action on the sea" but begged the commander to take a chance on him, calling on a "higher power" to persuade Forbes to accept his request to sail. Williamstown's Samuel Duncan also volunteered to make the trip as a surgeon but was willing to perform other duties as well, for which he could provide highly favorable "factory references." The town fathers of South Dennis, on Cape Cod, dispatched Daniel Sears to sign on as a seaman. Boston's Marcus Huntley said he would be a competent cook, "and could procure the services of some others . . . if you should wish them." And a twenty-three-year-old law student from Cambridge, Eugene Batchelder, who had participated in securing food and supplies for the *Jamestown*, told Forbes he would now "like to assist in distributing them to the Irish"—he volunteered to be the ship's secretary.

Groups offered their assistance, too. On behalf of the pilot captains of Boston, whose job was to transfer captains from shore to the large vessels they commanded, Henry Gurney told Forbes it would be "a duty and a happy privilege to be of service to you," including offering Forbes use of the group's offices. Moses Grant, benefactor to and member of the board of directors of the Boston Farm School for indigent boys, donated a "package of books, tracts, and pamphlets" for *Jamestown*'s crew members to peruse in their idle moments. "They are of small value in money, but may be interesting to some of the seaman," he said, adding: "Never did a ship leave our harbor under more delightful and gratifying circumstances . . . [the *Jamestown*] is a U.S. Ship of Peace."

And of course, food contributions arrived from all over New England, most of them from within Boston city limits, but many from elsewhere—towns, societies, individuals—transported free of charge on several railroads that also joined the wave of generosity that the mission engendered. Local Irish immigrants even hand-carried sacks of potatoes and flour to the dock for workers to load.

From gardens and farms in and around Boston, from the hills and hollows of northern Vermont, from the Rhode Island coast and the wheat fields of Connecticut, from the mountains of New Hampshire and Western Massachusetts, generous deliveries arrived in Charlestown with remarkable speed for loading aboard the *Jamestown*: meal, corn, bread, beans, beef, pork, peas, hams, oatmeal, dried apples, flour, potatoes, rice, rye, wheat, fish, clothing, and other supplies. Committees around New England wrote letters of support to Forbes even as they announced their contributions. "Our committee is free to forward about twenty-five hundred bushels of corn and other grain," reported the Portland, Maine, relief committee, and was pleased to do so "with sentiments of high respect for the truly philanthropic and generous course taken by yourself on this mission."

Forbes was astounded at the level of generosity. "Every sort of facility, wharfage, dockage, labor, pilotage, storage, chronometers, stores, and last, not least, sympathy and approbation have been offered most abundantly," he wrote. Further, any expenses incurred "will be of no consequence compared to the good feeling which will fill the hearts of our brothers in other lands."

He had no doubt that in years to come, he would look back on the mission as "the *most prominent event* of my life."

Forbes spent only about $1,700 of the $3,000 allotted by the committee to retrofit the *Jamestown*, which included the removal of all but two of the ship's deck guns to make room for stowing provisions.

When loading was complete on March 26, Forbes signed a receipt promising to return the *Jamestown* to the Navy Yard in Charlestown "as soon as the contemplated voyage can be accomplished—the dangers of the sea—enemies—pirates—detention by foreign powers, and other casualties excepted."

On March 27, the eve of departure, the navy formally released the *Jamestown* to Forbes, and the ports of Boston and Charlestown cleared the ship through customs.

The next morning, Sunday, at 7:30 a.m., Forbes hugged Rose and said good-bye to their three "chicks"—ten-year-old Bob, four-year-old Edith, and two-year-old James Murray.

Rose had opposed his going on the journey. She understood the humanitarian importance of the *Jamestown* mission, and Forbes knew she was proud of her husband for leading it. But she remembered those dark days almost a decade earlier when Forbes had embarked on his miserable two-and-a-half-year excursion to China at the worst possible time in their young married lives, when they were still recovering from financial ruin and the loss of two children. While the worst of her emotional distress had abated, she also recalled his short voyage to England in the spring of 1841 while she was with child, a son who was stillborn in the fall. It seemed the saddest times in their lives occurred when Robert was on a long voyage far from home.

Rose tried to dissuade him from leaving the family again—as Forbes put it, she "rebelled against my leaving home, until rebellion could not change my course"—but she had to know the chances were slim that her husband would succumb to her entreaties. The family friend who wrote a letter to Rose imploring her to assent to his leading the mission to Ireland suggested she send Forbes on his way "with an erected spirit and a serene countenance." It was one of several letters Rose received asking her to consider the magnitude of what was at stake. It is unlikely Rose's public opposition prompted these letters; more likely Forbes sought the assistance of allies in his efforts to convince Rose of the virtues of the journey. Forbes understood Rose's reaction, even sympathized with it.

But for him, his domestic situation had changed when disaster struck Ireland. This was an opportunity to combine a commitment to duty with good works and worldwide accolades. A man could go an entire lifetime without the opportunity to command such a mission.

An hour later, standing at the helm of the *Jamestown*, cap pulled low, his face already reddened by the bright morning sun and raw northwest wind, Robert Bennet Forbes surveyed the vessel that would transport him, his crew, and 8,000 barrels of food to Ireland.

Built in 1843, she was sleek and long, 157 feet from bow to stern, constructed of live oak, reinforced with copper, and fastened together with bolts. The *Jamestown* had three decks; the berth deck, where the crew ate and slept; the gun deck, now missing all but two guns; and the spar, or upper, deck. Forbes's cabin was aft, and the ship carried staterooms along the sides for other officers. Her three main masts seemed to stretch to the sky on this brightest of days. The *Jamestown* was a fine vessel, and the work done in recent days by riggers and stevedores and crew members had prepared her ably for this historic voyage.

At exactly 8:30 a.m., the ship pulled away from the pier. Forbes dutifully recorded her dramatic departure: "All things being ready, sails set, the fasts single, the breeze fresh, the ship struggling to be free . . . I cried 'let go!' and off she went."

Amid the hearty cheers of hundreds of people lining the wharves, Forbes guided the *Jamestown* out of Navy Yard waters, her stores laden with cargo and her three topsails unfurled. From her mizzen peak flew the Stars and Stripes, and from her magnificent royal mast snapped a white flag emblazoned with a wreath of shamrocks encircling a thistle. The revenue cutter *Hamilton* lowered its flag in salute as the *Jamestown* passed, and as the ship cleared Long Wharf, the towboat *R. B. Forbes* joined the ship, carrying cheering members of the New England relief committee.

How appropriately fitting, Forbes thought, that the steam-powered tug named for him accompanied the *Jamestown* as she left the harbor. The first iron vessel built for mercantile purposes in New England, the towboat had been a familiar sight in Boston Harbor for the past two years. As early as 1838, Forbes had urged underwriters and bankers in Boston to build a steam-powered tug, and after appointing a committee—of which Forbes was a member—to research the possibility and design the boat, the 300-ton *R. B. Forbes*, complete with twin propellers and a large steam engine, was financed, constructed, and launched. Forbes had concluded, only half in jest, that the tug was named for him with a view of "punishing him," since it was generally expected the steam experiment would fail. As his namesake tug accompanied the *Jamestown* on this Sunday morning in 1847, Forbes had no way of knowing that the *R. B. Forbes* would become one of the most successful ships he designed; for the next decade and a half, she towed most of Boston's famed clipper ships to sea.

Now the *Jamestown* sped down the harbor "like a racehorse," clearing wharves and moored ships and small boats at nine knots, the tug hugging her starboard side astern. About an hour later, the *R. B. Forbes* fell away from the *Jamestown* amid roars of approval from committee members on board. After measuring wind and swells, and conducting one final inspection of the ship, Forbes finally signaled to his crew that the *Jamestown* would take its leave from Highland Lighthouse on Cape Cod.

Without escort and under way, Forbes "launched our gallant bark on the broad Atlantic" toward Cork, Ireland, a "voyage full of hope and pleasure, and blessed with the appropriation of many kind hearts at home."

CHAPTER 16

"CONTRIBUTIONS...
ON A SCALE UNPARALLELED
IN HISTORY"

More than 5,000 ships would leave Ireland during the famine era carrying passengers who were fleeing utter destitution in their home country. The *Jamestown* was the first to travel in the opposite direction, laden with food and supplies for Ireland, and its celebrated mission provided the catalyst, the symbolic and physical impetus, that injected further momentum into the nationwide American famine-aid movement that had begun in February.

As spring bloomed and temperatures warmed, as frozen canals thawed and snowdrifts melted from rutted wagon trails and dirt-packed roadways and clogged railroad beds, most communities in the United States, large cities and tiny frontier towns, shifted their plans into action.

They set aside religious, racial, social, economic, and political differences to collaborate on an unprecedented countrywide demonstration of voluntary philanthropy on behalf of Ireland. The plight of a ravaged foreign country and its desperate people pierced America's hardest hearts and opened its most obdurate minds; the desire to relieve Ireland's suffering touched Americans of every stripe—rich and poor, men and women, from all backgrounds and religions and ages and races, from north and south, from the coast and the interior.

Not in the sixty years since the U.S. Constitution was adopted and the United States was established as a republic had the country expressed, or acted upon, near unanimity on *any* topic, let alone a peacetime endeavor that involved aid to a foreign country. When Americans turned their attention to Irish assistance in the spring and summer of 1847, the contentiousness that had permeated the national debate for decades—on issues such as slavery, the War of 1812, sectionalism, government policy toward Native Americans, the Mexican War—dissipated like morning fog.

Time and again, political and community leaders, journalists and clergy, farmers and bankers cited a similar theme as they collected food and shipped it to Ireland: the United States had been blessed by God with rich, productive land and teeming oceans that provided its residents with seemingly endless abundance, and in exchange for this bounty, its people had a duty and obligation to help others suffering for want of food.

It was a universal tenet, a spiritual one for certain, one that political opponents found impossible to argue with—virtually all Irish relief efforts were nonpartisan in nature—and one that was shared by all major religions and denominations. In addition to the obvious desire of Roman Catholics to help, other religions and sects eagerly sought to offer assistance. Jews, Quakers, Methodists, Presbyterians, Lutherans, Episcopalians, Congregationalists, Unitarians, and others all set aside their fears of Irish "popery," at least temporarily, in the name of humanitarianism.

It was an unlikely, even remarkable, causal event: famine in Ireland evoked a spirit of brotherhood across America.

What made the fellowship even more impressive was the nature of the contributions. Yes, people of all economic means sent money, but for the most part, Americans contributed food to the Irish relief effort, crops they had planted and harvested and livestock they had raised and slaughtered and cured, food they had planned to feed to their loved ones, or sell at market to purchase other goods for their farms and their families.

Through July 4, 1848, fifteen months after the assistance began, Americans donated a massive amount of food, more than 9,900 tons, to sustain Ireland. They sent barrel upon barrel of corn, peas, wheat, meal, flour, rice, biscuits, oats, oatmeal, barley, rye, bread, breadstuffs, hominy, hops, beans, arrowroot, vinegar, pork, bacon, beef, ham, venison, dried peaches, dried fish, and—yes—potatoes. And beyond that, Americans donated nearly 650 crates of clothing that they had sewn and tailored by hand, as well as supplies such as soap, candles, hats, eating implements, pots and pans, and other sundries. American ships sailed with their precious cargo into the Irish ports of Belfast, Cork, Donegal, Dublin, Galway, Limerick, Londonderry, Sligo, and Waterford, and also to Liverpool, England, from which food and supplies were distributed to Ireland and Scotland.

Newspapers across the United States urged local communities to join in the national cause to help Ireland, publicizing meetings, tracking total contributions, tugging at heartstrings, and appealing to the consciences of their subscribers, sometimes encouraging competition between communities in contributing food, other times shaming readers outright. "Pittsburgh has not contributed one half of what, of right, ought to be its share towards the relief of the sufferers of Ireland," declared the *Morning Post* in one typical editorial. The editor at the tiny *Hollidaysburg Register* in Pennsylvania noted that Americans across the country had given to Ireland "without distinction of sect or party." In New York, one Albany editor noted that other cities, such as New York, had moved more quickly on famine relief, and asked his readers: "Are not we here to have a share in this movement?" Another Albany publication encouraged abolitionists to exhibit the same compassion to the starving Irish as they did to slaves, pointing out that both groups endured brutal hardships and should be similarly pitied as "miserable sufferers."

Response was rapid and overwhelming. With the *Jamestown*'s departure on March 28, the floodgates opened wide.

The wellspring of direct aid from the United States to Ireland became a first-ever national deluge of generosity that shocked the world and, in many ways, changed it.

New York City and Philadelphia, respectively, emerged as the two largest and most active ports of embarkation for food and provisions (more than half the supplies that reached Ireland went through the port of New York alone). Relief supplies from all over the United States were channeled to their wharves and loaded onto ships bound for England and Ireland. Boston and Baltimore were major embarkation ports as well, and New Orleans remained the most active port for communities in the interior and along the Mississippi.

Most committees sent their contributions in care of the Dublin Quakers—as a whole, Quakers, formally known as the Society of Friends, contributed enormous levels of time, expertise, and manpower in Ireland ministering to the starving. And because Quakers were perceived as apolitical and neutral in their relief efforts, American committees found them easy to work with and honest, non-controversial brokers through whom to distribute food donations. In the United States, the Quaker organization Friends in America provided some of the earliest and most generous donations to Ireland.

Some committees, Boston and Providence among them, chose intermediaries such as British consuls in American cities or American representatives in England. The *Jamestown* mission worked mainly through William Rathbone, the British merchant and lawyer with extensive connections in both Ireland and Scotland. One Albany donation of fifty barrels of wheat flour went directly to Father Mathew, who was friends with the city's newspaper publisher and politician, Thurlow Weed.

In New York City, Irish-born Quaker Jacob Harvey served as secretary of the General Irish Relief Committee, collaborating with chairman Myndert Van Schaick—neither a Quaker nor of Irish heritage—to collect food from New York and twenty-three other states and send it along to Ireland. Harvey and Van Schaick, along with the rest of the committee, decided that unless a donor specified otherwise, all contributions handled by the New York committee would be entrusted to the Friends in Dublin. Philadelphia boasted two assistance operations, a "public state committee" made up of business and civic leaders, and a Society of Friends group under the leadership of Thomas Cope. The public committee accepted donations from around the state and from Maryland, Virginia, Ohio, New Jersey, Illinois, Kentucky, and Missouri. Cope's committee served as a central collection organization for Quakers residing in Philadelphia, in the rest of Pennsylvania, and nationally.

Donations came from Americans far and wide, from farms and mines and factories, from cities, towns, villages, and the vast frontier. Days after the *Jamestown* departed, the Irish Relief Committee in Newark, New Jersey, filled the brig *Overmann* with supplies, and momentum for the direct-aid relief effort gathered like a snowball rolling downhill. Shortly thereafter, the residents of Cincinnati shipped more than 4,000 barrels of flour and cornmeal via the Mississippi River and the port of New Orleans after deciding at a community meeting that "all receipts of money should be converted into provisions, and that a ship-load should be sent to your suffering poor." Organizers asked the Friends to verify that the food reached "the home of the hungry and the cabin of the starving," to assure donors "that their contributions have done good" and to encourage additional charity, "the noblest of our virtues." The citizens of Brooklyn loaded the *Patrick Henry* with food in the hope that it would "arrive in time to alleviate the miseries of a few of the many sufferers in Ireland," and the New York City committee shipped 2,000 barrels of kiln-dried cornmeal aboard the *New Jersey*.

Unsurprisingly, large cities donated the vast bulk of food shipments from the United States. New York led the way with more than $180,000 worth of goods shipped to Ireland, followed by Boston with just under $175,000 in contributions and Philadelphia with more than $80,000. New Orleans, Baltimore, Brooklyn, Pittsburgh, Newark, Charleston, Providence, and Washington, D.C., also contributed substantial amounts of food, clothing, medicine, and other supplies.

In addition, shipowners in these large cities, recognizing the momentum of the Irish relief effort and the goodwill that could spring from it, made more vessels available from April through the summer of 1847. During these months, the Philadelphia committee alone sent eight ships to Cork, Londonderry, Dublin, Donegal, Limerick, Galway, Belfast, and Liverpool.

But in some ways, the most symbolically impressive U.S. donations came not from the big cities, not from the wealthy and the merchants and the business owners, but from those who struggled and scraped to make ends meet, those who lived and worked throughout the nation's largely untamed interior—farmers and mill hands, hunters and trappers, saloon workers and shopkeepers, furriers and farriers. They most exemplified the spirit of giving during America's humanitarian outpouring to Ireland—they could least afford to contribute food, but did so without hesitation.

It is perhaps not shocking that New York City—big, brash, bustling, and boisterous even then—took credit for the generosity of America's smaller cities and towns that dotted the interior. In late June 1847, Myndert Van Schaick credited his city for encouraging donations from other American locales, especially small communities from the "great far west," then stretching to about the Mississippi River, and to some frontier outposts beyond, including those established by people who had traversed the Rockies and established residence as far away as California (before the Gold Rush). "The note of alarm and preparation which was sounded in this city no doubt produced a sympathetic pulsation throughout this country," he wrote, pointing out that more than 40,000 barrels of cornmeal from numerous small locales had passed through New York on their way to Ireland.

Whether contributors from outside New York would agree with Van Schaick is highly debatable. Virtually everywhere, Americans responded with startling generosity, sometimes with specific instructions reflecting the thoughtfulness they had given to Ireland's plight. Nashville, Tennessee, residents sent $4,000 to New York with instructions to purchase food and ship it to Ireland for distribution "in such a way as . . . may be productive of the greatest relief." The committee in Milwaukee, Wisconsin, specifically asked that the Friends request "Roman Catholic and Protestant ministers" in Ireland to distribute its donated flour as follows: "50 barrels to Dublin, 50 barrels to Belfast, 50 to Cork,

75 to Waterford, 100 to Galway, 60 to Valencia in Kerry, and 50 barrels to Westport, County Mayo." The Relief Committee of Steubenville, Ohio, located about seventy miles south of Pittsburgh on the Ohio River, requested that its 350 barrels of flour be distributed in the north of Ireland, since some of its contributors hailed from the northern region or were "descendants from those who emigrated from that quarter."

The chairman of the Richmond, Virginia, committee wanted the people of Ireland to know that his city's contribution of cornmeal came from people "whose sympathies have been painfully awakened by the awful calamity which has befallen your country."

For reasons of sympathy, kinship, or simply a realization among small farmers and trappers in America's interior of "there but for the grace of God go I," food contributions poured in from far-flung geographic locations, places where Americans depended almost exclusively on the crops they grew and the game they shot to sustain themselves and their families.

The relief committee from Detroit, then a frontier town and the capital of Michigan until mid-March 1847 when the state government moved to Lansing, contributed more than 2,300 barrels of food and "four packages of clothing" for Ireland's poor. "We represent a population of less than 300,000 souls, who are scattered throughout a territory embracing more than sixty thousand square miles," the committee wrote, "and a large part of them live in places so isolated and remote as not to have allowed their cooperation in this contribution." This geographic dispersion, coupled with the fact that "many of our citizens are poor . . . and have little accumulated capital," would seem to argue against Detroit's generous donation. But settlers in Detroit and Michigan were grateful that they were "blessed with abundant harvests," and Ireland's wants and needs were "met with sympathizing hearts" and a cooperative relief effort. In addition to generous donations from farmers and other residents, the committee noted that "the proprietors of our railroads, our warehousemen, and the owners of vessels have generously aided in affording the means of gratuitous transportation to Buffalo and New York [City]."

The Detroit committee assured the Friends in Ireland that "although many miles of land and ocean intervene between us," Michiganders considered the Irish their "suffering brethren" and sympathized with their pain. "Our home is more than eight hundred miles from the Atlantic, but the tale of your misery has reached us," the committee wrote, "and we are happy in being able . . . to contribute to your relief."

Some rural outposts despaired that they could not be more generous. From Zanesville, Ohio, the Muskingum County committee confessed it could only spare limited amounts of food, but assured the Friends that donations were given in "heartfelt sympathy" for Irish suffering. Residents of tiny Elyria, Ohio, acknowledged they had "done what we could" when they shipped twenty-five barrels of cornmeal and a "box of garments." The Madison, Indiana, relief committee apologized that it could ship only 135 barrels of cornmeal and 13 barrels of flour, but assured the Friends that residents gave "liberally according to their means," pointing out that "although this is a land of plenty, still we have some *here* who want [need] assistance."

And from Ottawa, Illinois, in LaSalle County, relief committee treasurer William Cushman hoped the Friends would not "despise the gift" of a mere $300 in cash that his settlers contributed, a "small pittance" for Ireland, he understood, but a gesture that proved "we will always be your friends in adversity."

He apologized for not sending direct food aid, but asked the Friends to remember that "the whole north part of the state was in the possession of the Indians until fifteen years past, and [is] of course, uncultivated."

Residents of small towns everywhere, including Rochester, New York, made Irish relief a community-wide civic exercise.

In late March 1847, in front of the Monroe County courthouse on Main Street, members of the Rochester Irish Relief Committee tallied contributions from the city and the county: nearly 200 barrels of cornmeal plus flour, corn, wheat, and clothing were ready to ship to New York City. From there, the schooner *Europe*, set to sail on March 31, would transport donations from upstate New York to Liverpool,

England, and on to Ireland. Levi Ward, chairman of the committee, observed that the Rochester contributions "have been most cheerfully made," along with prayers of the donors for the Irish people. There was little doubt in his mind that the ties of brotherhood between America and Ireland would be "strengthened fourfold" by famine assistance to Ireland.

The food shipment from Rochester was the culmination of a series of grassroots activities to benefit the Irish, beginning with a mass meeting at the courthouse on February 8, "the largest gathering of concerned and giving citizens we have ever seen," Ward recalled, "embracing all classes of citizens." Rochester residents quickly selected an executive committee and committees for each of the city's nine wards, and divided those wards into districts; over the next weeks, volunteers strove to "visit each family" in Rochester to solicit contributions. Committee members drafted circulars and visited nearby farmers seeking donations; others made the rounds of nearby communities in Monroe and Ontario counties—Ogden, Greece, Irondequoit, Batavia, Canandaigua—encouraging contributions.

A group of Rochester men organized a St. Patrick's Day gala for Irish relief. Volunteers visited schools seeking donations and asked clergymen to use their pulpits to urge parishioners to give generously; those efforts gained momentum when William DeLancey, Episcopalian bishop of the Diocese of Western New York, called upon Episcopalian clergy to make special collections for Irish and Scottish famine relief.

Members of the Rochester committee repeatedly emphasized the severity of the crisis. The "famine in Ireland has no parallel in modern history," remarked one in a newspaper article. Americans had an obligation to help, said another, "especially we of the Genesee Country, who are surrounded with an inexhaustible supply of nature's bounty," referring to the fertile Genesee Valley in upstate New York. Still another pointed out that the farmers of Monroe County had a moral responsibility to assist since wheat prices had increased dramatically overseas and had become a "source of great profits" to farmers across the valley.

Response was swift and widespread. Area farmers contributed livestock, corn, and other grains. Railroad managers and shippers along the

Erie Canal agreed to transport goods free of charge to New York City, and many local businesses, including the Savings Bank of Rochester, contributed money and goods and services. Before the Rochester relief committee disbanded in November 1847, it would ship nearly 1,000 barrels of cornmeal alone to Ireland.

"It is a delightful employment to feed the hungry and to succor the perishing," Levi Ward wrote.

Official Irish relief committees handled most of the contributions, but inspired by the national wave of giving, groups of citizens, workers' groups, and members of organizations across the country also took it upon themselves to donate on their own. Most of these donations were in the form of money, with contributors asking relief organizations in Ireland to purchase as much food as they could with the funds.

In Albany, members of the Labor Mutual Benefit Society contributed $100, with pavers, secretaries, and machine tenders each giving $1. Mill employees in Wilkes-Barre, Pennsylvania, raised $153 for Ireland and $51 for Scotland; most noteworthy and remarkable, according to a local newspaper, was that "every hand in the mill gave something, which was creditable to them . . . considering that they have been idle for some weeks, owing to the Mill undergoing some repairs."

Military personnel also felt the desire to give. Officers, mechanics, and laborers employed at the city fortifications in Charleston, South Carolina, sent a cash donation. Officers and cadets at West Point sent money to New York City, and members of the U.S. Navy serving on the west coast of Africa aboard the USS *United States* collected funds for Ireland, with one-quarter for Scotland. The crew, sent to its location to suppress the by then illegal slave trade, came forward to contribute "without being prompted," according to Captain Joseph Smoot, a hero from the War of 1812. "We are aware that it is but a 'widow's mite' when compared with the amount subscribed by our kind-hearted people at home," Smoot wrote, "yet we trust that it will effect some good."

Among the most poignant and heartwarming gestures on behalf of Ireland were the contributions made by the young, the marginalized, the enslaved, and the incarcerated. African American churches in

Philadelphia and slave churches in Richmond, Virginia, and other southern states sent donations, as did inmates in New York's Sing Sing Prison. Children enrolled in a pauper school in New York sent money to Asenath Nicholson, who described it as "an offer richer than all"; she gave the money to "a school in the poorest convent in Dublin that was in the greatest state of suffering." Boys and girls in a New York City orphanage raised small amounts for the Irish poor; in Newburgh, New York, two small boys gave $1 each from their earnings at a local manufacturing plant. Schoolchildren in many American communities brought coins to school that were donated to Irish relief.

A number of Native American tribes also sent donations to the Irish poor. By far the most magnanimous of these was the gesture by the Choctaw Indians, who just sixteen years earlier had suffered their own catastrophic event. In 1831 they were forced by U.S. government policy to endure a 500-mile death march from their home and ancestral land in Mississippi to the wilds of Oklahoma Territory. Unprepared for the grueling journey, which began in December during one of the most severe winters in the American South, more than half of the tribe died of starvation, disease, and exposure along what would infamously become known as the "Trail of Tears." Perhaps recalling their own suffering during the march, the Choctaw, during a meeting at their capital in Skullyville, Oklahoma, in the spring of 1847, collected money for Irish famine victims. The *Arkansas Intelligencer* reported that "a meeting for the relief of the starving poor of Ireland was held at the Choctaw Agency . . . after which the meeting contributed $170."

According to one Irish schoolteacher who fled the famine in 1847 and visited the United States, the Choctaw donation was "singularly appreciated . . . these noble-minded people, sometimes called savages by those who wantonly released death and destruction among them, raised money from their meager resources to help the starving in [Ireland]." The teacher's diary entry continued: "This is indeed the most touching of all the acts of generosity that our condition has inspired among the nations."

Established and cemented in 1847, the bond endured between the

Irish and the Choctaw. A century and a half later, during the commemoration of the 150th anniversary of the Irish famine, the lord mayor of Dublin unveiled a specially commissioned plaque to commemorate the generosity of the Choctaw. In return, Irish president Mary Robinson was given the title "Honorary Chief of the Choctaw Nation" by the Choctaw delegation who attended, the only woman so recognized in the history of the Choctaw.

In 1995, President Robinson visited Choctaw headquarters in Oklahoma and said: "We will always remember with gratitude . . . the compassion and concern displayed by the Choctaw Nation, who, from their distant lands, sent assistance to the Irish people at that sad time."

The Irish responded to this outpouring of American generosity with all the mixed emotions that recipients of kindness often feel: immeasurable gratitude for the generosity bestowed upon them; deep shame for the impoverishment that forced them to require assistance in the first place; and seething resentment toward those they held most responsible for their predicament—in this case, the British government and the bureaucrats who carried out its policies.

Using food contributions from the United States as a cudgel to criticize the Crown, the *Cork Examiner* opined: "A nation which owes us nothing [the United States] . . . should be a model to a nation that owes us her pre-eminent greatness." Even the *Times* of London, long antagonistic and unsympathetic toward Ireland, confessed to a "passing sensation of wounded pride" that English subjects in Ireland were helped far more by the United States than by the British government. "But if we are unable to rescue Ireland from the grasp of famine, as confessedly we are," the paper admitted, "it does not become us to resent the assistance of a generous kinsman and friend." The *Times* stopped short of overt criticism of the British government, but acknowledged: "Whoever is to blame, most true is it that Ireland does not prosper in our hands. We must therefore submit to be . . . helped in our task."

Jonathan Pim, secretary for the Friends' Relief Committee in Dublin, gratefully acknowledged America's "unparalleled manifestation of sympathy and liberality" and added that "we were not prepared for so large and general an [outpouring] of sympathy and such immense supplies as have already flowed in upon us." But at the same time Pim was embarrassed and humiliated by Ireland's dependency on charity. Capturing the bleak mood of the dispirited Irish people in a long letter to New York relief committee secretary Jacob Harvey, he wrote: "It is sad to think how much our country is demoralized. We are a nation of beggars." The psychological effect of such dependency was debilitating and exacerbated the "prostrated and demoralized state of the poor people under the influence of gratuitous relief."

Still, the overwhelming feelings from Ireland were thankfulness and hopefulness for the future. Late in 1847, Pim and his fellow secretary wrote to James Reyburn, treasurer of the Irish Relief Committee in New York, and conceded that Ireland owed virtually all of the food at its disposal "to the bounty of the citizens of the United States." The people of Ireland would never forget the gesture. "This country owes much to your countrymen," Pim wrote separately, "and we trust they will produce permanent effects, by cementing the bond of union between two nations."

The official report of the Society of Friends cited the "munificent bounty of the citizens of the United States" and concluded that American food "contributions to Ireland were on a scale unparalleled in history." The writers hoped that such generosity would be held "in grateful remembrance, and form a lasting bond of friendship and esteem between the United Kingdom and the great Republic of the West."

Father Mathew concurred, adding that the benevolence of the United States "has inspired every heart in this island with ardent gratitude."

Never before had the people of one nation offered assistance to those of another on such a grand scale.

The humanitarian transatlantic convoy from the United States that began with *Jamestown*'s unprecedented voyage did not stop for all of 1847, during which 114 ships from U.S. ports delivered food, clothing, and provisions to starving Ireland. U.S. citizens shipped so much grain to Ireland that corn prices dropped on the British market, which further (though only marginally) assisted the poor Irish as the year went along. Dozens of additional ships brought food and supplies to Ireland in 1848.

The sheer volume of food transferred from one country to another, coupled with the near-universal support and participation of the American people, made the Irish relief effort an unprecedented international event. New York committee treasurer James Reyburn captured the mood in the United States when he called the contributions "a glorious demonstration of a nation's sympathy for poor suffering Ireland."

For the Irish, the most enduring symbol of this broad charitable initiative—the one for which they were most grateful, the one that involved both private contributions from U.S. citizens and the appropriation of a warship by a foreign government for a noble humanitarian purpose—was the mission that started it all, the mission the whole world watched with curiosity and wonder, the mission with potential to profoundly change the way nations interacted with and behaved toward each other: that of the *Jamestown*.

PART V

IRELAND

"The noblest offering that nation ever made to nation"

The USS Jamestown *arrived in Cork Harbor on April 12, 1847. The ship was greeted by thousands of people who lined the hillsides and wharves, cheering wildly and weeping openly at the sight of the American vessel.*

CHAPTER 17

"You must have seen the tear drop of joy . . ."

For the first ten days of the voyage, Forbes and his officers worried that the *Jamestown* might not even reach Ireland.

Snow, sleet, dense fog, ice, howling gales, and then "rainy dirty weather and variable winds" made navigation risky, especially with the ship's inexperienced crew, and slowed the *Jamestown*'s progress early in the journey. The men struggled with new riggings stretched by constant dampness, and several of the sheets—the ropes attached to the lower corners of the sail—parted in the gale-force winds, keeping the crew busy night and day reattaching them. The *Jamestown*'s large square sails were difficult to set amid drenching rain and unpredictable gales; unwilling to trust his green crew in the rough weather, Forbes often ordered the main sails reefed, a process of rolling a sail in on itself to reduce its area and stabilize the ship, while reducing its speed.

Crashing waves, freezing temperatures, the spray of salty spume encasing ropes in a veneer of ice—all dangerous enough, Forbes knew, but even more so with a skittish crew. He had taken a quick inventory early in the voyage: of the forty-nine men on board, only thirteen were decent seamen, another fourteen were "fair ordinary" sailors, and Forbes estimated he had, at most, "31 effective men to go aloft, including one mate" and three petty officers. "The number is quite sufficient if they were really smart boys," he wrote, but most were "not very efficient." Forbes identified four laggards—"sick, lame, halt, and blind," he called them—and one aging seaman "fit only for the Insane Hospital."

Moreover, because the ship leaked so badly, something the crew had discovered early in the voyage, constant pumping was required and drew manpower that Forbes badly needed on deck and aloft. He and his officers kept constant vigilance about the leakage, since the ship rode three feet deeper than normal when fully laden with supplies.

For several consecutive days early in the voyage, temperatures hovered around freezing, and for all of their good planning on short notice, Forbes and his crew had forgotten to bring a cabin stove—so they improvised. Cooking was done over deck fires, but to heat the cabin and keep their clothes dry, Forbes invented a makeshift stove by hanging two fire-heated thirty-two-pound cannonballs from a cot hook—a "cheap and safe" way to radiate heat. It also further emblemized the peaceful nature of the voyage, Forbes noted, because like the conversion of the ship itself, using the cannonballs as a stove "carried out the idea of turning weapons of destruction to charitable ends."

Throughout the early foul weather of the voyage, Forbes's steady hand and leadership, along with the experience of his officers, kept the *Jamestown* moving, albeit slowly. Finally, on April 8, which Forbes described as "the first really pleasant day since leaving home," the *Jamestown* encountered temperatures of sixty degrees Fahrenheit and a "fine southwest breeze" that enabled her to travel up to eleven and a half knots (a little over thirteen miles per hour). Over the next couple of days, the ship made runs of 240 and 265 miles per day. On Monday, April 12, Forbes maneuvered his vessel alongside another ship and spoke to the captain; the other ship was bound for Liverpool and had departed from Philadelphia twenty-five days earlier. Forbes took pride that the *Jamestown* was only "14½ [days] exactly from the Navy Yard" when the difference in longitude from the two ships' departure points accounted for only "3 hours, 55 minutes."

Notwithstanding its green crew, leaks, bad weather, and early voyage delays, the *Jamestown* had performed admirably. Late in the day on Monday, April 12, exactly fifteen days and three hours after leaving Boston, the *Jamestown* came to anchor off the lighthouse in Whitebay, in the outer part of Cork Harbor. Forbes estimated that, manned with an experienced crew and encountering more favorable weather, the ship could have made the trip in thirteen or fourteen days. Still, all things considered, the *Jamestown*'s trip to Cork was remarkably fast.

The ever-competitive Forbes took even greater satisfaction when he found out later that he had piloted the *Jamestown* into Cork Harbor a full twelve hours ahead of the Philadelphia steamer's arrival in Liverpool.

Like almost every captain, Forbes had relished the idea of piloting his vessel into Cork Harbor, the deepest and one of the largest in all of Europe—some said large enough to accommodate the entire British navy. But Forbes discovered to his dismay that it would be impossible for a large sailing ship to enter the inner harbor against a strong ebb tide and stiff northerly winds. He waited at Whitebay overnight until the steam-powered British ship *Sabrina* arrived early on Tuesday morning, April 13, attached her towrope, and tugged the *Jamestown* "slowly and peacefully" across the broad expanse and bright waters of the inner harbor. "Never did we see our beautiful harbour to such advantage as at that moment," the Cork *Examiner* proclaimed.

From the *Jamestown*'s decks, gliding behind the *Sabrina*, Forbes and his crew stood in awe at the scene before them. Thousands of people lined the hillsides and the wharves. Men and children cheered wildly, women "waved their muslin," and many people wept openly. An Irish band onshore played "Yankee Doodle," while men in small boats waved their hats and shouted their greetings as the *Jamestown* passed. The town of Cove and County Cork had *expected* the arrival of the *Jamestown*, but to actually *see* the big American sloop, the first foreign warship to enter a British harbor since the War of 1812, produced a mixed reaction of joy, gratitude, and disbelief. When news reached Cork city that the *Jamestown* had dropped anchor, bells rang out across the city to welcome the American vessel. Forbes and his crew were greeted by a jubilant reception committee "before the anchor had fairly bitten the soil."

Maurice Power, Cove attorney and chairman of the local relief committee, recalled the scene at Cork Harbor in his own evocative way: "You must have seen the tear drop of joy . . . stand trembling in the eye of many a widow and matron, while a thousand lips pale with woe, and a thousand tongues half-paralyzed with hunger, uttered the feeble but still distinct exclamation, 'God Bless America.'" The name of Robert Bennet Forbes, Power declared, was "already engraved on the grateful hearts" of 8 million Irish.

Press accounts focused on the magnanimity of Forbes and his crew, who crossed an ocean "of their own free will, and at their own special cost . . . leaving their own homes and occupations to feed our starving poor." Without a doubt, the *Advertiser* declared, the *Jamestown* mission was "the noblest offering that nation ever made to nation." The ship, "crammed to the decks with corn and meal and flour," was more than a vessel bearing desperately needed and lifesaving sustenance; it also symbolized "the *feeling*, the *kindness*" of the nation that dispatched it—"a feeling and kindliness that pervaded the whole population" of the United States.

Never hesitant to chide the British government, the *Advertiser* added that *Jamestown*'s arrival also served as "an example and a rebuke" to London's inertia and inaction in dealing with the famine. Indeed, the very speed with which America acted to dispatch a "magnificent" vessel took less time than it would "to get an intelligible answer from the Board of Works, or comprehend . . . one of our bewildering Acts of Parliament."

After anchoring late in the day, Forbes and the *Jamestown* received a steady stream of visitors, including clergy, civic leaders, and military dignitaries.

The official Cove deputation, led by Judge Robert Hare and consisting of fifteen leading citizens, arrived around 5:00 p.m. to express its "sincere and lively gratitude." Reading from a proclamation with some difficulty because he had forgotten his spectacles, Hare said: "The cry of Irish suffering has gone across the waters of the Atlantic, and has been promptly and nobly responded to by the kindly heart of America." Hare and the committee commended Forbes for disrupting his home life and volunteering his services to lead the mission of mercy, the people of Massachusetts and New England for their food contributions, and the United States government for making a navy vessel available to transport "this most welcome cargo to our famishing people."

U.S. generosity and the *Jamestown's* arrival had provided a nation otherwise "filled with sorrow and dismay" its first feelings of consolation and gratitude in months, even more so since the generosity came from a country "which we look up to with so much respect and admiration." Thousands were fleeing Ireland's famine and boarding ships bound for the United States, Hare continued, and the kindness of the *Jamestown* mission had convinced the Cove committee to conclude— though, as it would turn out, with misguided exuberance and more than a little naiveté—that emigrating Irish could count on a "warm and hospitable" reception in America.

Forbes was touched by the Cove committee's reception and, now that he had reached Ireland, further inspired by the entire mission, admitting to the committee that he was "entirely unable by any adequate expression to transmit to you the feelings under which I drop anchor at Cove."

Forbes assured them of the deep resolve of the American people to help the Irish—"the sympathy created in America is of no ordinary character," he assured the Cove committee. The *Jamestown* relief mission, and the additional ships on their way with more provisions, "convey but in faint language the prevailing sentiment of Americans."

That night, from the *Jamestown's* deck, Forbes and his crew marveled at the scores of bonfires blazing upon the hillside, and the hundreds of lamps that shone from virtually every cabin window onshore, the light spilling across the water and illuminating the bay with a soft golden glow. Musical tones—"fairylike," one townsperson would describe them later—and the cries of rejoicing children, both carrying well on this clear night, drifted toward the ship, sounds of hope at last from a community whose citizens had subsisted on little more than despair for nearly a year.

⟨⚬⟩

CHAPTER 18

"I SAW ENOUGH IN FIVE MINUTES TO HORRIFY ME"

When Robert Bennet Forbes and the Reverend Theobald Mathew shook hands and embraced outside of the American consul's office in Cove, it was a providential moment for the starving residents who witnessed it. Both men had achieved nearly saintlike status among the poor Irish: Mathew, tending to his flock, sharing his bread and coin, opening his kitchen and bedrooms, praying over the fever-ravaged, risking his own health—his very life— for families he had long known and loved, a gladiator leading a relentless and courageous fight against famine and fever, from altar and alleyways, from hovels and hospitals; Forbes, the benevolent, mysterious, "illustrious" stranger—the "Merchant Prince," one publication called him—a man of accomplishment and high standing in his home country, convincing his government to loan him a warship, persuading Americans to donate food, volunteering to lead the mission that took him thousands of miles from hearth and family, risking his own life on the high seas for people he did *not* know.

Who could say which man and which gestures were more virtuous? For the Irish, whose religion had instilled in them the value of sacrifice, generosity, and gratitude, the question was superfluous and unanswerable. Both men warranted the highest praise; both deserved near-canonical adulation. Mathew and Forbes—the local and the foreigner, the clergyman and the captain—were fighting for Ireland when no one else was. Despite the deplorable condition of the country and its people, "the national heart yet can throb with gratitude for real kindness," one journalist noted.

While the rest of the world remained silent or turned its back, while the British government harrumphed and dithered, Mathew and Forbes—with, behind Forbes, a seemingly inexhaustible supply of food from the United States of America—were doing everything in their power to save Ireland.

Father Mathew had made the sixteen-mile trip from Cork city to Cove accompanied by his brother, his nephew, and his longtime dear friend John Francis Maguire, founder of the Cork *Examiner*, later a member of Parliament and mayor of Cork. Mathew and Maguire had known each other since boyhood—"the feeling which I entertained towards him at that early period of my life ripened into the strongest and truest friendship as I grew to manhood," Maguire wrote—and each became the other's trusted advisor.

Forbes would later say that he was struck by Father Mathew's humbleness. The priest who had achieved worldwide fame for his temperance crusade greeted the American sea captain in low, almost deferential tones, expressing his deep gratitude for Forbes's mission and the generosity of the United States. In turn, Forbes thanked Father Mathew for his long-distance support of the *Jamestown* mission through his letters to the United States, and emphasized how "impatient" the American people were for the clergyman, whose herculean efforts had been amply reported in the newspapers, to visit the United States. Forbes even violated a rule he had deemed ironclad at the outset of the voyage by offering to transport Mathew to the United States on the *Jamestown*'s return to Boston. The priest declined the invitation, despite his "long-formed wish" to visit the United States, due to "the state of his own country"—it would be an "unpardonable crime to desert her [Ireland] in the hour of her direst need."

When the two men finished exchanging greetings, a deputation of Cove citizens approached Mathew and requested his attendance at a dinner the following evening to honor Forbes, which Mathew accepted with enthusiasm (he would cancel at the last minute after "circumstances over which I have no control place[d] an insurmountable obstacle to my participation").

Then Mathew shared some bad news: Cork's Catholic bishop, John Murphy, had died on April 7, while the *Jamestown* was at sea, and the lord mayor of Cork was on the brink of death, both laid low by fever. For the downtrodden residents of a town bludgeoned by pestilence and famine, the deaths of two prominent leaders only served to further illustrate the hopelessness of their plight. The *Illustrated London News* headlined its account of Bishop Murphy's death "Melancholy State of the County of Cork," reporting that "the climax of mortality and misery has arrived."

When the two men finished their conversation, Forbes agreed to accompany Father Mathew back to Cork city. Mathew had taken it upon himself to serve as Forbes's near-constant companion and guide during his visit, and Forbes wanted to see famine conditions in the more crowded urban area.

It would be a visit that Forbes would never forget.

Breathless, Forbes and Father Mathew dashed into a Cork neighborhood store and made their way to the back door to get away from the starving crowd that had surrounded them outside the front entrance, begging for food. It was near the end of their depressing walk through Cork and, hoping to provide some relief to the poor but perhaps not yet understanding their desperation, Forbes had distributed a few pieces of silver that he had brought from home. Within minutes, the throng swelled and aggressively pressed in on the two men, dozens of voices pleading and clamoring for help. Soon the money was gone and Mathew and Forbes feared they would be crushed. The doorway of the store offered their only escape from a once-hopeful crowd whose desperation had transformed it into a mob.

For a stunned Robert Bennet Forbes, the incident was the culmination of a day that had shaken the well-traveled man deeply. He had seen poverty and hopelessness in other parts of the world, but nothing like this. He had read about the dire situation in Ireland and perhaps imagined the horror as the *Jamestown* plowed through the Atlantic waves toward Ireland—but there was simply no way to prepare for the horror he encountered.

"I saw enough in five minutes to horrify me," he wrote later, "hovels crowded with the sick and dying—some called for water . . . and others for a dying blessing." At one point, he and Mathew ventured off a main street into an alley, which he later described as "not the Valley of the *Shadow* of Death" but the "valley of death and pestilence *itself.*" Forbes was aghast that "every street corner is filled with pale, careworn creatures, the weak leading the weaker; women assail you at every turn with famished babies imploring alms." Father Mathew, like Dickens's Ghost of Christmas Present, next led Forbes to a Cork soup kitchen, where he witnessed a scene that staggered him: "Hundreds of spectres stood without, begging for some of the soup which I can readily conceive would be refused by well-bred pigs in America," he wrote.

Like others who visited Ireland at that time, Forbes kept the worst visages of the famine to himself. He noted that he could easily expound upon his descriptions of the "horrible tales of suffering" but the facts were "too revolting to human nature to be recorded on paper." One fact he was clear on: the newspapers were not exaggerating their stories of the famine. If anything, they were *understating* the Great Hunger's disastrous impact on Irish society for fear of offending or disgusting their readers.

"You will find the truth" in newspapers, Forbes wrote soberly, but "not the whole truth."

Forbes also knew that Mathew had spared him from viewing the worst "haunts of misery"—the urban cellars and dark, fetid apartments in which entire families perished. What he had seen on the streets of Cork today are "*nothing, absolutely nothing,* compared to what I might see had I the courage to go with Rev. Mathew" into these cursed dwellings. Mathew, of course, had spent months venturing into these "haunts of misery"—appalled, dispirited, disheartened, by what he witnessed each day, but never dissuaded from his mission to provide aid and comfort to the afflicted.

Forbes wondered where the priest found the strength to persevere.

As dockworkers were unloading the *Jamestown* at Cork Harbor in Cove, as Forbes shook his head in sadness along the byways of Cork city, conditions among the Irish were worse than ever. Surely the reason for the unbridled enthusiasm of the Irish—and the British—at the *Jamestown*'s arrival was that it coincided with the most fragile and desperate weeks of the entire famine tragedy.

Evidence of despair was everywhere. From Galway, a relief worker noted that "people are heartless and depressed, and in many instances lie down and die by whole families." From Mayo came a report that peasants were desperately trying to gain entrance to any workhouse still open because if they died there, their corpses would be buried in coffins, which they could no longer afford. People were dying so quickly in counties across Ireland that virtually no one attended funerals—normally a sacred rite among Irish Catholics—either because family members of the deceased were already dead or because burials were so commonplace that they no longer warranted prayerful reflection, especially from mourners whose singular focus was on finding food to survive.

Friends and loved ones clinging to life had neither the energy nor the desire to seek spiritual deliverance for those already gone.

CHAPTER 19

"NOT SO MUCH SOUP
FOR THE POOR
AS POOR SOUP"

To make matters worse, the British government's delay in launching the soup kitchen program was exacerbated when London decreed faster layoffs from the public works programs. British taxpayers were not interested in funding two expensive relief operations simultaneously.

In early March, Trevelyan wrote that the cost of public works has "attracted the attention of the Chancellor of the Exchequer and other members of the government." Later, he declared that the rate of expenditure on public works was "fearful," and that if the government continued to hemorrhage money on the program, "we shall add national bankruptcy to famine."

Accordingly, on March 20, just a few weeks before the *Jamestown*'s arrival, the government reduced the public works labor force by 20 percent; another 10 percent of the workforce was scheduled for dismissal on April 24, a total of 200,000 laborers in all. Still, that was not fast enough. Some in the British government were calling for *all* public works to be shut down as of May 1 unless otherwise instructed. Even Trevelyan thought this was too drastic; as many as 700,000 workers and their families—nearly 3 million people—would face starvation.

These threats spawned terror among the starving Irish. Appeals poured in to British government officials, up to and including Prime Minister Russell, begging that the public works programs remain intact for a few weeks longer. On the eve of the 20 percent reduction of workers in March, Sir Lucian O'Brien of County Clare asserted that if the works were closed down, 1,200 men would starve just in Ennis and Newmarket alone. As one discharged worker put it, there was "nothing to do but bar the door, lie down and die."

But the pleas fell on deaf ears. The result: in March, April, May, and much of June, thousands of Irish peasants found themselves with no way to earn money and almost no food of any kind.

By March 10 only around a hundred committees were actually operating soup kitchens in about 12 percent of Ireland's communities, and many of those efforts were tiny, inefficient, and wholly inadequate to feed their parish or town. By April 10, one soup kitchen administrator reported that the new system was still "getting on very slow indeed." It wasn't until April 5, 1847—a full eight months after the blight destroyed the potato crop and while the *Jamestown* was on its way to Ireland— that a replicable, model soup kitchen, designed to feed thousands of people as quickly as possible, opened in Dublin amid much fanfare.

Conceived by French chef Alexis Soyer, the wood-framed canvas building was forty-eight by forty feet, with an entrance at one end and an exit at the other. Rows of tables, about eighteen inches wide, had holes cut in them to hold enameled quart basins, to which metal spoons were attached by chains. One Irish author described the feeding process: "When a bell rang, the first one-hundred people would enter the main apartment and occupy benches at the one-hundred bowls of soup set in the tables." After grace was said, "they would use the chained spoons to consume the soup, until another bell signaled that their soup time was over, whereupon, as they filed out the exit in the rear, they would each be given one-quarter of a pound of bread or savory biscuit." About a minute later, just as the bowls and spoons had been rinsed and another quart of soup poured into each bowl, "the bell at the entrance would invite another hundred people in."

One British official objected to peasants being served like "wild animals," but of greater concern was the questionable nutritional value of the soup itself, which had been watered down to stretch as far as possible. One London chef wondered in a *Times* column whether the almost meatless soup had *any* nutritional value, much less enough to save the "destitute poor" of Ireland. Nor was he alone. England's famous medical journal, the *Lancet*, did its own scientific analysis of Soyer's soup and declared it worthless. Labeling as "soup quackery" Soyer's repeated contention that the broth contained sufficient nutrients, the *Lancet* said that the proportions of beef, fat, flour, sugar, and water provided "less than three ounces of solid nutriment to each quart of soup," whereas a healthy body required twelve to fourteen ounces. The gentry and the politicians might be satisfied with Soyer's soup, the journal wrote, but "that satisfaction . . . will never reach the public stomach." One historian described Soyer's concoction as "not so much soup for the poor as poor soup."

Even Queen Victoria's physician, Sir Henry Marsh, decried the reliance on "soups and other semi-liquid articles of food." The problem: "These pass away too rapidly from the stomach [and] are swallowed too hastily . . . food, to be at once sustaining to the labourer, and preventive of disease, must have bulk . . . [and] all the staminal ingredients of nutriment." Others agreed. A commissariat officer in West Cork complained that soup "runs through them without affording any nourishment," and a doctor in the devastated town of Skibbereen claimed the soup was "actually injurious" to the large number of residents suffering from dysentery.

Trevelyan welcomed and applauded the *Jamestown* and other ships from the United States because their cargoes provided the famine-stricken Irish both with food staples after the works programs began to shut down—"bridging the fearful interval between the system of relief by work and relief by food"—and, once kitchens finally began operating, with much-needed calories and nutrients that the watery soup lacked. Yet, while Trevelyan glowingly commended the United States for its "earnest and universal sympathy" and its "generous and munificent" contributions, he had two deeper reasons—one practical and one ideological—for gratefully accepting aid from "this land of plenty" to benefit the Irish, and by extension the British Empire.

Both, he hoped and firmly believed, would have a beneficial long-term impact on the future of Ireland.

The practical reason was simple: thousands of Irish peasants who worked the land were so weakened by hunger, disease, and lack of basic nutrition that the British government feared they would be unable to till the soil and plant the summer 1847 potato crop. This situation was worsened by the thousands more who had emigrated or were preparing to leave the country, many of them Ireland's youngest, strongest men, who would normally be hard at work in the fields. An insufficient potato yield, even if the crop was healthy, could result in another year of famine. Economic realities also prevented many Irish from tilling the soil. As one Galway citizen noted, many Irish were one or more years behind in rent, or in debt for "meal and manure advanced last season," and thus were afraid to till because "their entire crop would be seized for their debts."

Trevelyan's second deeper reason for welcoming U.S. aid was an extension of and influenced by the first, and went directly to his belief in the laissez-faire role of government. In their current weakened state, he believed, the Irish were already too dependent on the government for sustenance. Another year of crop failure could render that dependency irreversible. Therefore, private and direct food donations transported by the *Jamestown* and dozens of other ships that sailed to Ireland during the spring and summer of 1847 provided both physical and ideological nourishment by preserving the "necessary harmony . . . between the operations of the Government and those of the private associations."

This philosophical reasoning—not so different from the concern Jonathan Pim expressed to Jacob Harvey in New York—drove Trevelyan's policies and recommendations throughout the spring and summer of 1847. He mandated that soup kitchens begin ceasing operations in August, and wind down completely by 1848. He feared that "gigantic efforts" sponsored by the government would not only "exhaust and disorganize society throughout the United Kingdom" but also "reduce all

classes of people in Ireland to a state of helpless dependence." Ireland
had to solve its own serious problems—overreliance on a single crop,
lack of industrialization and modernity, and, most decadent of all, the
"habitual dependence . . . upon the government." For Ireland to survive
in the long term, it would have to learn to fend for and support itself in
a sustainable way. Relying on British government aid, or the largesse of
foreign nations, was a recipe for ongoing disaster.

In his account of the famine, Trevelyan claimed that the cultivation
of land in spring 1847 was "suspended" until landlords and tenant farmers
alike saw what "encouragement the Government would give—or, as it
was sometimes ingenuously expressed, 'We expect the Government to
till the ground.'" He later stated that in some parts of western Ireland
in 1847, many people "neglected . . . to lay in their usual winter stock of
turf" to burn for heat, believing the "popular expression that the Queen
would supply them with coals."

It is unlikely that virtually any of the thousands who cheered the
Jamestown's arrival in Cork Harbor shared Trevelyan's concern about
economic dependency. For them, the story was far more basic: the
holds of the U.S. ship contained an opportunity for renewed health
and vitality, a chance for survival. Forbes and his crew, and the captains and crews that followed, tantalized Irish peasants by delivering
a rare and elusive spark of hope, something their landlords and the
British government seemed intent on snuffing out.

It explains why, from the moment he set foot on Irish soil, Robert
Bennet Forbes was welcomed as a hero.

⌇━✦━⌇

CHAPTER 20

"I BECAME ENLISTED IN BEHALF
OF THIS GOOD CAUSE"

R obert Bennet Forbes prided himself on his communication skills—to entertain his friends, to persuade his adversaries, to settle disputes. He had conducted successful high-level business transactions on multiple continents with personalities of all stripes; he had ordered men to set sails in howling gales and climb riggings slick with rain in the black of night; and he was a prodigious and sensitive writer whose words comforted his distraught wife from thousands of miles away during her darkest days.

But for all of his communication talent and the early age at which he achieved many of his accomplishments during what he described as his "varied life"—first crossing the Atlantic at age six, first visiting China at thirteen, commanding his own ship at twenty, amassing a fortune at twenty-nine and then losing it at thirty-three—Forbes had never before spoken in public to an assembled crowd until he stepped to the rostrum on Thursday evening, April 15, 1847, in the large Coffee Room at Cove's Kilmurray Hotel, the first of two public dinners to honor him and the other *Jamestown* officers. The second event, hosted by Father Mathew, was scheduled for Monday, April 19, at the Cork

Temperance Institute. There, Forbes would address a crowd of nearly 300—this time with women among the invited guests.

In between, Forbes received public deputations aboard the *Jamestown* representing both the citizens of Cork, who wrestled with how to avoid ostentation in their efforts to honor Forbes in the midst of famine and suffering, and the Tenant League, which delivered a scathing indictment of British landlords in a controversial address aboard the *Jamestown* that Forbes wished had been done "in private"—his goal was to avoid political displays to the greatest extent possible.

It was the Coffee Room event that kicked off celebrations to honor Forbes, the *Jamestown*, and the United States. Decorated by Cove citizens, the room was aglow with a "profusion of wax lights," its walls festooned with rich drapery, olive and laurel wreaths, flower arrangements, and the British and American flags displayed at opposite ends of the hall. It was here, among the festive trappings and the excited crowd, that Forbes fully realized the extent of Irish gratitude for his mission, and instinctively understood the importance of acknowledging their gracious appreciation.

Still, he was decidedly uncomfortable at the rostrum. In the golden age of orators—the Websters, the Clays, the Everetts, and others who had inspired Americans to support widespread Irish relief efforts—Forbes communicated best by putting quill to paper to convey his arguments in a thoughtful and organized way. Public speaking had simply not been a part of his repertoire and, in fact, was at odds with his personality. In his view, a successful, well-bred businessman was defined or measured not by his flair and bombast and zeal, but by his quiet earnestness, sober intelligence, enduring perseverance, and unassailable integrity. His word was his bond; as such, he seldom had to raise his voice, a credo that had guided Forbes for most of his life.

But the people of Cove and Cork would have none of Forbes's natural humility. They practically *demanded* to hear from the ship's unselfish captain as they would from a conquering hero—or, in this case, a savior whose presence reminded them that their plight had not gone unheeded in other parts of the world. After a flattering and obsequious introduction by Maurice Power, chairman of the Cove committee, who called for a toast to Forbes "and the great country of which he is the distinguished representative," Forbes stood up, pulled a sheet of paper from his pocket, and began with his customary humility: "Those who do not well know how to collect their ideas in their heads are apt to put them in their pockets—"

The adoring crowd interrupted with roaring laughter.

"—and as I am one of those," Forbes continued, "I shall take the liberty of reading to you what I have to say."

After great cheering, Forbes visibly relaxed, the captain now in firm command of the room.

Though self-effacing in manner and a novice at public speaking, Forbes was a born storyteller with a sharp sense of humor—his extensive writings show us that—and he knew how to read people. The speeches he delivered at the Kilmurray Hotel and a few nights later at the Cork Temperance Institute were not remarkable for their rhetorical flourishes or inspirational passages. Instead, Forbes concentrated on substance over style to delight his audiences: first, by involving the already eager and fawning crowds in the improbable tale of how he came to travel to Ireland; next, by making it clear how fully he and the United States understood the calamity that had befallen Ireland; and then, perhaps to blunt any resentment the Irish might feel toward their benefactors, by thanking *them* for the gracious welcome afforded him and his crew.

Forbes apologized to the audience in Cork city for his cargo being "so inadequate to relieve the distress of the County of Cork; I wish it had been ten times as great." In Cove, he reassured the crowd of the deep sympathy "which prevails among all classes of people in America" for suffering Ireland. When Americans heard the full extent of the Irish catastrophe, they responded swiftly and generously; the result was a bond between the two countries that Forbes predicted would remain strong and deep for generations. When the audience cheered him repeatedly in Cork, Forbes interpreted the applause as "nothing more than a manifestation of the feeling of the people of Cork and of Ireland toward the people of the United States . . . I became enlisted in behalf of this good cause."

He described in detail the events that led up to the *Jamestown's* arrival—the big Faneuil Hall meeting in Boston where the idea was hatched to use a warship to transport food to Ireland; congressional support for the mission; the generosity of New Englanders and people across the United States who donated provisions; his answer to the critic who objected to the use of the *Jamestown* for a humanitarian purpose ("it is not an every day matter to see a nation starving")—and he was interrupted with cheers and shouting throughout.

He assured them that the *Jamestown* delivery was only the beginning. Word from the New England relief committee in Boston was that the *Tartar* and *Reliance* would soon sail for Cork, and that the *Morea* was bound for Glasgow, Scotland. And, as yet unaware of the delays that plagued the *Macedonian's* departure from New York, Forbes portended its imminent arrival in Cork: "I should not be surprised, if by the time I get home, the contributions amount to a fifth cargo," an announcement that was met with a thunderous ovation at the Cork gathering. While Forbes knew that widespread relief efforts were organized in the United States, he was not yet fully aware of the vast number of American ships that would follow with food and provisions for Ireland.

Throughout his remarks at both events, Forbes offered his thanks to his hosts, injected his trademark humor wherever appropriate, and above all, remained humble. The Cove audience cheered themselves hoarse when Forbes told the citizens of Cork that he had been "killed by kindness" during his time in Ireland, which only made him more satisfied that he represented the American people on "this beautiful errand." He was so moved by his warm reception that he had difficulty finding appropriate words of gratitude. He begged the audience to "spare me from any [further] public demonstrations of your kind regard—enough has been said and enough done to cancel all your debt to me, were it tenfold what it was." The Temperance Institute crowd laughed along with him when Forbes quipped: "You call this a temperance meeting; I must say that you are very intemperate—*very* intemperate in your good wishes."

The Cork mayor then presented Forbes with a lithograph engraving of the *Jamestown's* arrival in Ireland, mounted in a gilded frame. Forbes said he hoped to "hand it down to his great-great-great-great-grandchildren."

Visibly moved by the generous gift and the audience's response, Forbes endeared himself further to his hosts when he added: "If I shall live to the age of Methusela, I shall never forget my reception."

For their part, Forbes's hosts used the two celebratory events and a series of written declarations they presented to the *Jamestown* captain as an opportunity to thank the people and government of the United States.

Attorney Maurice Power, chairman of the Cove event, began the string of plaudits when he told Forbes: "You have added a new glory to the land of your birth, the land of Washington and Franklin. . . . Ages yet unborn will pronounce with reverence and respect your honored name." Ireland would never forget Forbes or the gesture by the United States; more specifically, no Irishman—"whether in the old world or the new"—would forget. Ireland pledged its full support, in the present and in the future, to the United States. The *Jamestown* mission had taught the Irish about the generosity of the American people even as they witnessed firsthand the failings of the British Crown to rescue them from starvation. "Wherever there is to be found an Irishman," noted the chairman of the Cove dinner to honor Forbes, "wherever his free heart beats, *there* America will find a natural ally and an unalienable friend." The theme was repeated by the Tenant League committee, which asked Forbes to assure the U.S. government and its people that "their one unarmed 'sloop of peace' has won a nation . . . and won an ally on every sea."

Citizens at a County Cork meeting about the *Jamestown* referred to Forbes as a "zealous and enlightened philanthropist" and said America's "philanthropy, benevolence, and humanizing charity should be graven on the mind of every grateful Irishman." Most magnanimous of all was that America's donations were made "unclogged with any condition and unalloyed by any selfishness . . . in the annals of self-devotion to the cause of the poor and the suffering, there is no brighter example."

For these people, who crept through Ireland's streets like "shriveled skel-etons full of sorrow and dismay," it was America's *gesture*, as much as or more than the actual food donations, that helped save their souls and revive their spirits. The *Jamestown*, said the official message from the Cork Temperance Institute to the U.S. government, was regarded by Ireland as an "angel of peace and love; as a dove of promise, bringing an olive-branch of hope" across the Atlantic to a "helpless and sinking ark."

At the Temperance Institute event, Father Mathew said he could never have imagined such happiness in a region so stricken with sorrow and bereft of hope—the gathering was "a sublime and beautiful one."

Praise and words of thanks also poured in from beyond Cork and Cove. Elected officials from Dublin wrote to the president of the United States expressing gratitude for the "unparalleled extent of the ef-forts now being made on [Ireland's] behalf" across America and the "unprecedented conduct of your government" by making a warship available while the United States was engaged in its own war. Again, Dublin officials emphasized, the *Jamestown*'s cargo certainly was wel-comed and needed, but worthy of greater gratitude was the "flattering good will evinced in conferring it." Forbes was particularly gracious in his response to the message from Ireland's capital, saying of his role in the mission, "I shall ever look back to it as one of the rare privileges to which few attain and as an honor, greater than which, few can aspire to."

Well aware of British-Irish tensions, Forbes tried to refrain from overtly political declarations in his remarks, but the residents of Cove, Cork city, and beyond were bound by no such strictures.

Time and again, their gratitude toward Forbes and the United States was laced with antipathy—and worse—toward the British gov-ernment. Whereas America had moved swiftly, with enthusiasm, and without conditions to help Ireland, the British government was sluggish and unresponsive during the most crucial famine months; where the United States donated food and a navy ship with no questions asked, the British government complained that refitting a warship was pro-hibitively costly and that wholesale shipments of food to Ireland would disrupt corn markets; where the British government and her landlords "despised and hated" the Irish laborer "as vile and infamous," the United States encouraged and counted on laborers, farmers, shopkeepers, fishermen, and dockworkers—many of them of Irish heritage—to contribute to Irish relief, people who "feel for [our] national suffering" and give their "unbought labor to hasten our succor."

Perhaps the most demonstrable example of a public expression of loathing toward the British government occurred at the end of a meeting among the citizens of Cork. A group put forward a resolution that commended Forbes, the United States government, and the American people for their generosity and charity, but chastised the English government, "whose duty it was to take measures to meet the fearful exigencies" of Ireland, for being guided by "a false political economy and petty government expediency." The chairman balked at whether to put the resolution to a full vote, saying he was reluctant to propose anything "in which there would not be the greatest unanimity," and because the phrase "expressed political opinions," some at the meeting might not agree with it, but "if it were the wish of the meeting it should be put, he would do so—"

The crowd interrupted him and roared, "Put it, put it," and the chairman called for the vote. The resolution passed unanimously, with resounding applause.

The *Jamestown* mission had provided the people of Ireland with food and—for the first time in the eight months since the potato crop failed—a voice.

Robert Bennet Forbes and Father Theobald Mathew had not known each other before meeting in Cove, but their like-minded toughness, generosity, sense of duty, and sometimes roguish behavior, and even the parts of their personalities that sought acclaim and occasional martyrdom, helped to cement their friendship quickly. Savvy about the power of symbolism and imagery, the two men understood the importance of being seen together working to alleviate some of the suffering in and around Cork; it reassured the Irish peasant population that men of prestige and importance on both sides of the Atlantic recognized their plight, and perhaps could influence the British government to do so also.

Mathew also seemed intent on providing Forbes with more pleasant memories of Ireland. Although Forbes declined invitations to London and Dublin on the grounds that they would distract from his mission, he did accede to Mathew's request to spend a few hours touring the Cork countryside. On Sunday, April 18, the priest escorted Forbes to Blarney Castle and watched approvingly as his guest adhered to Irish tradition and kissed the stone. The next night at the Cove Temperance Institute meeting, Forbes coyly suggested to the crowd that he had little to say, but then added: "I went yesterday to Blarney [loud laughter]—I suppose I must say something to you, or you will not believe that I kissed the stone [louder laughter]."

Later in the day, Mathew escorted Forbes to the 100-foot-tall temperance tower, built atop Mt. Patrick, several miles outside of Cork, to commemorate Mathew's enthusiastic reception from the people of London during his first temperance visit to England's capital city in 1843. The tower was constructed and funded by William O'Connor, a merchant-tailor, and was opened to the public on November 9, 1846, after the potato crop had failed. Despite the onset of famine, a grand event marked the tower's opening; hundreds attended the ceremony and climbed the spiral staircase to view the magnificent landscape of the valley. O'Connor and Mathew both spoke, and the tower was brilliantly illuminated at night by more than a thousand variegated lamps, creating a "grand and imposing" effect from its elevated location.

As he stepped onto the tower's balustrade on April 18, 1847, Forbes enjoyed "one of the finest views I ever had the good fortune to look upon," but he was well aware that the lush, sloping, verdant valley before him belied the pervasive despair he had witnessed on his trip—he would not be deceived. "I must not dwell on this and other views about Cork, and between it and Cove," he said. Yes, "they are surpassingly beautiful," but looking down from the tower "on the landscape apparently teeming with life and health and beauty," he could not help exclaiming: "Is this the land of famine and pestilence; and if so—why is it so? This is a question the wisest cannot answer."

Sandwiched around Forbes's Sunday respite and his visits to the Blarney Stone and the temperance tower were Saturday and Monday afternoon meetings that would not answer the question of *why* Ireland suffered famine and pestilence, but would determine practical steps of how to alleviate a portion of the suffering. These sessions were about the crux of Forbes's mission—how best to distribute the *Jamestown*'s food to as many starving people as possible.

They would be long, tiring, and emotional meetings. And because the very nature of their agenda was a matter of life and death, they would not be without controversy.

⟨—✦—⟩

CHAPTER 21

"The food should be distributed as soon as possible"

Perhaps human nature dictates that otherwise well-meaning people who are deprived of life-sustaining necessities long enough will clash about how to divide limited quantities of that sustenance once it finally arrives.

Or perhaps conditions in Cork city were so bad that reasonable men turned confrontational and reached diametrically opposing views on how to alleviate the suffering.

Most likely, it was a combination of the two.

In any case, two warring factions quickly established themselves when county leaders, clergy, elected officials, and Robert Bennet Forbes gathered at the Cork Institution to discuss the distribution of the *Jamestown*'s cargo. While both Irish and U.S. officials had decided before the ship left Boston that none of *Jamestown*'s foodstuffs would be distributed beyond County Cork's boundaries because the worst of the suffering occurred there, the issue turned heated among Cork leaders when they debated how to parcel out provisions within the county. The *Jamestown*'s cargo could feed thousands of people for a period of weeks, perhaps even a few months, but not indefinitely. Plus, the hard geography of the county—its lack of roads, rutted cowpaths, and muddy bogs—meant it would be exceedingly difficult to transport food to the interior regions.

Hard decisions were required.

Now that food had finally arrived, who would receive it—and how much?

The first group, led by Father Theobald Mathew, wanted virtually all of the food distributed within the Cork city limits, where thousands of people from the countryside had staggered, many ravaged by fever, in search of food scraps. Distress was so great in Cork city—just the previous day, for example, Father Mathew had visited an apartment in which sixteen people, delirious with fever, were dying in a single room—that he begged the committee to ensure that the "seven parishes in Cork [city]" received their share of food before anyone else.

He told the group that he had buried 300 corpses in his cemetery just the previous week, victims of fever and starvation, some with no family members alive to mourn them, and others whose loved ones were too weak to organize funerals. Who could be more desperate? Father Mathew stunned the group when he argued vociferously for a police cordon around Cork city to prevent any other country travelers from entering. The rural areas of the county needed to fend for themselves; or at least the committee should devise a different means to serve them.

The priest reminded others at the table that the city was cracking from the stress and desperation of the Great Hunger, and while he did not share his personal burdens with the committee, it was clear that the awesome weight upon his shoulders to provide famine relief was taking its toll. In all of Father Mathew's words and deeds during his lifetime as a priest, he had never turned his back on any group, let alone the poorest and most desperate. Through his years of alleviating the suffering of cholera victims, warning of the dangers of alcohol consumption, encouraging his flock to sign the temperance pledge, administering soup to famine victims, tending the sick, praying for the dying, and burying the dead, the meetings in Cork to discuss the distribution of the *Jamestown*'s cargo were the only times he suggested neglecting or outright abandoning *anyone* in favor of anyone else.

Living each day amid the suffering of thousands in a teeming, squalid city wracked by starvation, Father Mathew could see no further. He seemed unable—or unwilling—to consider the plight of untold thousands who suffered piteously in bogs and filthy mud huts across the blighted countryside of County Cork.

Tensions heightened after Father Mathew spoke.

The opposing point of view was most vehemently articulated by forty-six-year-old William Fagan, a Cork city writer and soon-to-be member of Parliament who argued that *none* of the *Jamestown's* food supply should reach Cork city; rather, all of it should "be sent to the most distressed districts" across the county. At this point, more than half the population of County Cork, and perhaps as much as three-fourths, depended totally on the potato, compared with about 30 percent dependency nationwide. Fagan went on to argue that once word circulated that the city would receive no supplies, people from the countryside would have no incentive to travel to Cork, "which would result in a diminution of the number of strangers coming into the city." Wasn't that what Mathew and other Cork city leaders wanted?

After all, Fagan pointed out, the *Jamestown's* food supply designated for the city would be, in the best of circumstances, "a drop in the ocean compared with the amount of destitution," which was "fifty times greater than the relief that could be afforded." Did it not make sense to concentrate relief efforts outside of the city?

Nonsense, said Father Mathew. Fagan couldn't be serious. His proposal to bypass Cork city entirely neglected the most desperate people in all of Ireland. And perhaps it would be a deterrent to *future* travelers from the countryside to flock to the city, but the priest wanted as much relief as possible "for the people who were already in the city." On this point, Father Mathew was resolute.

Looking to break the tension and the impasse, highly regarded Cork physician Dr. Robert Lyons posited that the "high quality of *Jamestown* food" compared with what residents had been ingesting—mostly seaweed, grubs, and the occasional turnip—might provide an opportunity to stretch it further and accommodate residents across the county. "Some of it [the food] was of so very superior a kind as to be impracticable for the use of the extreme destitute," he said. "It would be for the Committee to adopt a mode of rendering it double its present amount." Put another way, because Cork's starving residents were un-accustomed to quality food, they would be grateful for any amount put in front of them, even if were insufficient to satiate their hunger; this would allow the committee to stretch *Jamestown*'s cargo. If the goal was to feed as many as possible—and that most assuredly *should* be the goal, Lyons argued—wouldn't his approach be most equitable?

But Father Mathew and Fagan did not budge; they had made their positions known, and each rejected Lyons's compromise, which would likely shortchange every starving peasant across the county.

Others in the room remained silent, unsure of how to proceed, perhaps appalled at the committee's inaction at this seminal moment. After citizens of the United States had contributed thousands of barrels of food to the *Jamestown*'s mission and an American sea captain had successfully transported it across a wide ocean to a starving Ireland, was it possible that distribution would be stalled because of bickering and indecision? Was it possible also that Cork's most renowned clergyman and a future member of Parliament—men who had committed to serv-ing others less fortunate—could be intractably opposed on how best to distribute food when their constituents needed it most?

Another leading Cork citizen, attorney William Rathbone, who was intimately involved with the *Jamestown*'s mission, being the man with whom Forbes had worked during the planning of the mission, had an idea on how to move the discussion forward.

Rathbone suggested that the committee hear Forbes's wishes for dis-tribution. This was something of a masterstroke—it would be nearly impossible for the committee to oppose the wishes of the American sea captain who literally had made possible the bounty from the United States.

Forbes waded into the discussion gingerly, focusing on logistics and symbolic gestures first. He pointed out that the donations came from all classes of Americans, representing all religions. They did not expect that the food would solve Ireland's problems, "but they wished to sow the sentiment broadcast throughout the nation." In short, "they wanted the world to know the aim they sought in sending a vessel of war on a mission of mercy." He suggested the committee call itself the New England Committee for Irish Relief; this would reinforce and improve upon the message printed on the bags of food, marked "Boston Relief Committee"—it was important that Irish residents know from where in the United States the *Jamestown*'s donations originated.

His salutatory remarks complete, Forbes moved to the crux of the matter. Here, despite his experience with the starving mob in Cork city, he disagreed with both Father Mathew and William Fagan. Forbes favored the distribution of sufficient quantities of food "throughout the county of Cork." He pointed out that the *Tartar* would arrive in Limerick soon to supply the counties of Kerry, Limerick, and Clare. He believed more widespread distribution of food throughout County Cork, to city and countryside alike, appropriately reflected the "sentiments that influence[d]" Ireland's "American brethren." The purpose of the *Jamestown* voyage was to deliver as much food to as many people as possible to prevent starvation.

Forbes's declaration settled the debate. Fagan and Father Mathew put their objections aside, the full committee agreed with Forbes, and it appointed one of its members, Captain William E. D. Broughton, an inspector for the Irish Poor Law Commission, to draw up a distribution plan that would satisfy all the concerns expressed—and to do it fast.

Forbes held his tongue on the speed issue, but Rathbone informed the committee that Forbes was "anxious that the food should be distributed as soon as possible." The *Jamestown* had crossed the Atlantic in only fifteen days, Rathbone pointed out, and Forbes believed "that it should not take more than a second fifteen days before it [food] got into the hands of the poor."

When the committee reconvened on Monday afternoon, April 19, to hear Broughton's plan for distribution, Rathbone first asked for permission to read a letter he had received from Sir Charles Trevelyan earlier in the month. Whether to assuage the Crown's guilt or merely to fulfill his bureaucratic obligations, Trevelyan assured Rathbone that the British government would do as much as possible to assist with the distribution of the *Jamestown* cargo. For example, "Her Majesty's vessels would be employed to any necessary extent in . . . the conveyance of provisions" throughout Cork, and "every expense connected with their distribution will be defrayed by Her Majesty's government up to the point of the provisions reaching the parties in each locality." In this way, Trevelyan hoped to "preserve the integrity of the Boston donation" and make it more likely that the *Jamestown*'s bounty would find its way "in a more direct manner to the hearts as well as the stomachs of a portion of the sufferers."

Again the committee was divided, and Trevelyan's offer was met with a flurry of debate. Some members wanted no part of the British government's help in distributing food at such a late date, but others argued that taking such a confrontational stance at this critical juncture was spiteful, shortsighted, and counterproductive. Lord Mountcashell pointed out that many in his district were "poor men and would be benefitted by the conveyance of the food to the different parts of the country." The committee finally settled on accepting Trevelyan's offer wherever distribution help was required, and also agreed that "clergy of all persuasions" should administer relief in each district once the provisions arrived.

With the preliminaries out of the way, Captain Broughton spread out his map of County Cork as the other committee members, both wary and weary of each other, gathered around to hear his plan.

Given the sorrow he had witnessed in the past few months as an inspector of public works, Broughton must have experienced his first sense of buoyancy in a long time. For weeks, the former captain in the Royal Navy had suffered from famine fatigue, a debilitating condition producing pronounced anxiety and an exhaustion deeper than any he had known. The sights he had seen among County Cork's starving had brought him to the breaking point.

"Things, I regret to say, are in a most deplorable state, the poor people dying by half dozens at a time," Broughton had written two months earlier in a report that found its way into an evidentiary document published by Parliament. "I do not know how to meet the wants and exigencies" of the people. After a week in Duhallow, in the northwest of the county, despondency had overcome him. "There were six coroner's inquests held there on Friday; the verdicts for each were starvation." Then, just when it appeared things couldn't get worse, Broughton visited Douglas, a suburb of Cork city, and reported grimly: "I observed two men burying coffins as fast as they could place them alongside of each other, and met a cart containing eight others—on its way to the same field."

Whether Broughton felt any professional guilt about the failure of the works program is a matter of conjecture, but if he sought atonement, the plan he devised to distribute the *Jamestown's* provisions was serious yet simple enough to offer him at least a measure of it. Broughton had traveled far and wide across the county—from Duhallow to Douglas and then into the southwest to Middleton—and knew the suffering firsthand. Like Forbes, he was convinced that relief needed to flow rapidly and countywide; and because all residents of County Cork had suffered, Broughton also believed equity and fairness must anchor any distribution plan.

The map he created to illustrate his plan reflected both, as well as a sense of order that stood in stark contrast to the chaos, the near anarchy, that had befallen Ireland.

Broughton devised a grid system whereby he divided County Cork into 160 districts, each encompassing about three square miles. He proposed that the *Jamestown's* 800 tons of provisions be divided equally— five tons of food to each district—and because Cork city encompassed four of the districts, it would receive twenty tons of food, an amount that should satisfy Father Mathew's concern about rapidly feeding the most destitute of his flock. Broughton also suggested that hams and other high-end foodstuffs be sent to Cork city, where perhaps they could find a buyer and be sold "at a profit and more food bought for the people."

As for the most rapid distribution to the interior, Broughton recommended transporting food by ship to ports along the coast, and the "parties to whom it was allotted" in the surrounding interior towns could be informed "through the medium of the press" that it had arrived; they could make arrangements to travel to the port and retrieve their five-ton supply. "In this way, the food would be distributed in a few days," he told the committee.

Despite their previous contentiousness, the group responded with enthusiastic, immediate, and unanimous approval. "We all feel that we owe much to Captain Broughton for his plan," said the relieved vice chairman, N. Ludlow Beamish.

One final piece of business remained, and William Rathbone addressed it. While the committee had decided to accept Trevelyan's offer for ships and other related assistance, Rathbone wanted to avoid relying on government help wherever possible. He couched his suggestion as one of fiscal responsibility: eschewing government help and relying on Irish volunteers for food distribution would help the British Treasury avoid unnecessary expense.

But most in the room were well aware that Rathbone, an Englishman, was calling on the group to exert a sense of Irish pride that perhaps had been awakened by the gift of the United States. He left no doubt about his meaning when he said: "The cargo was put on board the *Jamestown* on St. Patrick's Day, by the voluntary contributions and assistance of [Boston] Irishmen—it would be satisfactory to show that it did not require the American climate to induce such an act of generosity."

The committee agreed. A foreign nation had reached out its hand to help Ireland; as part of its gratitude, Ireland—dispirited and weakened though it was—should now do everything in its power to help itself.

Any expectation that the committee's decision would constitute the last word on the *Jamestown*'s food distribution proved unrealistic. News of the committee's decision spread quickly, and inside and outside the county, desperate and opposing voices rumbled and rolled like thunder across the mountains and valleys and glens.

Lord Mountcashell lobbied for a much higher proportion of supplies for the Kilworth district of Cork, at the northern extremity of the county, a mountainous region whose nearly 10,000 people were "exposed to a greater intensity of privation than any other." The vast majority of people had no idea from where their next meal was coming, typhus and dysentery were rampant, and bodies lay exposed in fields, along the roadside, and inside "miserable cabins." Coroner inquests had ceased due to the enormous volume of deaths. An additional portion of food "bestowed on the dying creatures around me, will not be badly employed," he wrote to Forbes.

Catholic clergyman P. D. O'Regan of Cove wondered if, in addition to the food supply, Forbes and the committee had funds that could be spared for the "many victims of fever and extreme penury." Exhausted and dejected, O'Regan was delivering last rites at a rate of *"ten victims of disease every day"* and had visited the dying "in their wretched hovels at the perils of my own life," while he witnessed "scenes of misery which cannot be known." From his own paltry funds, he had purchased coffins for fifteen victims in the past month. He appealed for additional aid on behalf of "the miserable parishioners" of Cove.

Reaction was even stronger and more strident outside of County Cork. The Reverend John O'Sullivan, from Kenmare in County Kerry, who had visited Cork after the *Jamestown* arrived, was crestfallen that "I shall have to return without the slightest assistance to my unfortunate parishioners." He urged Forbes and the Cork committee to visit Kenmare, "to see with your eyes and judge for yourself"—otherwise, "no one can adequately conceive the destitution that pervades the whole population."

Father O'Sullivan pleaded with Forbes for assistance, declaring that each morning he would find "four or five" corpses dead on the street. It was his opinion that *"a third of the population has been already carried away."* Starving people that "pursue me during the day actually haunt me in my dreams at night." As though cursed, he reported, a Kenmare merchant and two others, looking to purchase cornmeal from a depot ship, drowned when their small boat capsized on their way to the larger vessel—going to the bottom with them were the funds with which they were planning to purchase the grain. "We are now in a position not able to draw one sack of meal from the ship, previous payment being required," O'Sullivan lamented.

O'Sullivan growled with bitterness—"I am, then, disappointed, *deeply* disappointed"—that the *Jamestown*'s entire cargo would be distributed in County Cork, "while so much greater distress exists in the county of Kerry." He dismissed promises of later shipments from America, fearing that additional Kerry residents would die in the meantime. And there was no guarantee that ships crossing the Atlantic were bound for Kerry—"and should the next [delivery] be consigned to either Limerick or Tralee, we cannot get our supplies from either place." This was a few weeks before the great armada of U.S. merchant ships crossed the Atlantic on their way to Ireland. In any case, O'Sullivan begged Forbes to "bear Kenmare in mind" in the event the American captain had any influence in directing future food shipments from the United States.

Most of these letters were dispatched to Forbes, who referred them to the committee. He had no authority to alter previous decisions, or at this point even to suggest further changes. He had done his duty and carried out his mission. He had crossed the Atlantic with an inexperienced crew to deliver the food safely, had turned over *Jamestown*'s cargo to the residents of Cork on behalf of the American people, and, at the request of the committee, had offered recommendations on how to quickly get it into the hands of County Cork residents.

Further decisions were out of his hands.

Officially, at least, the Cork committee was not swayed by these protestations. The Broughton plan to distribute all of the *Jamestown*'s food supply exclusively in County Cork went forward as proposed, with about half the cargo transported by "her Majesty's steamers" and deposited at the main ports along the coast "for more convenient transmission to the interior." The day before Forbes departed for America, a grateful Vice Chairman Beamish informed him: "Thus, the whole of this munificent offering from New England will be spread over an area of 1,700,000 acres, and distributed amongst hundreds of thousands of our suffering poor." The *Jamestown* cargo, Beamish added, would bring "joy and gladness to . . . cheerless homes," and would engender profound gratitude toward the United States, and particularly New England, a lasting feeling of thanks "which will be indelibly printed in the hearts of Irishmen."

Days later, and still facing scattered criticism on the distribution plan, the committee relented slightly by adopting a resolution urging each Cork district to "take care to extend itself to the neighboring districts" if food supplies allowed, so that relief "should be extended as widely" as possible. Such a gesture of goodwill should help avoid any "misunderstanding" that the *Jamestown* food was "intended to be *literally confined* to the places named in the published list," and instead convince residents that committee members strove "to make the most extensive and impartial distribution possible."

Beamish also recommended that "any blanks left in the distribution of the *Jamestown* cargo be filled up" by the Society of Friends, who had received other donations from America; he would provide the society with names of localities "apparently passed over" once distribution was complete.

Beyond these steps, the committee simply could not satisfy everybody—it received a "mass of letters" from country districts, "nearly every one of which proposed a different plan for distribution of the supplies."

Writing from the Imperial Hotel in Cork on April 27, five days after the *Jamestown*'s departure and shortly before he returned to England, William Rathbone urged members to take pride in their efforts despite criticism. "The cargo of the *Jamestown* is now in progress to the hearts and stomachs of a portion of the distressed," he wrote. "Accept my . . . earnest prayer for the speedy deliverance of your native land from her present appalling calamity."

—◦✦◦—

CHAPTER 22

"Young America opens
a new page in its destiny"

W hen word spread that Forbes had set the *Jamestown*'s departure date for April 22, a grateful Ireland redoubled its
praise for him, his mission, and the United States of America. Residents, clergy, relief workers, and government officials wrote and
posted letters—some of which Forbes read after he returned home—or
hurriedly dispatched couriers to the Cove docks with messages of gratitude. It was as if all of Ireland, torn asunder by famine and disease and
turmoil and hopelessness, came together to thank and wish safe passage
to their friend and benefactor from across the sea.

When Forbes and the *Jamestown* crew entered Cork Harbor, they
"effected a . . . revolution," wrote Roman Catholic priest George Sheehan, "and united the two continents more closely." While Sheehan
found it a "melancholy task to chronicle the miseries of one's own country," he was grateful for the cosmic balance that guided a foreign ship
to Ireland's shores carrying both the gift of food and something more
precious: "the noble sympathies of a deservedly prosperous nation for
the most afflicted people under the sun."

Because the *Jamestown*'s food supply was being distributed in Cork,
Sheehan's sentiments were understandable, as were those of Mrs. E. B.

Boston, secretary of the Ladies Association of Ballydehob village in southwest Cork, which had exhausted its funds to help the poor and was jubilant about the *Jamestown*'s contributions. If Forbes and America knew how much their relief would benefit "creatures dying daily of starvation and disease," then it would "rejoice their hearts," she said. "Bless the benevolent friends who help them." From Monkstown, relief chairman John Irvine said the *Jamestown* mission proved "the kindly feeling pervading the United States towards this country." And the chairman of the St. Anne's Hill relief committee in Blarney said that the generosity of the American people "can never be effaced from the hearts of Irishmen." The *Jamestown* mission, he added, "will be duly appreciated as one more connecting link binding together two nations."

But most striking about these final messages to Forbes was the number and tone of those from people *beyond* Cork, who were receiving no direct *Jamestown* aid. Letters from outside the county lauding Forbes's mission far outnumbered the complaints directed to the Cork committee for its distribution plan. Clergy from Mayo recognized that the *Jamestown* donation was the "spontaneous offering of a free, a humane, a brave, and a noble-hearted people." Limerick city's mayor told Forbes that his citizens were so overcome by the U.S. gesture that, in attempting to express their gratitude, their feelings would "choke the utterance and paralyze the tongue." The chairman of the Limerick relief committee described Forbes as a "missioner of mercy to a famine devastated land." The president of St. Patrick's Monastery in the town of Tullow in County Carlow used his April 22 letter to thank Forbes as a "true son of that *glorious land* where freedom dwells and ripens to maturity every noble quality of mind and heart," and also to upbraid the British government. "[It] would not spare one vessel, although several of them lie rotting in the harbors, and manned with thousands of Erin's hardy sons, whose parents, brothers, and sisters are dying of hunger!" scolded Serenius P. O'Kelly.

Forbes, who rejected both the hero's mantle and the cloak of virtue, was grateful for, although nonplussed and embarrassed by, the outpouring. His deference left it to others to place the *Jamestown* mission in full context, and many did on both sides of the Atlantic. Typical were the sentiments of American Elihu Burritt, who, while touring Cork and other regions in 1847, described the scope and alluded to the long-term impact of the charitable *Jamestown* mission. "Young America opens a new page in its destiny," he declared, "with revelations illustrated with golden promise, in this unprecedented act of philanthropy."

On Wednesday, April 21, twenty-four days after leaving Boston and nine days after arriving in Cork Harbor, the *Jamestown* was ready to return home. With most of his business complete, Forbes opened the *Jamestown's* decks to visitors from Cove, Cork, and neighboring towns from noon until 3:00 p.m.; several hundred people flocked to the ship. Forbes and his officers were "at home" with their guests, chatting, mingling, celebrating, and providing entertainment.

Recognizing that it would be in poor taste to provide his guests "a feast in a time of famine," Forbes offered them the *Jamestown's* "best bread, in the cask, flanked on each side by a huge piece of Fresh Pond Ice." The crew also made available "plenty of ice water, iced lemonade, with a little sprinkling of champagne," as well as gingerbread and additional bread baked on board. "The ladies partook of [these items] sparingly, but carried away with them in small bits to show what could be done in yankee land," Forbes noted. At two o'clock, the Temperance Band, which had been performing all the while, began playing a waltz, and soon "the ladies were sporting the light fantastic toe, with the red coats and the blue coats." Peasants and shopkeepers alike enjoyed a sense of gaiety and escape from their dreadful circumstances, and no one wanted the day to end. "It was only after I gave the *order* to disperse (4 o'clock) that they vanished to the shore after a most hearty farewell," Forbes recalled. But before they left, many of the departing women showered Forbes with poems, embroidery, hugs, and good wishes that they asked him to pass on to his wife.

CHAPTER 23

"OUR DELIVERER IN THE HOUR OF BITTER CALAMITY"

Thursday morning, April 22, broke clear, calm, and pleasant, an ideal day for departure.

Forbes made a quick trip to Cork to bid farewell to Rathbone and the committee, once again impressed with the "very high character" of members and grateful that they represented "all shades of politics and all creeds in Religion," united to bring relief to the Irish people. Such broad representation was the "best guaranty" that the seeds of the *Jamestown*'s cargo "will be sown to good account both in the hearts and stomachs of the poor Irish," as well as in the "remembrances of the better classes." He also hoped that the "lesson" of the *Jamestown* would be "charitably received in England," and that although London was doing much to alleviate distress "by running her steamers from port to port in Ireland with supplies" brought by the American ship, "that she will yet do more."

Forbes then purchased a public notice in the Cork *Constitution* in which he expressed his "unfeigned thanks for the many acts of kindness and the many offers of hospitality done and tendered" to his crew, before returning to Cove Harbor and boarding the *Jamestown*.

By 3:30 p.m., Her Majesty's steamer *Zephyr* had attached her towline and pulled the American warship clear of Haulbowline Island.

As they passed the town of Cove, the scene staggered Forbes. Thousands of Cove and Cork residents cheered and waved—the *Jamestown* was now as "familiar to Irishmen as household goods," one press account gushed. The U.S. consulate lowered its flag in tribute, and the marine detachment on Spike Island mustered and "gave us a *lot* of hearty cheers," to which the *Jamestown* crew responded. Forbes ordered the ship's flag lowered several times as a gesture of thanks.

Then the USS *Jamestown*, representing the United States of America—whom Father Mathew called "our deliverer in the hour of bitter calamity"—cleared Cork Harbor and, catching a light but steady breeze, turned toward home.

The trip began uneventfully enough. But after a few days of steady breezes and clear weather, the *Jamestown* encountered a punishing gale on the night of April 26, the likes of which Forbes had not seen since 1832, "except one off New York in December 1840." He was thankful that his vessel carried only ballast in her holds; other "corn and flour ships . . . will suffer tonight" from the deep troughs and hard squalls. Two nights later, at close to 2:30 a.m., again in the midst of a squally gale, an eastward-bound ship passed close to *Jamestown*'s bow. Sudden wind shifts and rough seas made collisions more likely and setting sails more difficult. "I have no anxieties excepting for a change in wind," Forbes wrote in the ship's log. The next morning, the weather cleared and the *Jamestown* moved swiftly, only for the wind to stop around noon on April 29. "We are a week out this p.m. and only one quarter on our way," Forbes lamented.

By Sunday, May 2, as the *Jamestown* laid up alongside the *Baltimore* traveling from the United States, Forbes recorded that his ship was now "10 days out" and still 1,880 miles and "*five weeks from Boston.*"

Early the next morning, the *Jamestown* and Forbes endured their worst day of the expedition, and suffered a painful reminder that the high seas could roil with unpredictable and unforgiving force regardless of the benevolence of a ship's mission. At 3:00 a.m., with the ship clipping along at eleven knots and pitching to and fro in darkness and rainy squalls, a deck officer ordered the jib taken in, and several crew members crowded onto the boom to furl the sail. Without anyone noticing, *Jamestown's* lone Irish-born crew member, John Hughes, apparently lost his grip and toppled overboard into the black Atlantic.

"He was seen no more!" Forbes recorded in the ship's journal.

Forbes acknowledged that Hughes's death was an "event which makes old men of us," and it rankled him that Hughes slipped from the jib-boom and fell into the ocean while his comrades remained unawares. Had he cried out? Had he struggled to stay afloat before dying alone in the darkness? Had he been knocked unconscious?

"It is aggravating to think that no hand was raised to save him," Forbes wrote.

With little recourse open to him, a despondent and frustrated Forbes inked his highest tribute to the lost seaman in his May 3 journal entry: "He was an excellent man."

By Sunday, May 9, with the *Jamestown* at sea for seventeen days, Forbes began to tire of the difficult combination of headwinds, crashing seas, and dead calm air. At 9:00 a.m. he noted that the weather was "dreadfully pleasant"—the *Jamestown* had yet to encounter any fair wind on her return voyage—and that his patience was "nearly threadbare." Short of spotting a whale the previous day, there was little to break the monotonous cycle of factors that inhibited *Jamestown's* progress. "I am getting heartily tired of this constant headwind," Forbes wrote, and then, with disappointment: "I shall not be able, I fear, to go to church in Boston next Sunday." Two days later, Forbes was "almost sick"—the *Jamestown* was stalled "with fair wind deferred." Still stung by the loss of Hughes, Forbes was more anxious than ever for the comfort of home and family.

The next morning broke with a smooth sea and light breezes. The packet *Virginia*, sailing from New Orleans to Liverpool, crossed *Jamestown's* path and dispatched a small boat and several crew members to greet Forbes and provide the *Jamestown* with newspapers from home. If the *Jamestown* sailors had forgotten that their warship was engaged in an unusual mission for the times, they were likely reminded by the front-page news of General Scott's victory at Veracruz, Mexico. The news buoyed Forbes's spirits and those of his crew, and their attitude improved even more on May 13 when the *Jamestown* encountered its first regular fair wind, a full twenty-one days from Ireland and 750 miles from home. Suddenly, "the ship steers perfectly and rolls so easy," Forbes wrote.

But his ebullience was short-lived. Temperatures plunged, and by early Saturday morning, May 15, with "the ship going like a racehorse," the shriek of gale winds and damp heavy fog rolled across the *Jamestown*'s decks. Forbes could barely see beyond the ship's bow. "*We can only guess at our latitude,*" he warned, sounding his bell repeatedly, and "guess[ing] at the horizon." Suddenly, his lookout screamed, "Sail-ho close aboard, hard up," as the *Jamestown* was about to collide with a brig sailing southward from Nova Scotia. Forbes jumped on deck just in time to shout, "Hard up, call all hands square after yards," and the crew whipped the *Jamestown* around just in time to avoid a potential disaster.

It was Forbes's last true test as captain of the *Jamestown*. By noon the fog cleared, allowing him a good sighting to establish latitude; the sun broke through the cloud bank, fair wind blew strong, and by 5:00 p.m., the *Jamestown* was 150 miles from Boston Light. Forbes took advantage of the favorable conditions and pushed the vessel throughout the night. By 6:00 a.m. on Sunday, May 16, the *Jamestown* had reached Cape Ann, located on the Massachusetts coast north of the Charlestown Navy Yard. Forbes would have the opportunity to attend Sunday church services in Boston after all.

Seven weeks and one hour after the start of its historic voyage, the *Jamestown* had come home.

PART VI

THE UNITED STATES AND IRELAND

"America has been our truest friend"

Desperate emigrants left Ireland by the thousands during the famine, most headed for the United States. This engraving by Henry Edward Doyle first appeared in the 1868 first edition of An Illustrated History of Ireland: From AD 400 to 1800, *by Mary Frances Cusack.*

CHAPTER 24

"The happiest event of my life"

A Boston newspaper reporter noted that the city's houses of worship were "thinly attended" this particular Sabbath, for thousands of Bostonians filled the wharves and lined the banks of the harbor to welcome the *Jamestown* home—many times more than had witnessed her departure. Men and women waved their hats and handkerchiefs and cheered loudly as the vessel anchored just off the Navy Yard at 9:30 a.m., twenty-three days after she left Cork and seven weeks and one hour from the start of her mission.

Hundreds boarded the *Jamestown* to pay tribute to Forbes and his crew, a throng so enthusiastic and adoring that Forbes joked that he had "hired a small spile driving machine to shake hands for me." Bostonians wanted to be close to Forbes, to hear him speak, to clap him on the back for his accomplishment, to share a pint with him and celebrate the success of his mission. Many of Boston's merchants and businessmen crowded onto the Charlestown docks to welcome Forbes and the *Jamestown*, but the city's wealthy elite and working-class poor were present in great number, too. The unprecedented nature of the ship's mission transcended class and social standing and financial wherewithal;

the *Jamestown* had captured imaginations and hearts across the spectrum. However, Rose Forbes apparently was unwilling to risk a trip to the chaotic scene with small children in tow; Robert Bennet makes no mention of their presence in Charlestown, and he likely would have recorded such a joyful reunion.

The celebration continued for hours. Luckily it was the Sabbath—otherwise, Forbes joked, the St. Patrick Society might have carried out its threat to waylay him on his arrival and carry him home "neck and heels with music."

His first mission upon leaving the ship would be to complete a report on the mission for the New England committee. The *Jamestown* voyage had attracted widespread national attention, and Forbes's opinions were eagerly awaited.

As always, he had a great deal to say.

Forbes had toiled on the report during the voyage and polished it the day after his return to Boston. On Tuesday, May 18, after a dinner of mutton and poultry, Forbes read his detailed report to the committee, describing the voyage and mission, as well as his thoughts about Ireland and the famine.

He began with the behavior of the English government, defending it from its harshest critics by citing supportive letters he'd received from Rathbone and Trevelyan, but also acknowledging its failures. In general, he held, London faced a monumental crisis that it was unprepared for—"carrying supplies and distributing them, through new agents and new channels"—and the process was necessarily complicated and "sometimes badly done." The scale of the famine was so broad and devastating that England's insistence in the early stages to label it a local problem left relief efforts far behind from the outset, and unable to catch up. Additionally, the British focus on process and paperwork created needless and unconscionable delays, and the hasty construction of the public works program meant that its foundation was inadequate to support even its rickety framework. Again, the government was late to recognize the inadequacy of the works program and thus late to establish direct soup kitchens to feed the Irish people. It was understandable, Forbes said, that the British government's failings led to "many complaints . . . in Cork and Cove of the want of sympathy" from the English of Ireland's plight.

On the other hand, Forbes read aloud, while he expressed "due respect and deference" to the people of Cork and Cove, he believed "they expect a little too much [from the British] and that they should forget political animosities and unite in the great work of regeneration in Ireland." Indeed, the *Jamestown* mission and the charity of the United States—even the famine itself, as distressing as it was—may have provided the impetus to unite people to work "shoulder to shoulder, and together act in concert and harmony in the cause of suffering humanity." Forbes had witnessed cooperation in Ireland between those "who never before met except to clash either in politics or religion." The terrible conditions in Ireland during Black '47 had, in some ways, awakened "kindlier feelings of the people." Catholics, Protestants, avowed supporters of Irish independence, and unabashed loyalists to the Crown— representatives of all of these groups were "forsaking all expense and luxury" and "uniting to palliate the general pestilence and famine."

Forbes lauded Father Mathew's support and cooperation throughout his Ireland visit, recommended that the committee recognize Rathbone and members of his family officially "for [their] personal sacrifices and . . . attention to your business," and offered profuse thanks to James Scott of Cove, "who entertained your servant with a home," and in addition had assured Forbes: "Call for anything and everything and it shall be forthcoming free." Scott had thereafter provided "every kind of aid and comfort" to Forbes and the *Jamestown* crew. Forbes also reminded the committee of the contributions of the *Jamestown* officers, "who so generously volunteered and went as my mates" and whose steady presence and expertise "harmoniously aided" in making the voyage a success. "I shall always owe them a debt not easily cancelled," Forbes offered.

Finally, Forbes looked to the near future by making an extraordinary recommendation to the committee, bolstered by his firm belief in *Jamestown*'s mission to help the suffering Irish and his admiration for the contributions of New England residents and those from around the country. Because the people of Boston had "use of the *Jamestown* for only 49 days, when it was expected that it would require 100," and because the *Jamestown* had never traveled to Scotland with relief provisions, as the initial congressional resolution allowed for, Forbes proposed that the secretary of the navy dispatch a "second *Jamestown*" mission to both Ireland and Scotland. His duties at home and the limitations of the original congressional authorization prevented him from leading a second mission, but Forbes offered to "open the subscription for the ship's cargo" by donating the "proceeds of the sale of this narrative . . . to that good end."

Forbes had no authority over whether the committee would put forth such a recommendation (it ultimately did not) or whether the secretary of the navy would agree with his idea. Regardless, the captain assured the committee as he closed out his report on the deck of the American warship: "I shall ever look back to the voyage of the *Jamestown* as the happiest event of my life."

After officially returning the *Jamestown* to the navy, Forbes over the next week participated in a number of activities related to the voyage, each meticulously and faithfully recorded by the press; it seemed Boston residents and readers could not get enough of the *Jamestown* story.

The May 22, 1847, edition of the *Pilot*, Boston's Catholic newspaper, carried a parody article entitled "Splendid Naval Victory," in which it colorfully described the *Jamestown*'s "attack" on Cork with its full arsenal of food and provisions, resulting in one of the most "brilliant exploits in the history of maritime war." The ship's shells—"in the shape of flour and . . . canisters of corn bags—found their mark again and again," taking the city by surprise. "Sometimes whole families would receive the contents of a shell which fell among them from the noble ship," the story proclaimed. The ship's crew continued to fire "shots" at the residents of the city, "directed mainly at their stomachs." The paper theorized that Forbes "is of the opinion that the whole of Ireland . . . may be conquered in the same manner." The *Pilot* also interjected its own antiwar view to conclude the spoof: "This brilliant affair will shed more glory on those engaged in it and on the country than all our victories in Mexico."

In the same issue, the *Pilot* informed readers that several copies of a lithograph engraving of the *Jamestown* that Forbes had brought home from Ireland were on sale for fifty cents each. The proceeds would benefit Irish relief, and "as there are only a few copies, those wanting them should apply immediately." The original, "splendidly framed," was presented to Forbes in Ireland by Cork mayor William Scraggs, who hoped Forbes could offer it as a gift to the president of the United States as part of Ireland's message of gratitude. Press accounts also informed Boston readers that Forbes delivered a daguerreotype and an oil painting of Father Mathew—"a splendid portrait," as he described it—to the Boston Athenaeum (these have since been lost), and sought a suitable location for a hand-painted lithograph of the temperance tower (now preserved at the Forbes Museum).

Boston citizens also read about a moving ceremony at the Mayor and Aldermen's Room at Boston City Hall that took place on Monday afternoon, May 24, when Captain Forbes presented Boston officials and citizens with a ceremonial flag from the people of Cork. Fashioned from fine white silk, the six-by-eight-foot flag was emblazoned with a harp at its center, surrounded by green shamrocks and topped with an American eagle—"making a beautiful appearance," in the opinion of one journalist, "emblematical of the assistance rendered from America to Ireland."

Forbes read an accompanying letter from Cork's mayor, saying that current residents of Cork and their descendants would remember always that "in our hour of deepest misery and desolation, America has been our truest friend, our most generous assistant."

In the days following the *Jamestown*'s return, stories appeared throughout the press of more relief ships reaching Ireland.

But one of Forbes's predictions to the people of Cork—that the other American warship, the *Macedonian*, would arrive with her relief provisions "two or three weeks" after the *Jamestown*—had failed to materialize. Whereas the entire *Jamestown* mission had proceeded fairly smoothly, Captain George DeKay had faced innumerable obstacles in New York. The *Macedonian* was stalled not by dead calm in the middle of the ocean, but by bureaucratic bellicosity, red tape, and infighting while the ship lay idle off the Battery in New York Harbor, still with only a mere 2,000 barrels of provisions on board.

Mindful of his promise to the Irish people, Forbes turned his attention southward—perhaps he could break the New York logjam and free the *Macedonian* for her own transatlantic mission of mercy.

⚬━✦━⚬

CHAPTER 25

"GOOD CAME *INSTEAD* OF EVIL"

O f all the components of America's massive relief effort on behalf of Ireland during 1846–47, the *Macedonian* episode was
the single fly in the nation's charitable ointment.

From the start, when Congress agreed to turn over the warships
Jamestown and *Macedonian* to civilian captains to transport food to
Ireland, Captain George DeKay, unlike Forbes in Boston, faced a wave
of political backlash, turf fights, and squabbling that stopped the mission in its tracks—a potential embarrassment to both Congress and
the president of the United States, who had blessed the vessel's voyage
to Ireland.

First, despite congressional approval of the *Macedonian* mission,
the New York relief committee declined to participate, arguing that
because the U.S. government had not appropriated funds for the ship's
"victualing and manning," the committee would need to expend an in-
ordinately large proportion of donated food and money to provision
the *Macedonian*. Though all the food was earmarked for the same destination, either egos, parochialism, or both carried the day—the New
York committee balked at disrupting its own relief efforts to join the
Macedonian's mission.

Perhaps some of the committee's hesitancy was due to misunderstandings. Disagreements had arisen over DeKay's reported desire to have either the British or United States government pay the freight on the *Macedonian*'s cargo. Secretary of the Navy John Y. Mason wrote to DeKay and claimed he had received word of "certain persons agitating" for the British government to pay the freight, a suggestion that would not be "entertained for a moment." The British government, Mason made clear, would not be asked to "pay one cent" for the *Macedonian*'s benevolent mission. DeKay defended himself, claiming the rumors were unfounded and were being fueled by "interested ship owners here, who deem it in their interest to keep freights up to the highest rate." Further, navy officers, unhappy about "not being allowed to go in the ship," had questioned DeKay's competence and are "incessantly agitating questions which neither this government nor myself have any control over."

And there was more. Some merchants opposed the use of the *Macedonian* because they thought—erroneously—that it was a former British vessel of the same name captured during the War of 1812. Forbes received wind of this while in Ireland and told one audience how laughable he found such pettiness. "You might with equal propriety suppose that I could not worship the God, common to all Christians, in your [Irish] cathedral, because you once prayed there that your enemies (the Yankees) might be smitten." Such logic was so convoluted, Forbes declared, that he wished he could "expunge this reason from the records before the public in the newspapers."

Others in New York, including the Society of Friends, objected to McKay taking control of the *Macedonian* because he had once served in the Argentine navy and Congress had expressly stated that the *Jamestown* and *Macedonian* missions would not involve naval personnel; despite the fact that he was not a current U.S. naval officer, some believed that DeKay's command would violate the spirit of the congressional edict.

Finally, DeKay engaged in a public feud with powerful New York newspaper publisher Thurlow Weed, who had become the harshest media critic of using American warships to provide Irish relief. In the *Albany Journal*, Weed argued that the federal government could do more to aid the Irish without the costly distraction of using warships that would actually reduce the amount of funds available to purchase food. "This appropriation of vessels of war to do what can be done at less cost without them will excite contempt rather than commendation," the *Journal* opined.

A frustrated DeKay had tried everything, including spending thousands of dollars of his own money and resources "in manning, equipping, and provisioning the ship," but he was thwarted in his efforts to secure sufficient funds or supplies—the 2,000 barrels aboard the *Macedonian* was embarrassingly short of the reported 15,000–16,000 barrels that DeKay had envisioned.

Weeks earlier, DeKay had anticipated "a full cargo as soon as the river opens" and a May 1 departure for Ireland, but neither prediction was close to accurate—his mission had veered badly off course. And there was little evidence that he could right the ship alone.

Forbes saw little chance to fulfill his promise to the Irish people unless two things occurred: the Boston committee stepped in to assume control of the *Macedonian*'s mission, and, as part of that maneuver, he traveled to New York to help DeKay.

On the surface his actions may appear presumptuous, but Forbes knew well that the *Macedonian* was now an orphan mission, shunned by New York elites, power brokers, and the Friends group that had organized most of the relief for Ireland. Unless the leadership void was filled, DeKay and his ship would remain stateside, the U.S. government's decision to make two warships available for humanitarian purposes would appear halfhearted and disingenuous, Forbes's promise to the residents of Cork and Cove would go unfulfilled, and most important, the Irish people would be deprived of additional food and provisions that the *Macedonian* would otherwise transport.

Forbes approached the Boston committee, which quickly accepted his proposal to assume management control of the *Macedonian* mission, and appointed Forbes, former state senator and secretary of the navy David Henshaw, and railroad director James K. Mills as a subcommittee to travel to New York, meet with DeKay to secure his agreement, and make arrangements to provision the ship and finally dispatch her to Ireland. Looking for any sort of lifeline, DeKay accepted assistance from Boston, even as the subcommittee agreed to "fill up his ship" only under the following conditions: that he should neither demand nor receive any compensation for freight charges from the British government; that the Boston committee send an agent—known as a supercargo—to travel aboard the *Macedonian* and take charge of the provisions it carried; that the whole enterprise be carried out "as a private matter, and without flying a pennant or wearing any navy uniform"; and finally, that DeKay report all particulars of his voyage back to the Boston committee. Forbes confessed that his eagerness for the *Macedonian* to travel to Ireland made him willing to "have her go on any terms," but Mills and Henshaw insisted on these "stringent terms" in order to lend their support.

Once DeKay agreed, Henshaw arranged through a New York firm for the purchase and loading of 4,000 barrels of cornmeal, rice, peas, and beans aboard the *Macedonian*. And nearly simultaneously, the Boston committee convinced famed Methodist preacher Edward Taylor of Boston, one of the most colorful and popular figures of his time, to make the voyage as the committee's supercargo and the *Macedonian*'s chaplain, maybe one of the only times a single person has held both responsibilities.

The committee offered no explicit reason for selecting Taylor, but from a political and populist perspective—as a way to engender support for a mission that had floundered badly—associating the *Macedonian*'s voyage with the beloved and nationally renowned "sailor priest" was nothing short of brilliant.

Born in Richmond, Virginia, on Christmas Day 1793, which many of his followers viewed as a fitting providential sign, Father Taylor—after running away from home at age seven—had spent much of his childhood and young adult years at sea, and he landed in Boston during one of the intervals between voyages. There he became a member of the Methodist Church and, eventually, began preaching to sailors, dockworkers, and other itinerants along the Boston waterfront, using nautical themes and colorful language and "making the truths of the gospel seem more real and practical to them than more refined phrases could have done," according to one account.

In 1832, Boston merchants, in their desire to support the religious training of seamen, built the Seamen's Bethel on one side of North Square and the Mariners' House on the other (the latter still stands today). For the next three decades, ministering at the Bethel became the great work of Father Taylor's life; there he conducted prayer meetings with and sermonizing to sailors and workers who made their living at or near the sea. He was, in the words of Ralph Waldo Emerson, "capable of doing wonders among the neglected class to which he was devoted— and soon awaked wonder and joy in hearers of every class."

Taylor's reputation as a spellbinding orator soon spread regionally, then nationally and internationally. Emerson compared his crescendos and flourishes to those of Daniel Webster. Walt Whitman pondered whether Socrates or Epictetus could have held their audiences in thrall as Taylor could. Charles Dickens, who described Taylor as a "weather-beaten, hard-featured man . . . with deep lines graven . . . into his face," visited Boston in the early 1840s and made a point of walking to the Bethel—which was tucked on "one of the narrow old waterside streets"—to hear Taylor preach. "He addresses himself peculiarly to seamen and . . . was once a mariner himself," Dickens wrote.

Regardless of his growing fame and popularity, Taylor always reserved the center seats in the Bethel for working sailors and other seamen—"strangers and ladies and gentlemen were ranged on each side"—and mesmerized them by linking scripture with the sea. With his knowledge of the sea and a gritty demeanor, Taylor spoke their language. When he described a ship, one parishioner recalled, he made "you feel (seated amid the press of a Sabbath congregation) that you were rocking amid the waves" and "smelt the salt sea air." Whitman, who when he visited the Bethel was struck by the pulpit, "rising ten or twelve feet high . . . backed by a significant mural painting . . . of a stormy sea, the waves high," was equally transfixed when Taylor spoke. "Soon as he open'd his mouth, I ceas'd to pay any attention to the church or audience, or pictures or lights or shades," he wrote, "a far more potent charm entirely sway'd me."

Emerson, also a visitor to Father Taylor's church, noted: "Everyone is cheered and exalted by him. How puny, how cowardly, other preachers look by the side of this preaching! He shows us what a man can do."

If leaders of the Boston committee were looking for the ideal combination of influence, energy, gravitas, and celebrity to infuse the moribund *Macedonian* mission and reignite enthusiasm among potential donors—and it appeared that was exactly their goal—they would be hard-pressed to find two men better equipped than Robert Bennet Forbes, fresh off a highly successful and widely publicized mission of mercy to Ireland that had brought him international acclaim, and Father Edward Taylor, whose love of sea and sailors and oratory made him a cause célèbre with the world's literati and an enduring and noble symbol of strength and camaraderie among mariners on both sides of the Atlantic.

The involvement of Forbes, Taylor, and the Boston committee resuscitated the *Macedonian* mission virtually overnight. Contributions poured in, first from New York sources and then beyond, and were added to the 4,000 barrels from the Boston committee. The Common Council of New York City donated more than 1,000 barrels of Indian corn, "to do the greatest good to the greatest number" in Ireland. The executive committee of New York's Independent Order of Odd Fellows contributed 300 barrels of cornmeal, acknowledging the donation was small, but expressing hope it would bring "temporary relief to a few" whom starvation had pushed "to the brink of despair and death." From Utica, New York, the Irish Relief Committee contributed 500 barrels of kiln-dried cornmeal to the *Macedonian*'s cargo, along with an undisclosed sum of money to purchase additional cornmeal in New York City that would then be loaded aboard the ship; the upstate cities of Rome and Troy also made donations.

Additional contributions "came from every quarter of our union," DeKay noted, "but especially from Boston." Moreover, unlike on the *Jamestown*, DeKay was willing to transport passengers to Ireland; he published a press notice offering passage for $100, of which $75 would be used to purchase food for Irish famine relief. And collections from churches of all denominations "poured in," DeKay noted, allowing him to buy additional provisions. Within two weeks of the Boston committee's involvement, "the ship began to be filled, the lower hold first, then the between decks, and so on up to the gun deck, and even the very cabins were filled to overflowing."

Finally, on June 19, 1847, George DeKay—beleaguered, besmirched, belittled, but unbowed and undeterred in his mission to deliver food and supplies to Ireland and Scotland—sailed the *Macedonian* out of New York Harbor. He was the living embodiment of an adage still decades from use in the American lexicon—"no good deed goes unpunished"—and before the *Macedonian* saga ended, he would suffer further humiliation and pay a steep price for attempting to represent the people and government of the United States in an honorable manner.

The *Macedonian* dropped anchor in Cove on July 16, "laden with 1800 tons of bread-stuffs . . . [and] a crew of 600 teetotalers," according to one press account. She was greeted by the mayor's barge, carrying Father Mathew and other dignitaries, and when the Americans spotted the famed Irish priest they unleashed raucous and "thundering" cheers. For the next twenty-five days, as his vessel was unloaded and its provisions distributed, DeKay was feted, toasted, cheered, and revered. "The man who came here in command of the *Macedonian* was a kindhearted, generous man," one speaker said of DeKay. "His heart is as large as the moon and as open as the sunflower."

On August 11, DeKay sailed for Scotland, arriving in Glasgow three days later, where he delivered the remainder of his cargo. While docked, the *Macedonian* took part in a review of ships by the young Queen of England, Victoria, who was making her first public visit to Scotland, greeted by "almost half the population of Scotland . . . on the shores and on the waters of the port of Glasgow." Later, at a public soiree to honor the *Macedonian* crew, Father Taylor told attendees he was honored to participate in a mission in which "they had exchanged bombs for buns."

DeKay wrote to Secretary of the Navy Mason on September 12 informing him that the *Macedonian* would sail for home "tomorrow or the next day," and two days later he wrote to Mason with a request that would again mire the *Macedonian* mission in controversy.

DeKay had purchased 700 tons of pig iron for ballast for the return voyage—he deemed the decision necessary to preserve the "safety of the ship and security of public property"—and, aware of his previous financial outlays, and hoping to be "saved from material pecuniary loss," he requested that Mason permit him to resell the pig iron in New York free of duty charges. With his request, he enclosed a letter from the *Macedonian*'s officers and petty officers who certified the need for the pig iron ballast to make the ship "safe and seaworthy," especially after the *Macedonian* had handled unstably following the delivery of provisions to Cork. Otherwise, the only other choices for ballast would be clay or earth, either of which would be "filthy and injurious to the ship."

Mason approved the request, and once DeKay arrived in New York, he wrote again to the secretary to confirm that the pig iron ballast had helped "save the ship in the heavy weather we experienced in the channel." On October 30, Mason congratulated DeKay on his safe return, asked him to deliver and sell the pig iron to the New York Navy Yard free of duty charges, and added: "It was a judicious precaution to increase the ballast of the ship, after delivering her cargo."

But Mason's permission for DeKay to sell the imported iron free of duty elicited vigorous press attacks against the navy secretary and the captain, accusing them of possible financial malfeasance and even profiteering from what was purportedly a charitable endeavor. "Could not Captain DeKay have as well loaded the *Macedonian* with a cargo of British woolens for an importing house in New York?" asked a Philadelphia paper in December. "What difference is there in principle?" Instead, the "little scheme" was little more than an attempt to "defraud the treasury of its just dues."

These attacks, plus the failure to be reimbursed the $30,000 of his own money DeKay had expended on the mission, took their toll upon the New York sea captain. Several times in the following months he requested Congress to reimburse him. "For a man with a wife and six children (and with a seventh expected in July 1848), this financial question was extremely important," wrote DeKay's granddaughter Phyllis more than a century later—but the process dragged on. In April, the House of Representatives authorized reimbursement of $16,000 to DeKay, prompting DeKay to send a letter in June asking Congress to refund "my actual outlay." DeKay stressed that events beyond his control "rendered it necessary that I should expend and risk a considerable sum, or make the country a laughing stock to the whole world." He had spent the money honestly and economically "in the most honorable service of the country." Congress, then, had to decide a moral question: "whether one citizen shall suffer a ruinous fine for faithfully executing its orders, or assume payment of the same." Another alternative, seeking reimbursement from Britain, amounted to "allowing a foreign power to interfere in your national charity," which "seems to be out of the question."

The fact that he needed to supplicate for reimbursements to which he was entitled continued to serve as a "source of anxiety and humiliation" to DeKay, according to his granddaughter. The stress proved too much—DeKay died suddenly on January 31, 1849, with his claim to Congress still pending.

Though the *Macedonian* voyage, in the end, was successful, this sad sequel left Forbes with a sour taste. "Commodore DeKay may be said to have sacrificed his life for the voyage of the *Macedonian*," Forbes wrote. "I made no sacrifice; all was smooth and pleasant from beginning to end."

Perhaps Forbes would have taken some solace from Father Taylor's marvelous tribute to him and DeKay during the priest's remarks in Cork, words that DeKay had heard in person. DeKay and Forbes, Father Taylor declared, "had united a whole empire, twenty-four States, into one great compact with Ireland, and had taken ships of that nation to carry bread to them who were in want of it."

That Forbes and DeKay inspired a nation to act as one was nothing short of remarkable.

"Who would have thought that two men could have compressed . . . a nation . . . and made them do this?" he asked. It was actions like this that would enable Ireland to flourish someday, actions like this that proved not "that good came out of evil" but that "good came *instead* of evil."

CHAPTER 26

"CANNOT BUT SOW SEEDS OF HATRED"

Like twin icebergs emerging from the North Atlantic fog in the direct path of an unsuspecting schooner, two prodigious forces loomed over Ireland in the late summer and fall of 1847, threatening to smash a country already enfeebled, demoralized, and clinging to survival after its yearlong fight against unrelenting hunger and disease.

First, in accordance with the Poor Law Extension Act approved by Parliament in June, the British government announced that it was ending all general relief and transferring responsibility and cost for aid to local Irish landlords. In mid-July, Trevelyan ordered government-funded soup kitchens closed by August 15, despite the fact that more than 3 million Irish, close to half the country, were receiving relief, the largest number since the onset of the famine. Loud protests from the most distressed regions of Ireland, especially from the south and west—Father Mathew's among them—persuaded Trevelyan to barely modify the schedule. On August 15, the government closed 55 of 130 soup kitchens; another 26 shuttered on September 12, and the final 49 on October 1, an overall grace period of six weeks. "It is my opinion that too much has been done for the people," Trevelyan said. "Under such treatment the people have grown worse instead of better, and we must now try [to see] what independent exertion can do."

In Trevelyan's view, the shocking number of Irish residents on relief, which included more than 750,000 children, was evidence not of a failure of the British government to ensure an adequate food supply for millions of its subjects but of a truly "benevolent operation," an astounding humanitarian feat—"the grandest attempt ever made to grapple with famine over a whole country." Trevelyan reached for superlatives in his prose to describe the British government's efforts to operate Irish soup kitchens but ignored the neglect and exploitation that led to Irish starvation—and thus the need for the kitchens—in the first place. "Neither ancient nor modern history can furnish a parallel to the fact that upwards of three millions of persons were fed every day in the neighborhood of their own homes," he wrote with satisfaction.

But enough was enough. The fact was, Trevelyan, the British Crown, Anglican churches, and the people of England had grown weary of talking about and providing for Irish relief and were anxious to be rid of it.

Trevelyan had read the reports of impending disaster if the soup kitchens were closed but saw no remedy beyond local relief measures, save for institutionalizing a system of perpetual charity supported by the Crown, which was out of the question for reasons both financial (the British Treasury was already straining to fund relief operations) and philosophical (indefinite central government aid would only serve to foster Irish helplessness). It was time for Ireland to devise a way to support itself, and continued assistance from London would only prolong and exacerbate the cycle of Irish dependence on external contributions. "Whatever the difficulties and dangers may be [of closing the soup kitchens] . . . I am convinced that nothing but local self-government and self-support . . . hold out any hope of improvement for Ireland," he wrote.

The British viewed with contempt and disdain Ireland's ongoing economic dependency, especially when coupled with consistent and boisterous cries for repeal of the Irish-British union—that is, a movement calling for Ireland's political *independence*. To hold these two concepts simultaneously demonstrated a sense of warped incongruity and appalling ungratefulness on the part of the Irish, according to the prevailing sentiment in Britain.

Repeal leader Daniel O'Connell's death on May 15, mourned deeply by the Irish even as the British government was providing direct famine relief, exacerbated this resentment among England's residents, clergy, and government leaders. If O'Connell's burning desire to bring about political disunion with England struck such a responsive chord among the Irish, was it not hypocritical for the same people to expect ongoing economic relief from Parliament and the Crown? How could Ireland in good conscience castigate Britain and condemn its leaders with one hand, while extending the other to beg for life-sustaining aid?

When Lord Clarendon, the recently appointed lord lieutenant of Ireland (replacing Lord Bessborough, who died the day after O'Connell), pleaded with Prime Minister Russell for additional Irish relief, Russell delivered an icy response: "The state of Ireland for the next few months must be one of great suffering. Unhappily, the agitation for Repeal has contrived to destroy nearly all sympathy in this country."

Even when repeal was not mentioned specifically, famine fatigue was draining the most generous wellsprings in England. When Queen Victoria issued a letter in the fall of 1847 seeking Irish charitable relief—an official appeal by the government to raise private funds to assist Ireland during the soup kitchen to Poor Law transition—her missive was met with intense resistance. Liberal newspapers such as the *Times* and the *Examiner* denounced the Queen's letter as an unacceptable imposition on the British people to support an ungrateful and overly dependent Ireland. One minister wrote to the prime minister acknowledging that his parishioners had been generous in the past, "but we must not have it again." An Anglican rector penned a hostile letter to the editor saying he refused to countenance a collection based on the Queen's letter, since "every penny we bestow [contributes] to the degradation of Ireland, and the perpetuation of beggary."

Ironically, Irish editorial writers also denounced the Queen's letter, but for different reasons; one labeled it a smokescreen for the overall "neglect and obduracy" of the British government. Irish opinion leaders demanded a repeal of the Poor Laws and a return to general relief to aid victims of the "absolute famine" that still ravaged Ireland.

In October 1847, a perceptive French journal pointed out that a year's worth of hearing about the Irish famine had squeezed almost all generosity from the English people, whose feelings "with regard to the Irish are every day expressed . . . with a bitterness, an acrimony, and a contempt." Their reaction "cannot but sow seeds of hatred in the heart of the nation thus outraged and insulted."

Even as England financially abandoned Ireland, even as many British residents spiritually cut ties with their brethren, the Irish were dealing with a second immutable reality brought on by a year of starvation, fever, weakness, torpidity, evictions, and emigration: although the summer 1847 crop was described as "superb" and "luxurious" in some quarters due to "magnificent weather," the acreage of potatoes planted was "miserably small."

A year of famine had produced a collection of gruesome numbers: thousands of Irish had perished, thousands had emigrated, and thousands had simply given up. Thus, an infinitesimally small number had engaged in planting. With so few healthy people available in the spring to till the soil, plant potatoes, and eventually harvest the crop, and with virtually no cash to buy seed, even a perfect harvest would not yield enough to feed the people of Ireland.

Relief officials sent crop estimates to Dublin that never exceeded one-fifth of the usual acreage, according to one report, and in many districts amounted to one-eighth of normal acreage. One report called the potato plantings "insignificant"—even a crop described as "abundant" in its own right was woefully insufficient. Nor did the small farmer dare to eat his grain crop, which, as one commissariat officer wrote to Trevelyan, "will go out of the country, sold to pay rent." As a result, the officer said, "the face of the country is covered with ripe corn while the people dread starvation."

When Trevelyan wrote that he heard crops were "magnificent," he was warned: "Nothing can take the place of potatoes."

The famine's deprivation had imprinted itself upon the Irish psyche, but the famine's lessons were more elusive to absorb and more difficult still to put into practice: the Irish still depended upon the all-purpose potato for their sustenance, nourishment, and way of life, and they would for decades to come.

Anticipating the meager harvest in the summer of 1847, beggars from the countryside continued to stream into Cork city in search of scraps of food. Father Mathew, who weeks earlier had proposed a cordon around the city to prevent starving countryside peasants from flocking into Cork's lanes and alleyways, now predicted "unutterable calamities" if the soup kitchens were closed on schedule.

Without enough food or cash in small towns and villages and countryside parishes, these nomads would continue to overburden Cork city, carrying with them disease and fever that would spread exponentially in close quarters. And once the "wretched creatures" reached Cork, they craved "a morsel of food from beings almost as miserable as they are." At night, "they lay themselves down to sleep upon the earth, exposed to wet and cold." In the morning, "these doomed beings . . . called vagrants" were loaded onto carts by authorities, driven four or five miles from the city, "and left there to perish." Many died in the fields, Mathew reported, while others stumbled their way back to Cork to repeat the piteous cycle.

The destitution—and sometimes the rage—that was all-pervasive in Cork served as a microcosm of overall conditions across Ireland; Father Mathew wrote of deep despair in Galway, Kerry, Mayo, Sligo, Clare, and Donegal. In many ways, the imminent shuttering of soup kitchens coupled with a sparse potato crop foretold a disaster that could well equal or exceed that of the previous year.

After issuing edicts and orders closing the kitchens and transferring responsibility for relief from Britain's central government to Ireland, Trevelyan viewed his job as complete—in fact, he believed he could relax "after two years of such continuous hard work as I have never had in my life." In August, he took his family on a two-week holiday to France.

Father Mathew spent the summer and fall feeding people in his home, burying the dead in his cemetery, and ministering to the fever-stricken across the city. "The famine odour was in his parlour on Cove Street, and at his door, and in the dwellings of the poor whom he daily visited," according to his friend and biographer. "Nothing, however, could intimidate him."

But even the indefatigable Mathew knew that with the soup kitchens closing, the cause he immersed himself in was a losing one—at least without the continued generosity from across the Atlantic.

On July 23, one week after the *Macedonian* docked at Cove, Father Mathew warned: "Should the charity of our great benefactors in the United States fail, it is horrible to anticipate the consequences of the stoppage of government relief."

CHAPTER 27

⌒⋅⋯⋅⌒

"THE MAGNITUDE OF THESE SUPPLIES ... IS REALLY ASTONISHING"

B ut charity from the United States did not fail. On the contrary, for several months, the United States continued its extraordinary beneficence to Ireland, then the single greatest philanthropic effort by one nation on behalf of another.

Food-laden vessels continued to arrive, most sailing on behalf of the Irish Relief Committee of New York and the New England relief committee.

The *Free Trader* and *Reliance* sailed into Cork Harbor, the *Saone* to Galway, the *Channing* to Dublin. The *Horatio*, *Rochester*, and *Mary Ann* docked at Liverpool with provisions for Ireland, and food supplies also arrived in Irish and English ports aboard the *Duncan*, the *Express*, the *Anne Maria*, the *Patrick Henry*, the *Minerva*, the *Malabar*, the *Boston*, and the *Newhaven*.

Sitting in Dublin, Jonathan Pim continued to express his thanks for U.S. support, pointing out that the transition from widespread government relief to local Irish Poor Laws would likely bring "a great pressure of distress, and [we] must endeavor to meet it." Pim reported that the western parts of Cork and Kerry were still suffering "severely," and that the west of Mayo and Galway were also in terrible straits. "The alarm of fever appears to some extent to have subsided," Pim said, though area hospitals were filled to overflowing. He quickly offered his reason for the apparent contradiction: "I don't think there is less fever, but we seem more used to it."

Americans continued to contribute to the Irish cause, especially from the interior. In mid-June, New York committee secretary Jacob Harvey assured Pim that "our canal is doing its duty—our daily receipts of flour and grain are enormous, and a large portion is at once shipped to Europe." Pim could count on continued deliveries until at least September 1. "I am more afraid of winter months," Harvey added, "when all internal navigation ceases" once rivers and canals froze. In late July, Harvey let Pim know that "contributions from the west are arriving every week." Pim wrote back that more than 3 million people—"not very much less than one-half of our population"—were receiving their daily food "at public expense." He was embarrassed by this "appalling state of things . . . how it is to end none can tell."

Pim emphasized that Ireland would continue to benefit most from direct food shipments rather than money, and also urged Harvey to send as many clothes as he could, "which to an almost naked population, is essential to the preservation of health." In late August Pim lamented that the Irish population had been "considerably diminished by emigration and death." After September, he reminded Harvey, no further English government relief would be available, so American contributions would become more vital than ever. Harvey again reassured Pim that "you will be receiving further supplies from us every month. Our [New York] Indian corn crop is now being cut and stacked . . . it has yielded abundantly." He said it would be ready to ship in three months. Further, "contributions from the far west are reaching Atlantic ports, and whatever we receive we shall forward."

All through the fall, Pim urged Harvey to encourage continued donations from the United States, since Ireland was far from able to stand on its own and there was no telling how long it would take for the country to recover. The continued arrival of U.S. ships at Irish ports with food and provisions impressed him—"the magnitude of these supplies, and the constant and quick succession in which they continue to pour in upon us, is really astonishing," he wrote—but the fact was, the famine had devastated Ireland's workforce. Ireland no longer contained enough healthy, intelligent people to work and rebuild the country; it suffered for "the want of a middle class," Pim wrote to his New York friend. "A long time must elapse before the traces of famine can be expected to disappear."

In November, Pim warned that food would run out before the first of the year, especially along Ireland's west coast, and that any hope the "prostrated and demoralized" country had to stave off a second year of starvation and fever depended "almost *wholly* . . . [on] the citizens of the United States."

He and his colleagues now concentrated on how best to distribute food to those who needed it most, and whether in some cases it was better to sell food and purchase other needed goods for the poor. In several townships, women were cooking rice and distributing it to children and ill adults. "We have had the most satisfactory assurances of its value when given in this way," he explained. In early November, fearful that "there is not food to keep the people until the first of the year," Pim's committee was limiting distribution almost entirely to "the sick, the convalescent, and young children." Even with the enormous American contributions, Ireland's food supply was still "utterly insufficient for any plan of general relief."

The committee also gave direct food aid and money to several schools, and was undertaking to distribute small amounts of cash in fishing villages to pay for "repairs of boats, nets, and lines." These advances would be "repaid out of the proceeds of the fish caught." In these cases, Pim was espousing the importance of the maxim that "teaching a man to fish" was more beneficial than providing him with food. Under the plan of advancing funds to repair nets and boats, he wrote, "much good will be effected; the people will be enabled to support themselves by their industry, and the quantity of food for the support of the district will be materially increased." Providing only direct food aid at this late date would "exhaust" supplies in a few weeks, "and the want would be as great as ever."

Responding from New York, Harvey sympathized with Pim, acknowledging that the "dismal prospects" in Ireland offered no easy answers. "All I can dare to hope is that the distress may not be nearly as extensive as it was last year," he said. "It is very difficult to know what is best to be done in such an unnatural state of society as exists in Ireland." In addition, would relief efforts truly make a long-term difference without wholesale changes—political, social, and economic—in Ireland? Until then, Harvey astutely noted that "every measure hitherto adopted seems to have been but a palliative, not a cure, and I can see no prospect of any radical change."

As the calendar changed to 1848, Pim confirmed Harvey's concern when he wrote in late February: "Want and misery are still rife in very many districts of our suffering country, and means provided for its relief . . . are far from arresting the progress of the destitution." Pim conveyed what he believed to be a spark of good news when he reported that most experts projected a healthier potato harvest in the summer.

Harvey wondered whether the news was positive or not. Wasn't absolute reliance on the potato part of Ireland's problem in the first place? "I do not know whether to rejoice or not at the improved prospect of the potato crop," he wrote to Pim. "If they should prove as prolific as formerly, what is to prevent the laborers and small farmers from falling back upon them as their only food?"

The last American ship filled with supplies sailed from New York in late June 1848, bound for Liverpool with flour and Indian corn. After more than a year of generous contributions, American farmers, merchants, and shopkeepers alike had reached their limits.

To be sure, the pace of shipments from the United States to Ireland had slowed since the end of 1847. There were many reasons for this. Harvey reminded Pim as far back as late November 1847 that frozen waterways would prevent western farmers from shipping cargo to the East Coast. "In a few years . . . we shall have one continuous line of railroad to the far west, and then we shall not mind the ice," he said, "but I trust you will not require so much foreign charity by that time."

But Americans also had other misgivings. Some were soured by the

British government's inadequate response to the famine—if the United States could engage in a broad-based national effort to attack starvation in Ireland, should not the British replicate it? Even exceed it? Harvey conceded that "it is painful to read in the Irish papers the bickering of political bodies; the repetition of old animosities; the abuse [by] those in power." Such squabbling caused Americans to wonder if the British and Irish alike, during a terrible crisis, "were losing sight of the only true union—one of brotherly love and kindness." Other Americans voiced concern about their own limited stores of provisions as winter approached. Often the length and severity of winter months required farmers to stretch their food supplies to feed their families—who knew how much could be spared, even for a cause as worthwhile as Ireland?

But one other factor above all else contributed to the slowdown of U.S. relief to Ireland as the calendar turned to 1848: Americans were growing increasingly frustrated and weary by the sheer numbers of Irish immigrants that flooded their East Coast cities. And while U.S. residents likely deduced *intellectually* that additional aid to Ireland might actually help stave off mass emigration from the suffering country, *emotionally* most Americans were unprepared for, and even repulsed by, the thousands of poor, sick Irish who arrived in the United States, and they expressed their displeasure by drastically limiting their donations.

Harvey pointed out that more than 60,000 Irish and an equal number of German immigrants arrived in New York alone in 1847; well over 6,000 Irish—a full 10 percent—wound up in hospitals when they set foot on U.S. soil because of illness, whereas only 380 Germans were hospitalized. "What a tale does this statement tell of the miseries of Ireland!" Harvey wrote. "The Germans are poor, but they come out better clad and fed, and bear the voyage well." It was not that Harvey was blaming the immigrants themselves, but the results certainly turned many New Yorkers against the arriving Irish. "It is a disgrace to the British government that her subjects should be such a tax to the cities where they land," Harvey said.

Long a champion of Irish immigration to the United States to provide much-needed labor to farmers, Harvey was emphatic that those arriving in January 1848 were hurting the Irish cause. "I am sorry to see so many poor emigrants arriving here this winter. We cannot find work for them . . . and many are taken sick of the fever soon after they land." Irish immigrants who arrived in the summer could easily fan out across the countryside and find work, he pointed out, "but they should let us alone in winter . . . all our [relief] houses are nearly full, and if they continue to come in the same ratio, we shall be puzzled what to do with them until navigation opens."

Black '47 also saw a stunning 37,000 Irish immigrants flock to Robert Bennet Forbes's Boston (including 1,000 on a single day in April), many of them stricken with disease and virtually all of them impoverished. The city, which had a population of only around 115,000, was quickly overwhelmed.

Fearful that immigrant Irish might be carrying contagious diseases, Boston officials required a bond from the ship's captain or the vessel's owner of $1,000 for each sick, aged, or incapable passenger. So great was the fear of typhus that Boston often refused ships that carried sick passengers direct entry to the port, and instead directed them to islands that dotted the inner harbor. In June 1847, around the time of Father Mathew's testimony before the House of Lords subcommittee, Boston authorities turned away the British brig *Seraph*, which was arriving from Cork; the vessel had 118 cases of fever on board, and her passengers were in such a state of starvation that the British consul had to go down to the pier with supplies of food. When *Seraph* was ordered to St. John, New Brunswick, or some other British port, heartbroken passengers made a rush and tried to "insist on landing," but were driven back into the ship by Boston police and militia.

In some cases, Boston required the captain to disembark sick passengers at a Boston Harbor island hospital before allowing the ship to dock at city wharves. A Massachusetts state senate report noted that one vessel carrying 657 immigrants—mostly Irish—came into port, and 60 people were immediately sent to Deer Island "in a very sick and filthy condition." Another 25 bodies, those of poor souls who died during the voyage, were removed and given a pauper's burial (in May 2019, a Celtic cross was placed on Deer Island as a memorial to as many as 850 famine-era Irish buried in unmarked graves there).

Despite these barriers to entry, thousands of Irish did come ashore in Boston, and by the early summer of 1847, the city was overrun with destitute, starving Irish immigrants; "groups of poor wretches ... resting their weary and emaciated limbs at the corners of the streets and in the doorways," reported the *Boston Transcript*. The Irish did not merely descend upon Boston; they *inundated* the city, cramming every nook, cranny, cellar, tenement, and shanty in the city's North End and in other waterfront neighborhoods. Some native Bostonians called the arrival of so many poor Irish the "Celtic locust swarm," and others despaired that the newcomers were transforming Boston into the "American Dublin."

Faced with a world into which they might never be accepted, the Irish initially avoided interaction with most other residents of Boston and kept to their own enclave; because of their poverty and lack of skills, they were forced into horrendous living situations that further appalled native Bostonians.

"The mason who finishes the cornice of the palace returns at night perchance to a hut not so good as a wigwam," Thoreau wrote. Dark tenements, rickety sheds, filthy shanties, and dank rat-infested cellars were all deplorable places that the Irish called home. The Irish built makeshift housing on any available plot of land. Before Paul Revere's house in the North End was restored, it was a tenement house, surrounded by other shabby tenements. By 1850, the North End averaged thirty-seven immigrants per dwelling, and in some houses in the Fort Hill neighborhood there were up to a hundred inhabitants in buildings of three to five stories.

And the Irish didn't just live aboveground. In his classic *Boston's Immigrants*, Oscar Handlin concluded that without the cellars, the Irish population pouring into Boston could not have been housed.

While these appalling living conditions dismayed Bostonians, most citizens could pretend they didn't exist by staying away from the Irish sections. However, general Irish poverty was something else entirely.

Many Irish began begging in the streets the day they landed in Boston, and officials warned that the Irish made up the bulk of Boston's pauper rolls and were fast becoming a burden to taxpayers and a strain on city resources. Sending money and aid to starving Irish in Ireland was one thing; it was quite another for city taxpayers to support thousands of unskilled, uneducated, undernourished, ill-equipped, and—perhaps most dreaded of all—Roman Catholic peasants whose presence was so jarringly out of place in Boston. In addition to the "destitution and wretchedness of these armies" of Irish immigrants, the Massachusetts senate reported in 1848, what was impossible to overlook was "their ignorance, and total inability, even when in perfect health, to adapt themselves to the requirements of society here." They clung to the inner city "with a tenacity commensurate with their moral debasement, want of self-respect, and abject and needy circumstances."

A city report on sanitary conditions provided the statistical foundation that supported Bostonians' anecdotal experience and fanned the alarmist rhetoric of city officials. In 1849, more than 7,700 people were listed as paupers in Boston, nearly 60 percent of them foreigners, and most of those Irish; that compared to only 2,700 paupers ten years earlier, an increase of 268 percent. During that decade, Boston had spent nearly three-quarters of a million dollars on their care.

In addition, the city had spent an annual average of $350,000 on its public schools, and half of that was for educating the children of foreign parents, "most of whom contribute little or nothing to the public expenses, in taxation or otherwise." Moreover, 90 percent of the "truant and vagabond" children between the ages of six and sixteen years were foreigners, who "from neglect and bad habits were unfit to enter the public schools."

Increases in contagious diseases, especially cholera, were also attributed to the Irish. In 1849, Boston was terrified by an outbreak of cholera, and because of their congested and unsanitary living conditions in crowded tenements in Boston's North End, the Irish not only suffered the worst, but were vilified for contributing to the near epidemic—particularly when the first death, on June 3, was an Irishman (as was the last, on September 30). More than 700 Bostonians died in the summer of 1849, and 80 percent of those were foreigners; perhaps three-quarters of those foreigners were recently arrived Irish immigrants, according to an 1850 report of the Sanitary Commission of Massachusetts.

As a result of the cholera deaths, the city's Committee of Internal Health investigated the Irish quarter of Boston and was horrified: "Your Committee were witnesses of scenes too painful to be forgotten and yet too disgusting to be related here . . . the whole district is a perfect hive of human beings . . . huddled together like brutes, without regard to age or sex or sense of decency; sometimes wife and husband, brothers and sisters, in the same bed." Mayor John Bigelow later complained that the Irish immigrants were living in "filth and wretchedness," crowded together in "foul and confined apartments."

What Bigelow did not say was the toll this took on the Irish themselves; for example, during this period, six out of ten Irish children in Boston did not live past the age of five.

Oscar Handlin bluntly concluded about the Irish in Boston: "[They] became a massive lump in the community, undigested and undigestible."

The fact was, if the *Jamestown* endeared Boston to the Irish, the reverse did not occur.

And beyond Boston and New York, as 1847 came to a close and the winter of 1848 descended, dynamics were changing.

U.S. generosity toward Ireland—inspired by political leaders, encouraged by churches, emblemized by ship captains, fed and replenished by citizens of all means and classes—so bountiful and expansive in late winter, spring, summer, and early fall, had all but dissipated, replaced at year's end by grave fears of the potentially crushing economic and social burdens created by thousands of poor Irish newcomers. One clergyman asked the question on the minds of many Americans when he wrote: "Must we submit to be overrun by the paupers of English government?"

In her classic book on the famine, *The Great Hunger*, Cecil Woodham-Smith captured this shift in U.S. attitudes in late 1847 into 1848. "By a curious piece of reasoning," she wrote, "the Irish starving in Ireland were regarded as unfortunate victims, to be generously helped, while the same Irish, having crossed the Atlantic to starve in Boston, were described as the scourings of Europe and resented as an intolerable burden to the taxpayer."

All through the fall of 1847 and into the winter of 1848, as U.S. contributions slowed and his own nation continued to starve, Father Mathew labored in and around Cork to relieve the suffering. Queen Victoria had issued him an annual pension of £300 in June 1847 (the equivalent of about $30,000 per year today) for his work in the temperance movement and during the famine, and Father Mathew used most of it to purchase seed and food for others; he had mixed emotions about accepting money from the Crown and eventually would receive blistering criticism for doing so.

In November and December 1847, he was as active and energetic as at any previous period of his priesthood. Even many of the poor he assisted urged him to slow down, telling him that he worked too hard, that he had changed, become "haggard and worn and sad." To one woman who expressed concern for his health, he replied: "My dear, I am the strongest man in Ireland."

But stress and frustration were grinding Father Mathew down, triggering in him uncharacteristic responses, even outbursts. Some of the frustration and anger he had expressed during the debates on how to distribute *Jamestown*'s food returned. On one occasion several hundred people gathered outside his home seeking food. Father Mathew asked another priest to divide the people into two lines, one on each side of the street, and Mathew came out of his home with a basket of bread, hoping to distribute it in orderly fashion, a minuscule amount to each person. For a moment, the crowd remained calm, but suddenly "in their eagerness to clutch at the bread," the gathering turned into a melee. "The two sides of the living wall closed upon [him]," the second priest reported, "and, blocking up the passage, held him a prisoner." Father Mathew pleaded for the famished souls to step back, to allow him room to breathe, but in their hunger, the sight of food had "rendered them insensible to all considerations of delicacy." Finally, Father Mathew was able to tear himself free, but in the process his best coat was ripped, "slit up from the waist to the collar."

Mathew erupted in a "towering rage," according to his fellow priest, vowing "never to have anything to do with such nasty and ill-behaved people," and declaring he was finished doling out further relief. But he calmed overnight and his outburst was replaced by his usual dedication to the poor. "He was at it again the next morning," the priest reported, "as fresh as ever, as if nothing had happened . . . kissing the poor little dirty children, and calling them all the tender names in the world."

But his grueling schedule and mounting exertions during the famine's second year, piled upon the punishing workload he had maintained during his temperance crusade of the previous decade, left Father Mathew physically exhausted. During Lent of 1848, in the midst of his customary fasting period, the priest awakened one morning, and as he stepped out of bed, he collapsed to the floor in a heap. The noise roused his secretary, who rushed to the bedroom, hoisted Father Mathew back into bed, and summoned his physician. When the doctor arrived, he asked his patient what was wrong.

"My dear doctor," Father Mathew replied softly, "I am paralyzed."

CHAPTER 28

⌘

"AN IRISHMAN LOOKS ON AMERICA
AS THE REFUGE OF HIS RACE"

Ireland tottered and stumbled forward throughout 1848 and 1849, desperate to stay ahead of a merciless and tyrannical famine that stalked the countryside and showed no signs of abating. By the summer of 1848, as Jonathan Pim had forecast, British government aid had all but ended. The Irish people were on their own.

In October, James Prendergast despaired to his children in Boston: "Distress is very great. . . . Many are deserting their farms and flying to America as fast as they can. Destitution is seen almost everywhere." By December, he had used all the remittances they had sent him just to pay for physician services during a long illness that left him bedridden for six weeks. "I am penn[i]less," he wrote. "The last of what I had is gone." Worse, the malady had brought him to the brink of death, and his doctor informed him that he could not "expect to hold out for long." His only regret would be leaving his wife, Elizabeth, alone and without sufficient funds to survive. "If I die, as I am sure I will before many days, there is not a shilling in the house to defray my funeral expenses," he wrote, while expressing his hope that neighbors might extend credit to their mother upon his passing. In a postscript obviously dictated to a scrivener, Prendergast let his children know that he tried to sign his letter himself but did not have the strength to do so. "I was unable to finish—nature is nearly exhausted," he said.

James Prendergast died on Monday evening, December 18, 1848. Elizabeth sent her children her first letter on Christmas Eve, informing them of their father's death. She reassured them that though James's illness had been long, "it was not painful." And while she had "not a shilling to bury him," the couple's daughter-in-law, Nelly, covered his funeral expenses in full. "Not a farmer in the parishes here was attended to the grave in greater decency than his daughter-in-law sent him to his long home," she observed. Relatives asked Elizabeth to come live with them, but she would abide by her husband's wishes that she "keep my own little house during my life." To do so, she was now totally dependent on her children continuing to send money back from the United States.

Elizabeth does not offer any overall assessment of the situation in Ireland, but her dependence on her children mirrored Ireland's continued dependence on outside contributions, which by this time were drying up. Untold thousands continued to die and thousands more emigrated; the Irish now looked longingly to the United States in their efforts to separate themselves from the British Empire in every way possible. Irish resentment toward and hatred of England had reached a fever pitch, and virtually no Irishman believed the British cared whether they lived or died. "An Irishman looks on America as the refuge of his race, the home of his kindred, the heritage of his children and their children," wrote Dublin novelist Thomas Colley Grattan. "The shores of England are farther off in his heart's geography than those of Massachusetts or New York."

The two men whose heroic actions during the famine would forever endear them to Ireland spent 1848 and 1849 in vastly different ways.

Father Theobald Mathew spent the first half of 1848 recovering from the stroke that had paralyzed his left side, while crowds surrounded his home to offer prayers and seek information on his condition. By July, he had recovered enough to travel to Dublin for temperance work. His doctor marveled at the priest's recuperative powers: "His mind was not . . . affected by the attack, and the weakness in his limbs soon diminished so much that . . . [we] could no longer prevent him from resuming his labours in the temperance cause."

Father Mathew, however, was haunted by the grinding hunger, the "misery which met him at every step" in Ireland's capital, and equally despondent that the famine had drained the temperance movement of much of its progress and virtually all of its vitality—out of despair and hopelessness, many Irish had begun drinking again and saw no point in stopping. "The famine had struck the [temperance] cause as well as decimated the ranks of its followers," Mathew's friend and contemporaneous biographer wrote. When Father Mathew informed Rathbone in August 1848 of, once again, "the total destruction of the potato crop," he also reported that the downtrodden "and wretched people" were now "bathed in tears," a condition that left him feeling impotent for his inability to help. For the first time, he admitted, if his health permitted it, "I would gladly abandon this land of horrors and misery."

Robert Bennet Forbes spent 1848 under more pleasant circumstances. He and Rose had their fourth living child, a daughter, Rose. Forbes spent much of the year at home engaged in business with his brother, "as consignees of shipments from China and as joint owners of vessels." For a time, Forbes's fame as the leader of the *Jamestown* mission took secondary status to his role as a husband, father, and entrepreneur.

But by the summer of 1849, both Forbes and Father Mathew once again made national and international headlines—Father Mathew for his first, highly publicized, and unexpectedly controversial trip to the United States; Robert Bennet Forbes for yet another heroic episode at sea.

—✦—

CHAPTER 29

"MY MISSION AMONG YOU CLOSES TODAY"

T housands of people, many of them Irish immigrants, lined the wharves of New York Harbor on Monday, July 2, 1849, to greet the packet *Ashburton*, arriving from Liverpool with several hundred passengers aboard, the vast majority poor Irish men, women, and children fleeing the famine. Thunderous cheers and applause from one of the "largest assemblages ever seen in [the] famous city" rang out across the water. Music played from bands onshore and ships from all nations anchored in the harbor flew their colors, which snapped in the smart breeze, to salute one special guest among the hundreds aboard the *Ashburton*.

Against his doctor's orders and the advice of friends who feared for his "broken health," Father Mathew decided in June to take his long-planned and ardently desired transatlantic voyage to advance the temperance movement to the United States and to thank Americans for their unprecedented famine relief to Ireland. The U.S. temperance movement was part of the worldwide effort, but was also incorporated into a larger set of social initiatives, including women's voting rights and abolitionism, encouraged by progressive reformers. Mathew believed the U.S. effort held great promise. Already, more than 300,000 Americans had joined the American Temperance Society, and in 1847, Maine became the first state to ban the sale of alcohol (several other U.S. states would follow suit).

The New York Municipal Council, arriving on the small steamer *Sylph*, welcomed Mathew aboard, and the group made its way to Staten Island, accompanied by more cheers from thousands on shore and hundreds more on ships anchored in the harbor. Mathew was humbled and fascinated by the scene; in contrast to the dreariness of his home country, here in the United States "all was bustle and animation, activity and life, betokening the power and progress of a great country in the first flush of its youthful energy."

For Mathew, no longer energetic since his stroke and hardly youthful at age fifty-nine, the trip from Ireland was long, tedious, and mostly unpleasant. Seasickness and gastric pain gripped him early in the voyage, confining him to his cabin for days. Despite his physical improvement since the stroke, his physician had noted just before he departed from Ireland that Mathew's "gait was every day more enfeebled," and "labor became a struggle." Mathew himself, just before he departed, had written to an American supporter and acknowledged that "friends in the States will find in me a mere wreck of what I was."

Progress at sea was excruciatingly slow; dead calms and intense fog delayed the ship for days, extending the monotonous voyage, and Mathew, a "man who . . . preferred bustle and excitement to repose," grew increasingly weary and fatigued, anxious to reach New York and the United States. The number of Irish emigrants who had traveled there linked the two countries, and Father Mathew believed the United States offered his people the hope and opportunity they had lost in Ireland. His fervent desire was that the Irish might be "sharers and helpers in the rise" of their adopted country, whose future prospects were "unparalleled," a country "destined to far outstrip the old, world-worn Titans as pioneers of progress."

If the Irish people were looking for a second chance, Mathew believed, the one and only place they would find it was the United States of America.

In addition to looking forward to his ministrations, Mathew

anticipated that a lengthy stay in the United States, a nation bursting with optimism and growth and plenty, would provide a recuperative respite from the three dark years of famine that had stripped Ireland of its sinew, its pride, its mirth, its very humanity. The United States possessed all of these attributes in abundance, perhaps enough to restore Mathew's own physical health and emotional spirits.

What he did not foresee was that, despite all of the good work he would do in the United States, he would wind up at the center of raging religious and social controversies that the country was grappling with, a position he neither sought nor was capable of managing.

Hampered by his own unwitting naiveté, Father Mathew initially antagonized the Catholic Church in the United States—whose leaders believed his temperance crusade was far too ecumenical and tolerant of other religions—before its leaders finally embraced him and his first visit. Then, despite his best efforts and much to his dismay, the humble, unassuming clergyman from Cork was thrust headlong into the American slavery debate, at which time he managed to infuriate both abolitionists and slaveholders alike.

The first few days of the visit were promising, a whirlwind of activity that energized Father Mathew and excited the crowds that came to receive his absolution or take the temperance pledge. He celebrated Mass at numerous churches around the city and spoke at chapels and public places. He trudged through miles of streets and slums to visit Irish immigrants in their neighborhoods and at their homes. He held his pledge events outside City Hall, and the crowds were so thick on the first two days that thereafter, to avoid congestion, he administered the pledge to men and women on alternate days. He was energized, buoyed by the people's response, and optimistic about their future in the United States.

The people loved him, but from the start, Church officials viewed with suspicion both his all-embracing manner and his willingness to accept a pension from the Crown, which they viewed as anti-Catholic and anti-Irish; one misstep and Father Mathew would find himself further alienated from the New York Catholic hierarchy. That inevitable stumble occurred when he attended a meeting of the American Temperance Union (ATU) at the Broadway Tabernacle, an enormous interdenominational church used for both temperance and abolitionist rallies. While the meeting was called by the ATU to officially welcome Father Mathew, Catholic leaders were outraged when they learned that Protestant ministers shared the stage with the Irish priest and offered opening and closing prayers. Mathew's participation under such circumstances bordered on blasphemy. New York bishops, and some priests—as well as clergy from other cities—accused Mathew of participating in an illicit faith service, not just a temperance rally. Baltimore archbishop Samuel Eccleston sent Mathew a stern reprimand and contacted other clergy for advice on how to handle the Irish priest. Eccleston wanted Mathew to issue a public apology for fraternizing with Protestant ministers.

Yet tensions between Mathew and other Church leaders remained private. During his stay in New York, Father Mathew administered the pledge to more than 20,000 people. His next stop was Boston, where similar difficulties awaited: Bishop John Fitzpatrick disliked and mistrusted him, while Protestant reformers were eager to welcome him.

But Church politics would be the least of Father Mathew's problems when he traveled to Boston. Instead, a public imbroglio in the aftermath of a meeting with abolitionist William Lloyd Garrison—and a letter Garrison subsequently made public—dragged Father Mathew into the vortex of U.S. slavery, threatened to sabotage his entire visit, miscast him as a purveyor of falsehoods, and filled the Irish priest with a deep and profound anxiety that further debilitated him and nearly ruined his health.

Father Mathew had longed to visit Boston, the city that sent the *Jamestown* to Ireland's shores, that held his friend Robert Bennet Forbes in the highest esteem, the community whose generosity launched the extraordinary and national American effort to supply Ireland with food and provisions during the most calamitous period in his home country's history.

Next to Cork, Mathew felt most affection for Boston; next to his followers and parishioners in Cork, Mathew felt most indebted to the people of Boston. The bonds between Boston and Ireland, strong for a decade, had grown all but unbreakable in the three years since the famine struck.

But Boston—smaller, more provincial, more homogenous, more quarrelsome, more religiously intolerant, more socially rigid, more politically impenetrable than New York—presented problems for Father Mathew from the outset in late July 1849. On his arrival, he was welcomed by Whig governor George Briggs, Whig mayor John Bigelow, and a cast of Protestant ministers, including Lyman Beecher, who—while a longtime temperance advocate—was also a virulent anti-Catholic. More than 15,000 devoted Mathew followers attended the main ceremony, but noticeably absent was Bishop Fitzpatrick, who was displeased with the Irish priest for sharing the platform with "sectarian fanaticks, calvinist preachers and deacons. . . . The appearance of fellowship between a Catholic priest and such men can hardly be without evil results."

Things got worse for Father Mathew on July 26, when renowned abolitionist leader William Lloyd Garrison and an associate visited the Irish priest. In addition to his staunch anti-slavery views, Garrison did not drink, was an ardent supporter of Irish nationalism, and was a longtime admirer of Mathew's. One reason for his affection was that eight years earlier, both Father Mathew and Irish nationalist Daniel O'Connell had signed an anti-slavery address sent to the Irish in America. The letter declared that American slavery was "a disgrace to the country" and "a sin against God and man." The moral question was clear, the two men wrote: "All who are not for it must be against it. None can be neutral." In addition to signing the anti-slavery letter, Mathew had welcomed former slave and abolitionist Frederick Douglass to Cork in 1845, another sign to Garrison that the priest was firmly and publicly on the right side of the slavery issue. In fact, Douglass later told Garrison he had been "entirely charmed by the goodness of this truly good man."

Mathew and Garrison began their Boston meeting amicably enough, but the pleasantries ended once Garrison got down to business. He had a small favor to ask, one to which he was sure Father Mathew would accede, considering Mathew's strong declaration against American slavery in 1841. He presented Mathew with a written invitation to a special event: Boston abolitionists were about to celebrate, on or about August 1, the ninth anniversary of the end of slavery in the British West Indies. Would Mathew be willing to speak at the event? In the invitation, which he knew was likely to become public, Garrison had written a reminder of the anti-slavery letter Mathew had signed eight years earlier, and requested that the priest use the West Indies commemoration to bear testimony against the "enslavement of *any* portion of the human family."

Father Mathew had no interest in becoming embroiled in the American slavery debate. He believed that it would detract from his temperance message, and especially diminish his influence in the South, home to thousands of Irish and a major part of his U.S. itinerary. Further, he knew full well that Irish Catholics and abolitionists were at loggerheads and had been for several years. Irish laymen and Irish Catholic clergy in the United States resented anti-Catholic attitudes expressed by many in the abolitionist movement, and they believed firmly, and generally correctly—and would throughout the Civil War—that abolitionists, in their zeal to end the injustices of slavery, ignored the plight of and injustices against destitute Irish immigrants.

As Garrison held out the invitation letter, which Mathew grasped "with some agitation and embarrassment of manner," the Irishman recognized the dilemma in which he found himself. He truly and thoroughly detested slavery, and attending the West Indies event would offer him a chance to reiterate his beliefs and send a message to Boston and America. But still fresh in his mind was the debacle at the Broadway Tabernacle, Bishop Fitzpatrick's repeated admonitions, his desire to focus on his temperance mission, and, perhaps weighing most heavily, his knowledge of the anti-abolitionist attitudes of Irish Americans. The latter group was his major constituency on this U.S. tour.

Garrison awaited an answer. Within seconds, Father Mathew declined Garrison's invitation—the priest would not speak at the West Indian celebration.

"I have as much as I can do," Mathew said to Garrison by way of explanation, "to save men from the slavery of intemperance, without attempting to overthrow any other kind of slavery." Furthermore, it would not be "proper" to participate in the anti-slavery event when he was in the United States to "promote the cause of temperance."

Later, after Garrison publicly ridiculed and derided Father Mathew's decision, Mathew wrote to his friend and eventual biographer, John Maguire, in Cork and complained that "Mr. Garrison . . . strove to entrap me." Maguire replied that the priest's response "ought to have satisfied any fair man," as he "did not visit America to accomplish the emancipation of the negro, but to advocate and promote the cause of temperance." Any attempt to join the abolitionist cause, Maguire asserted, "would have been in bad taste and in worse judgment."

But Garrison could not have disagreed more. His first reaction toward Father Mathew's decision was bitter disappointment, and his second was utter rage. For Garrison and many abolitionists, any goodwill toward Father Mathew for his temperance work, any admiration for his inexhaustible labors to assist Irish famine victims, dissipated overnight.

Slavery was still a few years from becoming a widespread moral issue in the United States; for most, it was still a political matter, and even in progressive Massachusetts, abolitionism was still the minority view. Boston was changing demographically, and despite differences with the Irish, abolitionist leaders such as Garrison for years had pointed to the anti-slavery writings of deceased Irish nationalist Daniel O'Connell and Pope Gregory XVI as a way to persuade Irish Catholics to oppose slavery. Father Mathew's attendance at the West Indies emancipation celebration surely would have bolstered that effort.

An angry and indignant Garrison perceived that Mathew was backsliding on the slavery issue, and viewed his decision as a sign of unforgivable cowardice and hypocrisy. At the West Indies event, with Father Mathew absent, Garrison recounted the clergyman's decision as the crowd shouted "Shame! Shame!" Then, over a six-week period in September and October, he published in his newspaper, *The Liberator*, five scathing letters to Mathew, along with Mathew's 1841 anti-slavery address. "It is with great sorrow of heart," Garrison wrote, "that I lay these facts before America, Ireland, and the world." Garrison blasted

Mathew for opposing American slavery from the comparative safety and distance of Ireland, but "now that you are on American soil you . . . give the slave no token of your sympathy, and his oppressor no cause of uneasiness!"

Garrison was not alone. Frederick Douglass, an erstwhile Mathew admirer, expressed himself in more measured language, but reached an equally devastating conclusion when he grouped Mathew with other foreigners who visited America and refused to condemn slavery. "We had fondly hoped . . . that he would not change his morality by changing his locality," Douglass wrote. "We are however grieved, humbled, and mortified to know that HE too has fallen."

Mathew's letter also became an issue for southern supporters of slavery, who accused Mathew of being a "wolf in sheep's clothing" when he visited Washington, D.C. A simple resolution by the United States Senate to seat Mathew "within the bar" of the Senate chamber, to honor his efforts during the famine and on behalf of the temperance movement, was passed only after hours of acrimonious debate. Southern senators, led by South Carolina's John C. Calhoun and others, balked at according the honor to a man whose letter had denounced the Confederacy and their way of life (the only other foreigner previously honored was the Marquis de Lafayette, a French hero of the American Revolution and the most revered non-American in the United States).

Most southern senators who voted against the resolution were not swayed by northern arguments that Mathew was being honored for his humanitarian work, not his political views on slavery, and, in any case, that the Irish priest had *repelled* Garrison's advances to speak at the West Indies emancipation event.

Shaken but undeterred by the hostility he faced from northern abolitionists and southern politicians, Father Mathew embarked over the next two years on an odyssey through American cities and small towns: down the Eastern Seaboard to Richmond and southern Virginia; into South Carolina; across the Deep South to Mobile, Alabama; New Orleans, Louisiana; Natchez and Vicksburg, Mississippi; and Little Rock, Hot Springs, and Sulphur Springs in Arkansas (it was in Sulphur

Springs that he spent the most enjoyable time of his U.S. tour); and through what would then be described as the American West (Tennessee, Kentucky, Ohio, and other portions of the Midwest today); then winding his way back to the East Coast. Along the way, he administered the temperance pledge to thousands, met and embraced Irish immigrants who had arrived in their new home within the past few months or years, and thanked Americans everywhere for their generosity to his flock in Ireland during the darkest days of the famine.

The stress weighed upon him. In late March 1851, while steaming up the Mississippi from New Orleans on his eventual way to Nashville, he suffered a near-fatal stroke. The attack was a warning that, after "twelve years of incessant labor—of heart, brain, and body—such as not one man in a million could endure," it was time to return home. Mathew was "shattered, broken down, worn out."

In a final address in Cincinnati, months after the stroke, Mathew acknowledged that "the growing infirmities of age, aggravated by repeated attacks of a dangerous and insidious malady, now demand retirement and repose."

On November 8, 1851, the sixty-one-year-old Father Mathew boarded the steamer *Pacific* in New York for his transatlantic voyage, exhausted, impoverished, more than a little disillusioned, and physically broken. His hair had turned from gray to white, his limp was more pronounced, and he often suffered loss of breath after even minimal exertion.

Yet his American tour had been a remarkable triumph. On his sojourn, he visited more than 300 cities and towns in twenty-five states, and administered the pledge to upward of 500,000 people, some of whom would remain true to it for the rest of their lives. The *New York Herald* estimated Mathew had traveled 37,000 miles to accomplish his goals, "which, when added to two voyages across the Atlantic, would make a total distance equal to twice the circumnavigation of the globe." Regardless of his health, Mathew repeatedly ignored his physician's warnings to rest, instead continuing in "the heavenly task of reclaiming his fallen brother [and] welcoming the prodigal son back into the bosom of society."

Just prior to his departure, Mathew published his "Farewell Address to the Citizens of the United States," people who had forged a bond with Ireland even as the rest of the world—including England—had all but turned its back. "My mission among you closes today," he wrote, and "I now bid you a reluctant, a final farewell . . . I carry with me, to the 'poor old country,' feelings of respect and attachment . . . that neither time nor distance can obliterate."

Father Theobald Mathew died on December 8, 1856, five years after his return to Ireland and, fittingly enough, on the Catholic holy day of the Feast of the Immaculate Conception. He was sixty-six years old and had served as a priest for forty-two years.

The sixty months after his return from the United States were not kind. Ireland was in the final throes of the famine (some historians contend that full recovery did not occur until 1855), but conditions were still difficult and the food supply was still insufficient to meet the nourishment needs of the people. The poor still lined up outside of Father Mathew's home, but they were often joined by charlatans and grifters who took advantage of the priest, whose diminished faculties had made him easy prey. His friends feared that he could no longer distinguish between "imposters and genuine cases," according to his grandnephew. Father Mathew, frustrated and "crushed by melancholy," did his best to stand as a pillar against which the poor Irish could lean, but he no longer was capable of doing so. "His own people found him looking old and tired," his grandnephew wrote. "The great activities of his life were over for him."

He suffered seizures and two more strokes before traveling in October 1854 to the Portuguese island of Madeira on the advice of his physician, who suggested that the warmer climate—and a break from his priestly duties—could improve his health. The weather helped, but his "lameness" prevented him from walking around the capital city, Funchal. He returned to Cork the next summer, and one day staggered and nearly fell while celebrating Mass. He was afraid to say Mass again, a deprivation that depressed him more deeply.

In the autumn of 1856, in an attempt to rest and regain some semblance of vitality, he ventured to Queenstown (known as Cove when the *Jamestown* arrived in 1847, but its name was changed in 1849; it remained Queenstown until it changed to Cobh in 1920). But residents nearly cried when they saw "the man who had swept half the world with his fiery will and energy" tottering through the streets, leaning on a boy's shoulder. "Old and broken, he was passing through the Valley of the Shadow," his biographer noted.

One December morning while dressing, Father Mathew suffered a final stroke and tumbled to the floor in his bedroom. The attack rendered him speechless and paralyzed except for some slight motion in his fingers, enough to administer the sign of the cross to well-wishers who lined up to visit the bedridden clergyman. The Sisters of the Queenstown Convent, who tended to him in his final days, asked, through a series of yes-or-no questions, where he wished to be buried. Mathew indicated he wanted to rest not in the family plot in Tipperary but in the Catholic cemetery in Cork, which he had started years earlier, and where his brother and the poorest souls who had perished in the famine were interred. Always cognizant of his role as a shepherd, he would enter eternity amid his flock.

Father Mathew died moments after he had made his wishes clear.

His body was brought to Cork and laid in state in the Church of the Holy Trinity, which he had built. On Friday, December 12, 1856, an estimated 50,000 Cork residents poured into the streets and jammed the alleyways and walkways to pay their respects, while a two-mile funeral procession wound its way solemnly through the city Father Mathew had served and blessed for decades. "Every class, every rank, every party, every creed had its full representation in that sad procession," one report described, with the rear of the crowd filled with "the truest mourners of all—the poor." At the entrance to the cemetery, more than seventy Catholic clergy received Mathew's body, his fellow priests treating him with far greater reverence in death than they ever had while he lived.

After a long and solemn service, "amidst the tears and prayers of his fellow citizens who that day represented a mourning nation," Father

Theobald Mathew—Ireland's Apostle of Temperance, a godsend to his people during their country's destructive famine, the greatest friend and protector the Irish poor ever had—was laid to rest near a large cedar tree, beneath a cross he had erected years before.

At that chosen spot, Maguire wrote, Ireland's most famous and beloved priest was "consigned to the grave for which his spirit had long yearned."

CHAPTER 30

⊂—✦—⊃

"Haul up! Haul up!"

On June 20, 1849, twelve days before Father Mathew arrived in the United States, Robert Bennet Forbes bid his family and his country farewell and embarked on the steamer *Europa* for England, the first leg in a long business excursion to China that would encompass a series of boat trips and a grueling eighty-five-mile overland route from Cairo to Suez across sand, dust, and gravel. Along the way the nearly forty-five-year-old Forbes would visit Alexandria, take a steamer down the Nile, and sail the Red Sea.

Forbes anticipated that the journey would take months; and again, he would leave Rose with the children, four of them this time, including her namesake, who had not yet celebrated her first birthday when her father departed.

Seven days into the journey, just as Father Mathew was traveling the other way toward the United States—their two ships likely crossed close to each other—the *Europa* was navigating through a dense fog, and around 2:00 p.m. Forbes went to his forward cabin to rest. Ninety minutes later, Forbes felt a "sudden shock" and heard a loud crash. Bolting upright, he threw open the door and raced to the deck. He knew at once, by the intensity of the vessel's shudder and the hideous sounds of violent crunching, that the *Europa* had collided with something.

Was it another ship or an iceberg?

When he reached the deck, he had his answer. He was looking at "a scene of horror and confusion which beggars description."

The *Europa* had collided at its port bow with the sailing ship the *Charles Bartlett*, which was traveling from London to New York. By the time Forbes reached the deck, the U.S.-bound vessel was already heeling over and about to sink, a gaping hole gashed into its side. The wreckage of the *Europa*'s fore-topmast—she had been running under full sail in addition to her steam power—with all the sails attached and unfurled, lay amid the debris caused by the violent crash, the wind still catching the toppled sails and pushing the ship deeper into the *Charles Bartlett*'s side.

Thick fog engulfed both ships, but Forbes could see that the *Bartlett*'s decks were swarming with screaming men, women, and children, and as he took in the scene, he heard the *Europa*'s steam "blowing off with a noise that drowned the shrieks of people." Other passengers were in the water, crying for help and struggling to remain afloat. Forbes raced aft on the port side to try to lower a lifeboat, and as he was clearing the rescue boat's lines, he spotted a woman and child floating nearby. He plunged into the water, crying out for a rope, but by the time one was thrown to him and he reached the poor souls he realized they were "lying facedown without any signs of life." Swiveling his head around, Forbes spotted a man clinging to a piece of timber; he tossed the rope over him and the man was hauled up, "more dead than alive."

Forbes climbed back onto the *Europa*—by this time the *Charles Bartlett* was sinking and dragging the *Europa*'s fore-topmast down with her—raced to the other side of the ship, and spotted another man in the water, gasping and barely keeping his head above the churning sea. Forbes snatched a rope, jumped back in, and grabbed the man just as the ship rolled windward and dunked both men. Forbes held on to the man with all of his strength, and, as the ship lurched the other way, they were jerked out of the water and Forbes secured a better grip on both the rope and the drowning man. Again the ship rolled in the opposite direction, and the men were swamped. When they resurfaced once more, Forbes screamed "Haul up! Haul up!" between ingesting mouthfuls of water. The line had become tangled, and by the time it was freed, Forbes was exhausted and coughing out seawater. Finally, crew members on board the *Europa* began hauling the pair up; the rope hitch was slippery and Forbes's arms ached from supporting the man's estimated 200 pounds and his own 175 pounds. As they were hoisted, the pair cleared the surface of the water and Forbes managed to wrap an arm around the man's neck. He reached for the ship's rail with one hand still gripping the rope. But then an assisting crew member, moving forward near the rail to get a better hold, accidentally stepped on Forbes's hands. Forbes could "hold on no longer and down went my man."

Forbes let go of the rope and plunged back into the water, going "far under," but could not reach the unfortunate victim. The nearness of the man's rescue only to lose him at the last moment haunted Forbes for decades.

By this time, a lifeboat swung around the stern, manned by the *Europa*'s third mate, other sailors, firemen, and stewards. They pulled an exhausted Forbes aboard, and he grabbed an oar as the boat made its way through the debris and a few other passengers still struggling to remain alive amid the waves. Forbes spotted a man who was about to go under, barely visible in the trough. He laid in his oar and, seizing a boat hook and reaching far over the bow, was able to fasten it to the man's clothing and pull him to safety. The lifeboat crew searched for more floaters nearby, but the boat had gotten turned around in the fog and— despite the cries and screams nearby—they could not spot any on the roiling surface. With the few people in the lifeboat needing immediate medical attention and with the *Europa* now nearly out of sight in the heavy fog, the small lifeboat crew made a decision: the rowers pulled hard, reached the collision scene, and pulled themselves and their victims on board the *Europa*.

On deck, the scene was chaos; some *Charles Bartlett* passengers clung to the *Europa*'s ropes and side rails after leaping from their doomed vessel; other victims who had reached the *Europa*'s decks were screaming and sobbing. Forbes heard the heartbreaking cries of one man "nearly frantic over the loss of his wife, six little ones, and all his earthly possessions."

The collision in the North Atlantic fog was catastrophic.

Of the 168 passengers and 14 crew members aboard the *Charles Bartlett*, 136 people died, including 3 crew members. Among the group of mostly German, Irish, and British emigrants on board, only one of forty women, Bridget Conroy of London, survived, hauled out of the water by several men who had tossed her a bowline. All of the more than forty children on board perished.

In his official report, Captain Bartlett described the dense fog that had settled around his namesake ship just after noontime, which caused him, at 3:00 p.m., to order "a good look-out from the top gallant fore-castle; also directed the man at the wheel to look sharp to the wind-ward." Both measures were standard practice when ships encountered heavy fog, which happened often in the North Atlantic. But a half hour later, Bartlett heard "a rumbling to windward like distant thunder" and he "turned [his] ear to windward and eye to the horizon." Emerging from the thick fog was what appeared to be a ship about 400 yards distant, traveling full speed ahead toward the *Bartlett*. "All hands shouted at the same time to alarm the ship and I ordered the bell to be rung and called to the ship to 'port her helm,' as I saw that was the only chance of escape," Captain Bartlett described. It was no use—one minute from the time Bartlett and his officers spotted the *Europa*, the steamer, traveling hard at twelve knots, struck the *Bartlett* full force. "The crash and the terrible scene that ensued I am not adequate to describe," he said.

But he tried to do so. In vivid language, Bartlett recounted the minutes after the collision. He was knocked down, and after righting himself, he shouted for every person to cling to the *Europa* "as their only hope." He caught hold of a broken chain on the bow and hauled himself aboard the *Europa*, while shouting for his passengers and crew

246 • Voyage of Mercy

to follow. Bartlett was not abandoning his ship, which was sinking fast, but trying to find a high point from which to direct rescue efforts. It was not until he climbed onto the *Europa* that he surveyed the terrible damage the collision had caused and the near-total destruction of the *Charles Bartlett*.

Bartlett also was torn emotionally by memories of the jovial scene aboard his vessel just prior to the collision. Some passengers were playing musical instruments on deck while women and children "danced and played." "Then came a shout, a crash, a bubble, and all went down— not one child, and only one woman saved."

Captain Bartlett credited the captain, officers, and crew of the *Europa*, as well as many of the steamer's passengers, for their rapid and valiant rescue efforts. But he saved his most heartfelt thanks for one man.

"I particularly observed one passenger using the most noble exertions," he said. "I saw him let himself overboard and clench a man in his arms. . . . I next saw him on the bow of a boat, hauling a man from under water with a boat-hook, who was afterwards restored to life on board. I afterwards found that person to be Capt. R. B. Forbes of Boston."

Shortly after the *Europa* reached England, the Liverpool Shipwreck and Humane Society presented Forbes with a medal for his "bold and meritorious conduct in leaping overboard" to attempt to save *Bartlett* passengers. The resolution noted that Forbes's action had come "at the risk of his own life." And the group reiterated its gratitude to Forbes for delivering "an immense supply of provisions" to Ireland as part of the *Jamestown* mission, "an act of generous humanity which never ought to be forgotten."

Forbes was also honored by Lloyd's Shipwreck Society of London and, in absentia, received a gold medal and glowing testimonial from the Humane Society of Massachusetts, of which he was a trustee. The modest Forbes was genuinely moved by both the society's words and the medal, which was the only one of its kind ever awarded. "The *first* will be gratefully remembered while my life continues," he wrote to committee members, "and the last, when my lamp shall be extinguished, will remain to stimulate my sons, and my sons' sons, to flinch not when the way is opened for them to do their duty, whether on the land or on the sea."

Forbes arrived in Canton, China, in mid-September 1849 and would stay until the following April. At one point during his stay he became so ill that he nearly died; at his weakest moment, he asked his doctor to ensure that his coffin was built from a ship's mast. To his surprise, and his doctor's, he recovered.

His physical ailment was bad enough, but in December, he received news from home that tragedy had struck the Forbes family again. His daughter, Rose, had died on September 5 at the age of fourteen months. With the death of their youngest daughter, Bennet and Rose had now suffered the loss of four children; and this time, unlike the other three instances, Rose handled the heartache of burying her namesake child alone, while Bennet was thousands of miles away.

This latest tragedy did not elicit a great outpouring from Forbes. It is unclear whether his muted response to little Rose's death was due to stoicism, past heartache, his up-close observance of suffering in Ireland, the numbing sense provided by great distances, or a simple understanding and resignation of the fragility of life among the vulnerable young, especially in a congested city like Boston (a cholera epidemic swept the city while Forbes was away).

In any case, his tribute to his deceased daughter was heartfelt but sparing, remembering little Rose simply as "a sweet child."

On Thursday, July 3, 1851, more than two years after he left home—and just a few months before Father Mathew concluded his U.S. tour— forty-seven-year-old Robert Bennet Forbes stood on the platform of a steam-engine train and prepared to jump.

He was approaching the Quincy, Massachusetts, stop, just outside of Boston, and Forbes learned to his dismay that the train made scheduled stops in Quincy only on Sundays. He begged the conductor to make an exception after his exhausting trip, but the trainman agreed only to slow down and allow Forbes to jump; from there Forbes could walk to his home in Milton.

Forbes agreed, and now, as the train slowed to about seven or eight miles an hour, Forbes measured the distance, clutched his bag, and leaped, landing hard on the station platform, feeling the pain shoot up his legs. "I trundled along some yards, feeling as if all my joints were coming apart," he wrote, "but I kept my legs."

Forbes acknowledged later that his decision to jump was probably foolish—"I resolved from that day never to leave a car while under such headway"—but, as he explained to the conductor, he had his reasons for deciding to leap from a moving train.

"I told [him] of my very long absence," Forbes recalled, "and of my earnest desire to get home."

PART VII

LEGACIES: THE IRISH FAMINE AND THE JAMESTOWN MISSION

"The links between our countries . . . have endured"

German children in West Berlin wave to a U.S. Air Force transport aircraft as it lands at Tempelhof Airport during "Operation Vittles"—the Berlin Airlift—in 1948. A century after the USS Jamestown *voyage, the United States used the same public-private partnership model to provide food to Berlin residents during a time of crisis.*

CHAPTER 31

"THE GREATEST SOCIAL CALAMITY . . . THAT IRELAND HAS EVER EXPERIENCED"

Elizabeth Prendergast finally emigrated from Ireland in late August 1850, excited about joining her children in Boston. "I have a good featherbed and plenty of bedclothes to take with me," she wrote, "and ye have sent me the means to procure the rest." She sailed to Liverpool, where she waited for seven days before boarding the *Niobe* for the United States. "I am more than joyful at the thoughts of [going] to my dear children," she wrote.

Thousands followed suit, departing their beloved Ireland. By 1851, the year both Father Mathew and Robert Bennet Forbes returned from their long foreign journeys, the worst of the Irish potato famine had abated, though its immediate remnants—severe food shortages, high incidences of contagious diseases, deep despair and discouragement among the Irish poor, and especially increased emigration—continued at least until 1856, the year of Father Mathew's death.

The human toll of the Great Hunger was devastating. In 1841, five years before the famine began, the Irish census recorded the country's population at more than 8 million people; the 1851 census report estimated that under normal conditions, with expected birth rates, the population that year should have reached approximately 9 million. But by 1851, Ireland's population had dropped to about 6.5 million people; in the words of the census writer, the "enormous number" of nearly 2.5 million people, or nearly *30 percent* of the nation's population, had disappeared.

The poor potato crop in 1845 followed by the totally blighted crop in 1846, in combination with the British government's apathy, neglect, incompetence, hostility, or active genocide—depending on one's historical interpretation and perspective—produced six cataclysmic years between 1845 and 1851. The numbers vary according to sources, and an exact count is difficult to determine, due both to the impoverishment and anonymity of so many who died, and to the failure of local governments to even record many deaths at the peak of the Great Hunger. But even using conservative statistics in the aggregate, it is safe to say that during the famine's duration, well over 1 million Irish men, women, and children died from starvation or attendant diseases such as typhus, other fevers, malnutrition, cholera, and dysentery, or from hypothermia due to post-eviction exposure to cold and wind and rain and snow.

During those same six years, a staggering 1.5 million to 1.8 million people fled the country—with few possessions and little hope, and more as refugees than as emigrants—and boarded lice-ridden, disease-festering famine ships in a mass outpouring from Ireland, a level of emigration unrivaled up to that time from any country.

Extend the time span to 1860, and over the preceding fifteen years, more than 3 million Irish departed their home country in search of something better, equivalent to more than one-third of the impoverished nation's people, an almost biblical exodus when considering the size of Ireland's population in the first place.

The Irish no longer trusted their land or their country. "The misery which they have for many years endured has destroyed their attachment to their native soil," the census report concluded during its discussion of emigration, an extraordinary admission in an official government document. "The numbers who have already emigrated and prospered remove the apprehension of going to a strange and untried country."

Ireland's population would continue to fall for decades, due mainly to "the relentless drain of emigration," according to a 2012 analysis by Irish president Michael D. Higgins, a migration prompted either directly by, or by lingering memories of, the frightful famine years.

From a high of 8.5 million people in 1845, Ireland's population plunged to *less than half* that number by the start of World War I. One historian noted that the famine was the worst tragedy visited upon Europe since the Black Death of the fourteenth century, and the "severest decimation of a single people" on the continent until nearly a hundred years later, when Adolf Hitler and the Nazis exterminated two-thirds of European Jewry during the Holocaust.

One hundred and sixty-five years after it occurred, President Higgins called the famine "the greatest social calamity—in terms of mortality and suffering—that Ireland has ever experienced."

That such a monstrously catastrophic event struck a major portion of the British Empire so close to London seemed to elude the writers of the 1851 Irish census summary, who—despite the grim statistics and observations embedded in individual sections of the report—produced a conclusion bordering on fantasy, surmising that the Crown would find it "gratifying . . . that although the [Irish] population has been diminished in so remarkable a manner by famine, disease, and emigration . . . and has been since decreasing, the results of the 1851 census are, on the whole, satisfactory, demonstrating as they do the general advancement of the country."

Virtually no one living in Ireland between 1846 and 1851, or since, would agree with such an assessment; in fact, such glaring disparities between official British reports and on-the-ground Irish suffering ensured that the injustices of the famine years would be ingrained in Ireland's psyche for more than a century and a half.

As one Irish scholar observed in 1999, "The Great Famine has been the unseen guest at every Irish dinner table since the mid-nineteenth century."

The Great Hunger seared itself into Irish folk memory and poisoned future political, historical, cultural, religious, and social relationships with England. Other issues inarguably played a part in ongoing British-Irish tensions—resentment about economic and social status, bitterness between Catholics and Protestants, rancor between nationalists and unionists, animosity between landlords and tenant farmers—but these were mostly symptoms whose underlying cause was British actions during, and the Irish's indelible memory of, Black '47.

For the remainder of the nineteenth century and most of the twentieth, the famine's ghost haunted Irish-British relations, draping a dark, heavy, and enduring pall upon both countries that smothered hope and conciliation and allowed smoldering distrust and anger and violence to fester.

From a second major famine in the late 1800s to the fatal hunger strikes of 1981; from Bloody Sunday in 1920 during the successful War for Independence that established the Irish Free State to another Bloody Sunday in 1972 during the "troubles" in Northern Ireland; from the Easter Rising of 1916 to the Good Friday agreement of 1998; from Ireland's state-sanctioned refusal to fight alongside England in World War I (though many Irish units did) to its declared neutrality in World War II even as England stood alone against the Nazi menace for much of 1940 and more than half of 1941—all of these, along with hatred and heartache borne of unforgivable deeds and actions, were offspring of the disastrous potato famine of 1847 and the unshakeable Irish perception, largely accurate, of Britain's negligence, indifference, and abandonment during the most terrible year in Ireland's history.

Ireland's decision to remain neutral during World War II is most troublesome and conflicting for many Irish, and well into the twenty-first century it caused debate among the Irish people. "From the moment this war began, there was for this State only one policy possible—neutrality," declared Irish prime minister Eamon de Valera in 1941. "Our circumstances, our history . . . made any other policy impracticable." Some historians have argued that hatred of England was so strong that more than half of Ireland's people expected and hoped that Germany would win the war.

But by no means did extreme Irish nationalism extend to the whole population. In fact, 60,000 to 70,000 Free State Irishmen—those residing in the southern twenty-six of Ireland's thirty-two counties—enlisted in the British armed forces when war engulfed the continent. More than 3,600 died (in addition to the 3,900 killed from Northern Ireland, which remained part of England), and 12,000 returned to Ireland when World War II ended in 1945. Returnees were reviled and scorned when they came home, according to historian Bernard Kelly, and many were viewed as anti-nationalists and even traitors. Kelly pointed out that several thousand more Irish combatants went further, deserting the home-country Irish Defence Forces to join the fight against Hitler; they were treated as pariahs and faced official sanctions when they returned, including being stripped of all pay and pension rights, and prevented from finding work by being banned for seven years from any employment paid for by government funds. Special lists were drawn up containing their names and addresses and were circulated to every government department, town hall, railway station, or any other public entity where they might find a job.

Those who received medals hid them, including one Irish soldier who took part in the D-Day landings and helped liberate the German death camp at Bergen-Belsen. As late as 2011, according to the BBC, he had nightmares that he would be arrested by Irish authorities and imprisoned for his wartime service. "They would come and get me," he said, "yes they would." (All such Irish "deserters" were pardoned in 2012.)

Moreover, many sailors in the British navy and mercantile marine went to watery graves off the west coast of Ireland during World War II—especially near Mayo and remote Clare Island—because Irish harbors were closed to British ships seeking refuge from German U-boats. In the words of Cecil Woodham-Smith: "From these innocents, in all probability ignorant of the past—who had never heard of failures of the potato, evictions, fever and starvation—was exacted part of the price for the famine."

The decision by Irish leaders to remain neutral while England fought against Hitler meant, of course, that after December 7, 1941, they were refusing to join America's fight, too. Not only did the vast majority of Irish people have no quarrel with the United States, but nearly a hundred years after the famine they still viewed the United States with deep affection and respect, both as their ancestors' savior during 1847 and as a close contemporary ally; the United States had delivered aid when Ireland needed it most, and later, opened its doors to thousands of Irish citizens who desired a better life for themselves and their children. Irish guilt—in large part a direct outgrowth of the 1847 famine—manifested itself among a large part of the citizenry because of their country's decision not to fight alongside American GIs during World War II. At a time of monumental crisis, Ireland's antipathy toward England caused it to eschew support for its strongest ally, the United States, a policy that many Irish struggled with for decades.

Even Winston Churchill's stunning offer of Irish reunification during World War II, two decades after Northern Ireland was partitioned by the British from the newly recognized sovereign Republic of Ireland, could not change official Irish policy. In a telegram to de Valera the day after Pearl Harbor, Churchill pleaded: "Now is your chance. Now or never. 'A Nation Once Again.' Am very ready to meet you at any time." But the British prime minister's overtures were ignored.

Across the Atlantic, Irish Americans were steadfastly opposed to Irish neutrality after Pearl Harbor, and were outraged later in the war when both German and Italian diplomats walked the streets of Dublin—as they were in May 1945 when de Valera made a condolence call on the German minister after Hitler's death. By then, even the *Irish Times* was critical of de Valera's neutrality policy, saying he "contrived to convince the people of this country that Irish neutrality had a high spiritual basis." Rather, the *Times* opined, neutrality was a policy of "national emasculation ... in the war which has just come to an end [in Europe] no man with a conscience could be really neutral."

Ireland's World War II neutrality posture illustrates most vividly the deep fissures and raw emotions the famine provoked between England

and Ireland. By the 1940s, the sentiments of an Irish labor organizer who grew up in New England in the 1890s and remembered stories her parents had related about the famine fifty years earlier were still widespread. "As children we drew in a burning hatred of British rule with our mother's milk," she said. "Until my father died, at over eighty, he never said 'England' without adding, 'God damn her!'"

If the Great Famine was the seminal event in modern Irish history, the resulting Irish diaspora also changed culture, religion, history, and demographics in the United States. More than 600,000 Irish arrived on U.S. shores between 1846 and 1851 (another 250,000 landed in Canada, and most made their way to the United States).

Their arrival and subsequent progress in Boston encapsulated the Irish experience in the United States as a whole. From 1846 through 1849, which encompassed the cruelest and most destructive years of the Great Famine, enough Irish arrived to irrevocably alter the city's profile, and transform it from an influential but quaint large town to a growing and overcrowded ethnic city. One official Boston city report estimated that 125,000 foreigners arrived during those years, three-quarters of whom were Irish laborers. By 1850, the city census showed a total Boston population of 138,700, of whom 63,300, or 43 percent, were foreigners, the vast majority of them Irish (this includes the 37,000 Irish who arrived in 1847 alone).

The Irish overcame religious and financial odds, recognized early the benefits of banding together to vote as an ethnic bloc, and soon made breathtaking progress. By the early 1880s, Boston elected its first Irish-born member of Congress; by the mid-1880s, the city elected its first Irish-born mayor. By this time, Boston's conversion was irreversible, if not complete: it had become both an Irish and a Catholic city, a remarkable transformation in thirty or so years. This Irish domination of Boston continued for well over a century; President John F. Kennedy, a descendant of post-famine immigrants, was exaggerating only somewhat when he made his highly celebrated 1963 visit to Ireland—the first ever by a sitting U.S. president—and said, "Nearly everyone in Boston is from Galway."

Nor was Boston alone in the growth and influence of its Irish population after the famine. By 1855, one in four people in New York City was Irish, and the Irish soon made up nearly half of all immigrants in the city; the Irish also accounted for a quarter of the population of Philadelphia and Baltimore. One historian pointed out that by 1870, of the forty-three most populous cities in the United States, the Irish were the largest first-generation immigrant group in twenty-seven, and second-largest in the rest. In San Francisco, due largely to the Gold Rush, the Irish constituted nearly 15 percent of the city's population and more than 20 percent of its labor force; ten years later, approximately one-third of San Francisco's population was of Irish descent.

In fact, the Irish famine set in motion a tradition of sustained emigration on a scale unmatched in the modern world. History provides many examples of famines that claimed more lives than the Great Hunger of 1847—in the twentieth century alone, tens of millions died in famines in Ukraine, Russia, India, Africa, and China. Yet it is the Irish famine that history has immortalized in song, poetry, plays, movies, and books. Two Dartmouth authors point out that more than a dozen U.S. states include the Irish famine in their high school curricula. The Great Hunger, the scholars wrote, "has gained a broader and more lasting fame than many other famines, perhaps because millions of Irish fled it to Europe and North America, creating a vibrant diaspora."

The potato famine of Black '47 endures as a cornerstone of the Irish American identity and storytelling, and was especially powerful in the formative years of the Irish assimilation and upward mobility in the New World. "The memory of the Great Hunger has faded," one historian noted at the end of the twentieth century, "but a powerful residue remains."

That residue has dusted so many aspects of Irish and Irish American character: the continued emphasis on family, including unwavering support when times are difficult; loyalty to and interest in the homeland; a distrust of Britain and its policies; a sturdy cultural bond with the United States; and a commitment to philanthropic and charitable causes. It is the famine's residue that today makes Ireland a leading global advocate in the fight against hunger; in 2012, the country committed to spending 20 percent of its overseas aid to support activities that improve access to food and reduce undernutrition in the world's poorest countries. With that commitment, President Michael Higgins said, Ireland not only drew on the lessons and memories of the 1847 famine to fight against starvation today, but also sought to emulate the example of the United States, which launched its broad and generous charitable tradition during Ireland's Great Hunger.

"The links between our countries, although forged out of tragic circumstances, have endured," he said.

That the Irish left their country in droves was due to the starvation and disease brought on by the famine; that they made the United States their primary destination was due both to what they viewed as near-limitless opportunity and bounty, and to a lasting and unbreakable kinship brought on by the wildly successful *Jamestown* mission and the unprecedented contributions of food and provisions by the American people in 1847.

The *Jamestown* became the stuff of legend in Ireland's mournful famine story, an act of benevolence that not only signaled a new spirit of brotherhood between nations but also forged a deep bond between people across an ocean. For years after the *Jamestown*'s arrival, Robert Bennet Forbes noted, Irish parents named their children "James" or "Forbes" or "Boston." According to one account, a thoroughbred cow with calf, put aboard the *Jamestown* by a resident of Cork, produced "numerous progeny," which were for years known around Boston as the "*Jamestown*" breed. Irish who fled the famine had certainly arrived by the thousands before the *Jamestown*'s voyage, but after Forbes and his crew delivered their precious cargo, the United States was viewed by residents of Ireland, particularly Cork, as a land of refuge, a place of safety, and, most important of all, a place where food was available.

John F. Maguire was prescient when he wrote of that sunny day in April 1847 when the *Jamestown* made its way across Cork Harbor. He described the moment as "one of those things which a nation remembers of another long after the day of sorrow has passed."

Put another way, to the Irish, the *Jamestown* represented more than the generosity of America—its bounty, its very presence, epitomized the *promise* of America.

⌘

And the *Jamestown* represented something more.

Beyond Ireland and outside of the United States, the American "warship of peace" had delivered—along with precious food and supplies—a message of fellowship to the rest of the world. For hundreds of years prior to the *Jamestown* and the overall U.S.-wide relief effort to Ireland in 1847, relationships among nation-states were marked mostly by the violence and savagery they visited upon each other, or the economic necessities that forced them to lay down their arms temporarily. The notion of one nation providing direct aid to another for altruistic and charitable reasons was unheard of, as foreign and out of place on the international geopolitical landscape of the mid-nineteenth century as a whale in the desert.

The year of Ireland's Great Hunger, Black '47, changed everything.

Wars and hostilities continued between countries, and will continue always, but the *Jamestown* and the United States' response demonstrated that it was acceptable, appropriate, and—as unlikely as it seemed before the voyage—perhaps even *obligatory* for countries to assist each other for purely humanitarian reasons.

Not only did the *Jamestown* mission and the widespread U.S. relief effort define the country's generosity and establish its emergence on the world stage, not only did it cement bonds between Ireland and the United States that remain strong to this day, but it also signaled a sea change in the affairs of nations—perhaps not "uniting all mankind as one family," as Father Mathew had hoped, but advancing the notion that gestures of philanthropy and brotherhood, rather than signs of a nation's weakness, were displays of quiet strength and moral certitude.

In his characteristically simple but eloquent language, Father Mathew at once captured the essence of the *Jamestown* voyage and the American people's response to it when he described it as "a God-like mission of pure humanity and brotherly love."

CHAPTER 32

⌒⟶⊸⌒

"TO . . . [OUR] FRIENDS AND KINDRED BEYOND THE SEA"

I f the *Jamestown* mission signaled changes in 1847 for the United States, Ireland, England, and the rest of the world, its greatest long-term effect has been the collaborative public-private blueprint it relied on that has guided America's international charitable relief for more than a century and a half—a model that has established the United States and its citizens as the leaders in international aid, enabling Americans to assist millions of victims of famine, war, flood, earthquake, and other natural and man-made disasters.

Countless times since the *Jamestown* sailed across the Atlantic in 1847 to assist Irish famine victims, the words of U.S. senator John J. Crittenden—"We can make the bounty *national*"—have inspired American philanthropy around the globe and even within U.S. borders. These donations—money, food, clothing, housing, medicine, machinery, technology, and expertise—usually involve a combination of government funding coupled with provisions, funding, logistical support, and sweat equity from citizens, companies, and organizations such as the American Red Cross, the Salvation Army, and dozens of other private, nonprofit charitable entities.

And even though bureaucratic disputes and political missteps have sometimes delayed the flow or distribution of contributions, the essential generosity of ordinary Americans has continued uninterrupted for more than a century and a half; time and again, they have rallied in the same way western farmers and eastern shopkeepers did in support of famine-ravaged Ireland in 1847.

It was the *Jamestown* mission, and the massive U.S. relief response that followed, that provided the precedent and pointed the way to the future.

It did not happen immediately.

After 1847, for three decades, with a few exceptions—including some organized relief for Ireland in 1863 while Irish regiments fought for the Union in the Civil War, and privately donated food items sent to France and Germany in 1871—the United States' international charitable contributions were all but put on hold. The country was beset with internal strife, beginning with the divisive Know-Nothing era and the increasingly acerbic slavery debates of the 1850s, followed by a catastrophic Civil War, a presidential assassination, and a Reconstruction era that ripped at the nation's fabric during the 1860s and 1870s.

But in 1880, the United States adopted the *Jamestown* relief model again, and again it was to assist Ireland during a severe potato famine. Though not as destructive and lethal as Black '47, blight and torrential rains in 1879 caused most of the potato crop to fail, particularly in the western counties and especially County Mayo; hunger was widespread and the ugly stain of mass evictions again splashed across the landscape.

In the midst of the famine, Irish nationalists formed the Irish Land League to wage war on landlords and their agents to bring a radical change to the status quo, end evictions, and allow tenant farmers to own their own land. It was during this famine that the word "boycott" was introduced to the English language—it was used as a tactic against Captain Charles Boycott, an English land agent in County Mayo. Tenant farmers refused to harvest his crops until they were treated to more just terms; after that, "boycotting" became a common practice during the

Land War of 1879–82, used against uncooperative and primarily British agents and landlords who refused to comply with nationalist demands.

Parliament would eventually enact the Land Act of 1881, which guaranteed fair rents and made it possible for tenants to buy the land they farmed, but the legislation was too late to stave off famine in 1879–80. Once again, the United States responded, and this time the efforts of citizens included thousands of Irish Americans whose families had emigrated three decades earlier during the Great Hunger. The American media not only provided significant coverage of the 1880 famine, but also organized fundraising drives. *New York Tribune* journalist James Redpath provided vivid descriptions of the misery in Ireland and urged the United States to help. *Harper's Weekly* featured major stories and assured its readers: "America is not slow to respond to a call for bread." The *New York Herald* was among the greatest advocates for Irish relief, organizing a fundraising effort that had collected more than $200,000 by late February 1880.

Following the *Jamestown* precedent, the United States government also responded with alacrity. Congress and President Rutherford B. Hayes approved the use of the warship USS *Constellation* to transport food for a second serious Irish famine. The vessel, under the command of Captain Edward E. Potter, left New York on March 30, 1880, with 3,300 barrels of food and clothing. After a "very anxious and boisterous passage" during which the ship fought its way through twenty-foot waves, the *Constellation* arrived in Queenstown (Cobh today) on April 20, and—just as the *Jamestown* had experienced—was welcomed by a cheering crowd of thousands.

The *Jamestown* mission also was very much on the mind of the recipients of American contributions in 1880. In a letter to Potter and his crew thanking them upon their arrival, the Irish welcoming committee remembered that "thirty-three years ago, in one of the darkest periods of our strange history, we had similar proof of the generosity of your nation." Despite the passage of time, "We have not forgotten it, we have not been ungrateful for it, and this other fresh proof of your sympathy for us shall bind us a thousand-fold more firmly to . . . [our] friends and kindred beyond the sea."

Like Robert Bennet Forbes, Potter was almost overcome by the gratitude expressed by the people of Cork and their political representatives. When he returned to the United States, he thanked the secretary of the navy for allowing him to command the *Constellation* mission, since "it has given me an opportunity to witness the . . . heartfelt gratitude of the Irish people to the United States government." Potter found the "attentions" given to him and his crew "bewildering in their multiplicity, and almost overpowering in their demonstration."

As the twentieth century dawned, America's humanitarian efforts became more widespread and generous, and public-private collaboration became more ensconced as the country's philanthropic blueprint— albeit with increased participation from the federal government.

In 1899, following the Spanish-American War, Congress appropriated $100,000 to be distributed by U.S. Army units to inhabitants of Cuba who were "destitute and in imminent danger of perishing," and private organizations and U.S. citizens also contributed food and supplies. Three years later, Congress appropriated $200,000 to charter privately owned vessels to transport privately donated foodstuffs and rescue inhabitants of the French West Indies after a hurricane.

A devastating earthquake in Messina, Sicily, in December 1908 prompted an outpouring of private donations from U.S. residents, particularly those who were Italian immigrants or of Italian heritage. It also convinced President Theodore Roosevelt to redirect several of the sixteen American warships carrying 5,000 U.S. sailors—who by happenstance were anchored at Alexandria, Egypt, on the last leg of an around-the-world tour to display American naval prowess—to Sicily to provide several thousand pounds of food. Sailors also built temporary housing for victims who had lost everything. Not to be outdone, Congress appropriated $800,000 in federal assistance.

In December 1917, when more than 1,000 people were killed and 9,000 injured after a French freighter loaded with ammunition exploded in Halifax, Nova Scotia's harbor—the largest man-made detonation prior to Hiroshima—Boston and the United States responded with extraordinary relief efforts. Within a few hours after the disaster, relief trains carrying medical supplies, food, clothing, and emergency personnel—doctors, nurses, engineers, repairmen—set out from the northeastern United States, fighting blizzard conditions. Long after the immediate emergency, supplies poured in from across the United States and Canada, collected by the Canadian Red Cross and the American Red Cross, community groups, and religious organizations.

The Massachusetts-Halifax Relief Committee opened a warehouse where displaced families could obtain, free of charge, household goods they would need to furnish rebuilt or temporary housing—a model similar to NECRIS, which was established for the Irish famine in 1847. The committee worked with Halifax for six more years to help survivors and improve health conditions in the city, as well as collecting more than $1 million in contributions. Halifax never forgot the generosity; to this day, Halifax annually donates a Christmas tree to Boston that is lit as part of the beginning of the city's holiday celebration. Thousands of Bostonians turn out for this traditional event.

And in two of the most celebrated international humanitarian efforts of the twentieth century—one at the outset of World War I and one shortly after World War II—the United States employed the public-private partnership that began with the 1847 *Jamestown* voyage for similar purposes, but on even grander scales—once again, in each case, to save millions of Europeans from starvation and deprivation.

In 1914, the United States and future president Herbert Hoover led a massive relief effort to provide food and supplies to more than 10 million Belgians trapped behind German lines, their food warehouses plundered by German forces. Because the United States was still a neutral nation (it would not enter World War I until 1917), German officials allowed safe passage for ships carrying precious, non-military cargo under the auspices of the Commission for Relief in Belgium (CRB), or the "Hoover Commission," a collection of U.S. businessmen, academics, and volunteers. The CRB's makeup and operation bore a remarkable resemblance to the 1847 New England relief committee.

Under Hoover's leadership, the CRB delivered 150,000 tons of food each month for Belgian relief, funded by private charities and the governments of the United States, France, and Great Britain. The people of the United States donated an impressive $35 million, which bolstered Hoover's effort to secure more than $400 million in federal funding. Private donations also helped Hoover emphasize the humanitarian nature of his work to foreign governments that were skeptical of charitable missions during wartime. "Benevolent organizations became our effective armor against periodic attempts of both the British and German militarists to suppress or restrict our activities," he explained.

Once Belgian relief was formally established, Hoover urged individual U.S. states to create Belgian relief committees of their own, another component of the relief effort that bore a striking resemblance to 1847. More than forty states did so (as well as nine countries). Many states—including Massachusetts, Virginia, Connecticut, Kansas, Oregon, and California—hired ships to transport goods. Reminiscent of the U.S. relief model during the 1847 Irish famine, service organizations around the country made appeals for funds and food, as did churches of all denominations; schoolchildren and university students made donations, newspapers organized relief drives, and even the poor made contributions. In one of the most touching episodes of the entire effort, young girls from a "charity home" in Cooperstown, New York, sent $1 a month to help Belgian children, donated from the meager payments they received for doing tasks well, such as sweeping floors or making their beds.

Belgian relief captured the imagination of Americans, many of whom saw it as their duty and moral obligation to save the starving people of Belgium, much as New England citizens had felt about the *Jamestown* mission in 1847. In words apropos to America's 1847 undertaking, a Stanford University professor who worked with Hoover on Belgian Relief summed up the importance of private donations both to the contributor and the recipient: "The giving has been so worth while; worth while to Belgium, saved from starvation of the body; worth while to America, saved from starvation of the soul."

As the Irish once had expressed their gratitude to Forbes, the *Jamestown*, and the United States nearly seventy years earlier, the Belgian people followed suit. Author and relief worker Robert Withington noted that "everywhere one went, [we] were overwhelmed with heart-felt expressions of gratitude from rich and poor, from young and old. The very children in the little villages waved their caps as the car with its CRB pennant went by." He noted that men and women saluted Americans as they passed. Schoolchildren stood up to greet Americans who visited their classrooms, and they sang "The Star-Spangled Banner" in the visitors' honor. "Time and again people said to us, 'If it had not been for America, we should all be dead,'" noted Withington. One Belgian Catholic cardinal suggested that a tablet be placed on the door of every church, so future generations would always remember Belgian Relief. The sign should read: "Remember the help which America brought in the Terrible Years."

Hoover himself copied the public-private format of the CRB when in 1919 he founded the American Relief Administration, which helped get food to starving millions in central and eastern Europe at the end of World War I; again in 1921–22 during the great famine in Russia; and again when he helped organize the United Nations Children's Fund (UNICEF) at the end of World War II. He even used the same public-private model domestically when he oversaw massive and successful relief efforts after the great Mississippi River flood of 1927.

The United States also borrowed from the *Jamestown*'s public-private relief model in one of the most remarkable and risky direct-aid human-itarian efforts in history; in 1948, the United States established the Berlin airlift to feed thousands of starving Berliners after the Soviets surrounded the city and cut off supply lines.

This time, it was military aircraft, not ships, that transported food to desperate people in need. American planes, which just a few years earlier had bombed Berlin to rubble to force Germany's surrender in World War II, now flew their own missions of mercy—a gesture that at first stunned residents of Berlin, who wondered aloud how former enemies could be so generous. The Berlin airlift, according to author Andrei Cherny, was "as much an American fable as that winter in Val-ley Forge, the last desperate stand of the Alamo, or the bus boycott in Montgomery. It was a turning point in the nation's history, the moment

America came to fully accept the mantle of leader of the free world." Cherny's language was not unlike descriptions of U.S. contributions to Ireland a hundred years earlier.

And like the *Jamestown* mission and the widespread U.S contributions to Ireland in 1847, the full scope of the Berlin Airlift "gripped the imagination of the Western world," as journalist Edward R. Murrow put it—the unprecedented rescue effort came against the backdrop of the 1948 U.S. presidential campaign and fears of a war with the Soviet Union. There was one particular aspect of the effort that made news around the world and prompted the extraordinary involvement of the American people in what was largely a military operation: In addition to delivering his regular cargo of food and supplies, American pilot Gail "Hal" Halvorsen took it upon himself on one flight to drop candy attached to "handkerchief parachutes" to the starving children of Berlin. He and other pilots quickly became heroes among Berlin parents and children, and the "candy bombers," as they became known, soon received worldwide fame and support and donations from across the country.

The town of Chicopee, Massachusetts, home to Westover Air Force Base and the launching point of planes headed to the airlift, volunteered to take charge of gathering candy and tying the parachutes. Contributions poured in to Chicopee from across the United States—candy from as far away as Walla Walla, Washington, and Corpus Christi, Texas. The Connecticut chapter of the Veterans of Foreign Wars provided 3,000 handkerchiefs. Walgreens drug stores provided 200 pounds of candy and gum. The Life Savers Corporation donated 4,000 rolls of candy. A Philadelphia clothing company donated 11,000 yards of linen to make the "parachutes." Chicopee schoolchildren cut the fabric into eighteen-inch squares, attached the twine and candy, and on each parachute stamped, in German, "This candy is sent to you from the school children of America." In all, Chicopee students would be responsible for collecting, sorting, and preparing 36,000 pounds of donated candy attached to 100,000 handkerchief parachutes for Halvorsen and the other candy bombers.

As impressive as the American effort was, it was the response of the children and adults of Berlin that touched the candy bombers the most. Nine-year-old Peter Zimmerman wrote to Halvorsen and enclosed a crudely made parachute, a map, and instructions so that he could drop candy right at the Zimmerman home. "Fly along the big canal . . . at the second bridge, turn right . . . I live in the bombed out house on the corner. I'll be waiting in the backyard at 2:00 p.m." Ten-year-old Helma Lurch wrote that she and her little brother were unable to compete with the older, faster children in the scramble for chocolate, "so please drop some chocolate on our street." She added: "Take care of yourself, and remember us children and we will remember you our whole life." American journalist and author William Shirer found that everywhere he went in Berlin he heard "expressions of gratitude," including from jubilant Germans who celebrated Lieutenant Gail Halvorsen Day on October 3, 1948.

In all, American pilots (later joined by those from Britain, Canada, Australia, New Zealand, and South Africa) flew 277,000 flights and delivered 4.6 billion pounds of food and supplies as part of the historic and successful Berlin airlift, which lasted for more than sixteen months. At the height of the operation, an allied aircraft landed in Berlin every minute; the unprecedented relief operation provided Berliners with an average of 2,300 calories a day, far above their paltry rations during and shortly after the war.

The Berlin airlift, Andrei Cherny concluded—again in language reminiscent of the U.S. relief effort to Ireland in 1847—"was the moment when America . . . was revered by people around the world who looked to the United States as a source of decency and good . . . it is a story of America at her best."

Each of these international relief programs carried out by the United States, and virtually every one since, is rooted in a mission that occurred more than a hundred years before the Berlin Airlift, when Robert Bennet Forbes piloted the USS *Jamestown* into Cork Harbor, Ireland.

The *Jamestown* set the example and provided the model for hundreds of American international relief missions since, as well as charitable work inside the United States. In addition to the Mississippi flood of 1927, the great Galveston hurricane of 1900 and the San Francisco earthquake of 1906 were two examples in which the American Red Cross was designated by the United States government as the private relief organization charged with organizing and delivering donations from across the country. In 2010, with the whole world watching, several American companies provided the technology and tools that were instrumental in rescuing thirty-three Chilean miners trapped beneath thousands of feet of rock.

Today, of course, organizations from the Red Cross to Catholic Charities to the Salvation Army and hundreds of others participate with the United States government in providing food, medical aid, and supplies to disaster victims inside the United States and around the world.

Decades after the historic *Jamestown* mission, Robert Bennet Forbes wrote that the expedition "will be remembered in the history of philanthropy; and as the servant of . . . generous people . . . who gave their mite to the alleviation of the suffering poor of Ireland." The *Jamestown* mission changed Forbes, his city, his country, and, to be sure and in many ways, other countries. It offered hope in the midst of agonizing despair. It united two continents. It began with the seedling of an idea and grew into a national mission of goodwill that left a lasting effect.

Simply put, millions of people through several generations have the successful *Jamestown* mission to thank for establishing the precedent that has been part of America's charitable and philanthropic model for nearly 175 years. The voyage marked the emergence of the United States as a world leader and forever altered the way the country would interact with other nations, governments, and people; after *Jamestown*, the moral righteousness of providing humanitarian aid for its own sake became marbled into both the national realpolitik and U.S. international relations.

The Irish recognized this in the moment. In 1847, the Cork Temperance Institute predicted that the *Jamestown* mission would become something the United States could always "look back with pride on . . . that most . . . glorious page in its history, when, in its lusty youth, it fed its ancient parents from its teeming fields; [and] removed from its war-ships their engines of destruction, and made them almoners of the nation's bounty."

EPILOGUE

Decades after he led the Jamestown *mission to Ireland,*
Robert Bennet Forbes looked back on it with "an honest pride."
Courtesy of Forbes House Museum, Milton, MA

On March 15, 1857, seven years after she departed County Kerry to join her children in Boston, Elizabeth Hurley Prendergast died at the age of eighty-seven. It seems fitting that she was buried at Cambridge (Massachusetts) Catholic Cemetery on St. Patrick's Day. Five of her six children lived to old age in the United States.

More than 100,000 people thronged the Cork city center on October 10, 1864, to witness the dedication of a bronze statue and the accompanying parade that honored Father Theobald Mathew, the Apostle of Temperance, the priest who also ministered tirelessly to victims of the Great Hunger.

Eight years after Mathew died, the priest's admirers flocked to Cork from across Ireland—by horse, by train, and by steamer—to participate in the event, filling roadways and scaling stone walls and climbing on rooftops to get the best vantage point. In the city center, residents peered from every window onto the streets below. Spectators waved flags, held bunting aloft, and cheered themselves hoarse as the procession traveled toward St. Patrick's Street, led by the carriage carrying Mayor John Francis Maguire (Mathew's biographer). Following close behind were other dignitaries, bands, and members of temperance societies from Cork and beyond.

Most impressive, though, was the group that followed, more than 4,000 tradesmen—cabinetmakers, housepainters, stonecutters, carpenters, blacksmiths, farriers, shoemakers, shipwrights, coachmakers, and plasterers—who marched under their respective banners. These were the workingmen of Cork and Ireland, the people who loved Father Mathew most and for whom he labored his entire life.

In all, the procession was nearly two miles in length, so long that by the time the first carriages had reached the statue some sections were just beginning their march; it would be close to an hour before enough of the procession passed for the mayor to begin his remarks. Amid cheers and shouts, Maguire pointed out that throughout the world's cities, statues honored great men—warriors, patriots, philosophers, philanthropists, poets, historians, painters, sculptors, statesmen, "great bishops and holy priests." But, he asked the crowd, "where is the name more worthy of honour than the name of Theobald Mathew? Where is the man more entitled to an enduring mark of public respect?"

Now, Maguire said, they had come to this spot to dedicate a memorial to Cork's "best and greatest citizen." At this point, the cord holding the veil was pulled, and the face of Father Mathew "looked out on the assembled multitude . . . once more, thousands felt blessed by [his] outstretched hand." The mayor noted that the statue faced northward at the St. Patrick's Bridge end of the street, so people entering the city, now and in the future, would be greeted by the face and the outstretched hand of the Catholic priest whose statue would serve for generations as an identifying landmark of Cork.

And so it did.

During the 150th anniversary of the unveiling in 2014, the lord mayor of Cork, Mary Shields, described the statue as "one of Cork's best-known and best-loved landmarks . . . when Corkians speak of 'The

Statue' they mean only one." The priest was both well remembered and "still loved" by the people of Cork. Local historian and author Roger Herlihy agreed. He grew up on Cove Street, literally around the corner from Father Mathew's old chapel. The statue was simply something he saw as part of his daily existence, a place he and his friends gathered as schoolboys and young men. "Nobody called it the Father Mathew Statue," he said, "it was just 'the Statue' . . . where the trams and the buses stopped." And even though Father Mathew hailed from Tipperary, his arrival in Cork as a young Capuchin priest meant that "he was just a part of Cork . . . there was never a time that we didn't have Father Mathew."

In July 2018, a visitor from the United States, obviously unaware of Father Mathew's reputation in or contributions to Ireland, noted on a travel website that visiting the statue is "probably not worth a mention as a separate thing to do" in Cork. "You will see it as you walk along St. Patrick's Street and maybe take a picture as we did," the reviewer continued, "but you wouldn't go out of your way to see this."

But in 1864, tens of thousands of thankful Irish admirers of Father Mathew did just that—as have thousands more since.

Eleven years after the dedication of the Father Mathew statue and nearly three decades after the *Jamestown* voyage, on an eighty-degree June morning in Boston, seventy-one-year-old Robert Bennet Forbes, his ruddy face scoured from years of windburn, finally put pen to paper, after struggling with his thoughts and mining the crevasses of his memory.

It was 1875, one year before the nation's centennial, and Forbes had lived his life in an America transformed. Born in September 1804—just two months after the duel between Alexander Hamilton and Aaron Burr, when Thomas Jefferson was president and Lewis and Clark were hacking through thick forests and fording swollen rivers—Forbes had lived through unprecedented progress and epic conflict: on the one hand, the creation of canals and railroads, the birth of the Pony Express, and the invention of the telegraph; on the other, the burning of the nation's capital by the British, the bloody annexation of the American southwest from Mexico, and a ghastly Civil War that had ripped the country apart even as it ended slavery.

Forbes was his own pioneer—in an age when few people traveled more than a few miles from home, he had visited five continents, hunted buffalo on the American plains, and, in 1870, joined a couple of hundred other members of the Boston Board of Trade on the first non-transfer transcontinental train trip from Boston to San Francisco. His love for the sea and sailors was deep and eclectic: he had built ships, sailed raging seas, written papers and pamphlets on nautical topics, worked to improve the safety of ocean travel, supervised the building of gunboats for the Union during the Civil War and also established a coast guard against rebel raids, and helped to establish a home for retired sailors in Massachusetts. He built businesses, suffered financial ruin, and rebuilt his personal fortune; and he did so in the midst of crippling personal grief. He received medals and proclamations for heroism and generosity—yet he never thought of himself as a hero or as overly generous. For all of his worldliness, he believed that the random and often mundane turns of everyday living, more than storybook adventures, defined one's health, wealth, and outlook.

But the *Jamestown* voyage, which had occurred twenty-eight years earlier, was anything but small. He had first written about the historic event in 1847, weeks after its conclusion, once the *Jamestown* and its crew returned to Boston. Ever prescient, he'd recognized the potential long-term impact of the mission. A few weeks after his return to Boston, he wrote to a grateful Irish official to say that he and his crew had been "rewarded, ten-fold, for the very small sacrifices made by us." Among those rewards, Forbes said, was the "grateful approbation" of the Irish people, but even more than that, "the great privilege of [carrying out] such a beautiful mission, which is to be remembered by us, and our children, with feelings of satisfaction until time is no more."

Now, in 1875, Forbes prepared to narrate the tale again, this time for his memoirs. He would focus on his personal thoughts and observations about the *Jamestown*, Ireland, Father Mathew, and the Irish people.

His razor-sharp memory undimmed by the passing of nearly three decades, Forbes recalled the astounding events of 1847 with verve, richness, clarity, and—in keeping with a man who often deflected praise even as he welcomed and appreciated it—an "honest pride."

Rose Greene Smith Forbes died in Milton, Massachusetts, on September 18, 1885, at the age of eighty-three, passing away, after a short illness, on her husband's eighty-first birthday. In the succeeding days and weeks, Robert Bennet Forbes and other family members received scores of bereavement letters, including one from a friend who observed how hard it must have been for Forbes to lose his wife of more than fifty years on his birthday, which he would likely remember as "the saddest of his life."

Among the most poignant of the letters was from Forbes's daughter Edith, who since 1864 had lived in Burlington, Iowa, with her husband, Charles Eliot Perkins, who had become president of the Chicago, Burlington, and Quincy Railroad. Obviously unaware of her mother's demise, she wrote on September 18 to offer her father happy birthday greetings. "I hope it is as fine a day as it is here, for it is perfect," she said. She reminded her father of his birthday celebration eleven years earlier when he had visited Edith and her husband on his way home from a hunting trip to Nebraska. She fretted that her mother was becoming exhausted and "handicapped physically" by caring for her sister, who had recently lost her sight. "I hope mother's cold is better and that she will not have another," Edith wrote on the day her mother died.

Then, in what served as an appropriate though unintended epitaph, Edith added: "There never was another woman like her and never will be."

In letter after letter, well-wishers pointed to Rose's kind and generous nature in ways that transcended the general niceties that accompany gestures of condolence. "Mrs. Morrison says she cannot remember when she 'did not know her' and she was always so kind," wrote John Morrison, a friend of James Murray Forbes, Robert and Rose's son. "Aunt Rose was my second mother and took the place she occupied while I was still but a child," Forbes's nephew wrote. "Her loving care and kindness I can never forget, and her loss is mine as well as yours."

Another friend urged Forbes to take consolation by remembering his wife's "lifelong devotion to you," and, perhaps alluding to some of the couple's early travails, "above all, her courage in all situations in life."

Indeed, Rose did not lead an easy life. The loss of four children was devastating enough, but Forbes's multiple and lengthy trips afar compounded her periods of loneliness. Judging from correspondence, she and Robert Bennet loved each other deeply, nourished each other with strength and support, and were reasonably happy; but it was Rose—by herself for long stretches—who cared for and raised their children, and endured the brunt of the couple's long separations through large portions of their married life.

Nonetheless, Forbes and Rose enjoyed a special relationship that their family and friends alluded to often in the condolence letters upon Rose's death. Almost all urged Forbes to remember his many blessings even in the face of such grievous loss. It was one friend's fervent hope that Forbes, a man "who has done so much for the good of others," could call on "many precious memories" to comfort him during his "solitary hours."

Robert Bennet Forbes died in Milton, Massachusetts, on November 23, 1889, at age eighty-five, four years after Rose.

To the end, he never stopped thinking about the *Jamestown* voyage. He wrote about it often, with passion and satisfaction, referring to it at various points in his life as "a very high honor," "the most prominent event of my life," one of "the most agreeable episodes," and the "happiest event of my life." No other event throughout his eclectic and accomplished life—filled with adventures that began at the age of six and did not stop until Rose's passing—occupied his thoughts for so long, made such an impression, or left such an indelible mark, on him and the nation. One eulogist said Forbes's role in the *Jamestown* "errand of mercy" was by far the most expressive example of the "chivalric side" of his character, engendering great "respect and affection . . . [for] a good deed well-conceived and carried out."

Forbes may have brushed aside the talk of chivalry and affection, but he likely would have approved of the "good deed" characterization of his celebrated voyage, which began America's extraordinary relief effort to Ireland.

Chiseled on his gravestone, set on a gentle rise and shaded by a canopy of trees at Forest Hills Cemetery in Boston—near his wife, near their daughter Rose, near several other family members—are his name and the dates of his birth and death. What's noticeably missing, however, is the inscription Forbes desired most on his stone, words he penned boldly, in all capital letters, near the conclusion of his auto-biography. Perhaps his loved ones did not interpret his wishes literally, perhaps they ignored them altogether, or perhaps they viewed a stone carved with understated starkness more in keeping with the bearing and reputation of the Forbes family.

None, though—not family, nor friends, nor anyone who knew even a little about Robert Bennet Forbes—would have disagreed with the content and spirit of the unchiseled phrase, the epitaph Forbes had cho-sen for himself, his lifelong creed that he believed defined him wholly. It was this character trait—before and above all else—that Forbes wanted the world to remember him for:

HE TRIED TO DO HIS DUTY.

ACKNOWLEDGMENTS

Since I published my first book seventeen years ago, I have been amazed by the number of people who have donated their time and talent to make my work easier and better. For this, my seventh book, the story is largely the same. I have many professionals, family members, and friends to thank for helping me get *Voyage of Mercy* into your hands; this book would not have been possible without their contributions.

Before I begin, I'd like to offer my deepest thanks to you, dear reader, because it's you who make this and all books possible. I'm honored by your support of my work. I'm humbled by your encouragement and inspired by your kind words. In so many ways, a simple thank-you seems inadequate, but I hope you can recognize the heartfelt manner in which I convey it. You have given me that rare and often elusive gift that all authors hope to receive—loyal readership; I hope you found *Voyage of Mercy* worthy of it.

Now to the others who have sailed with me on the *Voyage of Mercy* journey . . .

Peter Drummey of the Massachusetts Historical Society (MHS) helped me navigate through MHS's extensive Forbes Family Papers collection, which includes the Robert Bennet Forbes Papers. As I note in my Bibliographic Essay, this is a rich and indispensable collection of letters, notes, logbooks, diaries, copybooks, newspaper clippings, ledgers, and other documents that form the foundation for the Forbes character in this book. Peter's guidance helped me successfully mine the critical portions of this massive collection.

The Forbes House Museum in Milton, Massachusetts, also contained some treasures. Heidi Vaughan, executive director, expressed her enthusiastic support for this project, guided me on a private tour of the historic house, and introduced me to Phyllis Forbes Kerr, great-great-granddaughter of Robert Bennet Forbes (RBF), who authored the illuminating volume *Letters from China*, which proved essential in understanding RBF and his wife, Rose. Phyllis, in turn, introduced me to her first cousin, Robert B. Forbes, RBF's great-great-grandson. My conversations with Phyllis and Robert helped further my knowledge of their great-great-grandfather and the Forbes family in general. I'm also grateful to Gwen Labbe, assistant to the director at the Forbes House, for her help on a number of research matters. Heidi, Gwen, and the team at Forbes House also discovered, just prior to the deadline for this book, the "believed-to-be-lost" Robert Bennet Forbes Bible hidden in a drawer in the family's Milton home; pages within the Bible provided invaluable information about the deaths of the four Forbes children.

At the National Archives and Records Administration (NARA), I thank—as always—Archives Historian Jessie Kratz, who offered her initial expertise and then suggested I reach out to Tom Eisinger, senior archivist at NARA's Center for Legislative Archives. Tom provided me with the lengthy House of Representatives report that is used as the foundation for the portions of the book covering George DeKay and the voyage of the *Macedonian*.

My editor Tim Bartlett, at St. Martin's Press, has my deepest thanks for his support of this book. Tim edited my previous work, *American Treasures*, and brings to his work a keen eye, a professional's touch, and a desire to improve a book for readers. *Voyage of Mercy* is a better book because of him. I'm also grateful to St. Martin's Press assistant editor Alice Pfeifer for her assistance every step of the way, including her thoughtful reading of the manuscript and the helpful feedback she provided. Tim,

Alice, and the entire team at St. Martin's are a pleasure to work with, including the Art Department, which produced the book's stunning cover.

It's hard for me to believe that my agent, Joy Tutela, and I have been a team for nineteen years and that *Voyage of Mercy* is our seventh book together. Time flies. Joy's belief in me from day one and her passion for my first book, *Dark Tide*, launched my journey as an author, and what an adventure it's been. Through the years, I have always been impressed with Joy's enthusiasm, encouragement, loyalty, and professionalism—and have valued her friendship most of all.

I am the beneficiary of unwavering support from so many friends and family members whose interest and encouragement inspire me and make me a better author. It is impossible to list them all, but I would like to mention a few for all they've done.

My dear friend Paula Hoyt, who regularly edits my work, once again shared her talents to make this book better. She not only offered suggestions on the *Voyage of Mercy* manuscript, but throughout the year, she is the overall manager of my website (www.stephenpuleo.com) and my author Facebook page (www.facebook.com/stephenpuleoauthor). Her sound judgment, thoughtful insights, and excellent communication skills improve my work in countless ways—regardless of the medium—but I am most grateful for the constancy of her support and the depth of her friendship.

For more than four decades, my friend Ellen Keefe has selflessly offered my wife, Kate, and me a wellspring of support, encouragement, wisdom, and love that we've drawn from often. She helps us celebrate joyful moments and offers solace and support when times are tough. It's a bonus that she also assists me with research, edits my manuscripts, constantly spreads the word about my books to family and friends, and shares my love for history and reading. She is and always has been there for us. Kate and I are eternally thankful for a friendship so rare.

I had the great pleasure once again of working with my niece, Rachel Brevich, who assisted me with the research on *Voyage of Mercy*, just as she has with my two previous books, *American Treasures* and *The Caning*. Rachel holds a degree in history and is a thorough and intuitive researcher with an eye for what's important—when I trust Rachel with a project, I know her work will be excellent, and the records she gathers will be both compelling and well-organized. For this book, Rachel focused mainly on the Irish portion of the story, digging deep into contemporaneous newspapers and other documents for information about the famine. I'm immeasurably proud of the care Rachel brings to her work—and blessed by the love she shares with Kate and me.

My mom, Rose Puleo, can't believe I've published my seventh book, and, as always, provided her constant support, interest, and love throughout the whole writing process—as she has throughout my whole life. I greatly miss my dad every day, but feel his love and comforting presence always; when I'm writing, or doing anything else, he's on my shoulder and in my heart. I will never be able to thank my parents for all they have done.

Forty years ago, I married into a large Irish family when Kate Doyle did me the honor of saying yes and agreed to become Kate Puleo. This book pays tribute to Kate and her (our) family by offering them a sense of their own roots, a heritage forged upon a hearth of perseverance, resilience, hard work, loyalty, and love. Their story is the quintessential Irish American tale—ancestors who arrived around the time of the famine, overcame hardships, and built vibrant lives for themselves and their loved ones in America. It is an illustration of history's enduring impact that the bonds created between the United States and Ireland by the *Jamestown* mission in 1847 still link to the Doyle family—and thousands of other Irish Americans—in the twenty-first century.

And speaking of enduring bonds, the love and friendship Kate and I have shared for the last four decades is my greatest joy and most profound blessing. We are true partners in so many things, including book writing—she is the first to hear my ideas, the first to offer insights, the first to read my manuscripts. Her gifts are many, and she shares them constantly with me and countless others. She recently retired after forty-one years as a teacher and principal, during which time she inspired thousands of students to reach their full potential, but one job from which she can never retire is inspiring me every day. I am proud of all she is and all she's done, proud to share our dreams, and, from the bottom of my heart, thank her for everything—always.

BIBLIOGRAPHIC ESSAY

For some time, readers have asked me what historians a hundred years from now will do for source material since potential nonfiction characters no longer keep diaries or write letters, at least in great numbers.

My answer: I'm glad I won't be around to find out.

I mused often about that point throughout the research and writing of *Voyage of Mercy*—the major characters in this book wrote often, wrote vividly, wrote passionately, wrote descriptively, and wrote well. Robert Bennet Forbes, especially, wrote for his entire life: letters, logbooks, diaries, notes, reports, and a full-fledged autobiography. Moreover, he recognized the importance of preserving records: his decision to amass his comprehensive personal observations, along with every scrap of written correspondence, speech, newspaper account, citation, expense, and meeting minutes into a single volume about the *Jamestown* mission provided me with primary source material historians often just dream about. And his many letters to and from Rose provided invaluable insight into their hopes, fears, insecurities, and strengths.

To my knowledge, no one has attempted a full biography on Forbes—this book comes closest—but he does deserve one, and would-be authors will find a trove of primary source material thanks to Forbes's decision to write early, late, and often. He is that rare character: a prolific writer who also labored in the trenches, was not afraid to get his hands dirty, and had a near-unquenchable appetite to experience—not merely observe—life to its fullest.

And how often does a second such rare character play a pivotal role in a story? Across the Atlantic, Father Mathew labored during the day and drew from a reservoir of energy to write profusely, mostly at night. Not nearly as itinerant as Forbes—he spent most of his life in and around Cork—he had far greater influence in Ireland than Forbes did in the United States. His temperance work achieved worldwide fame (and a full book on *that* is also merited), but his efforts during the famine have been little noted until now. His constant stream of letters to Charles Trevelyan, pleading for help for his flock and famine victims across Ireland, were a thorn in the side of the British government; his correspondence to contacts in the United States helped raise awareness of the Irish plight. His testimony before the House of Lords on emigration from Ireland was as compelling and candid as you'll see in any sort of official government setting, and was particularly refreshing to read, especially when compared with modern committee hearings in which clarity and bold opinions are usually cloaked in caveats and bureaucratese. That this testimony was preserved by Parliament assisted me in drawing Mathew's character and in further understanding the desperate conditions in Ireland.

I was also greatly aided by the fact that the British and Irish governments maintained and published lengthy and meticulous famine records; that enough people—including Asenath Nicholson and Elihu Burritt—visited Ireland during the worst of times and recorded what they saw (though almost all refused to commit the worst visages to paper); that the Society of Friends compiled and organized hundreds of letters from towns, cities, and relief organizations in the United States; and that the official involvement of the United States government in the *Jamestown* voyage and the country's first charitable mission—a story told in full for the first time in this book—produced extensive congressional testimony (both in advance of the mission and, later, when Father Mathew visited the United States), as well as separate writings and speeches from the likes of Daniel Webster, Henry Clay, John J. Crittenden, and President James K. Polk. Further, Father Mathew's U.S. tour produced tumultuous U.S. Senate testimony within the context of the slavery debate, during which some of the most legendary and notorious Senate voices were heard: Webster, Clay, Jefferson Davis, John C. Calhoun, William Seward, Sam Houston, and others.

What follows is the approach I've taken in my previous books—an extensive and wide-ranging list of primary and secondary sources, and for certain ones, an explanation of how I used them in the narrative and why they were important. I have grouped them into topical categories and, when appropriate, in chronological order, for easy reference and understanding. I have received many favorable comments from readers that this approach is more appealing and revealing than a traditional bibliography in which sources are simply listed; I'd appreciate your thoughts as well.

It's important to let you know that in cases where there are several sources about a topic, I have done my best to give greater weight to the source chronologically closest to the event for greatest accuracy and veracity; for example, I leaned more heavily on Robert Bennet Forbes's 1847 in-the-moment observations about the *Jamestown* mission than his 1882 recounting in his autobiography. While both are rich and valuable sources, perspectives often change with the passing of time, memory lapses increase, and a desire to romanticize and aggrandize accomplishments is a natural tendency.

Finally, it's important to note that there have been hundreds—maybe thousands—of articles and books written about the Irish famine. The list that follows includes but a fraction of that number, but in my view, they are among the best and most important; they provided me with invaluable material for this work.

Robert Bennet Forbes and the *Jamestown* Mission

PRIMARY SOURCES

I am thankful and pleased that this portion of the story is based almost entirely on primary sources; a few secondary sources—particularly contemporaneous newspaper accounts—are important and add vivid color to the narrative, but primary source material provides the foundation and most of the framework for this section.

To build this part of the book, I relied most heavily on the Forbes Family Papers and the Robert Bennet Forbes Papers at the Massachusetts Historical Society, the latter a subset of the former, but the Forbes Family Papers also contain separate Robert Bennet papers pertaining to the *Jamestown* voyage. Together, these collections contain Forbes's letterbooks; the *Jamestown* logbooks; letters on the *Jamestown* expedition (including letters to President Polk, William Rathbone in Liverpool, and many others); letters to Rose and other family members; accounts and letters related to Forbes's early travels to China and other locales; articles and correspondence related to the *Macedonian* voyage; financial records of the *Jamestown* mission; correspondence with members of the New England Committee for the Relief of Ireland and Scotland (NECRIS); correspondence before and after the trip; correspondence from prospective crew members requesting passage on the *Jamestown*; the condolence letters Forbes received upon Rose's death; and general correspondence to, from, and about Forbes and his family.

In addition, I drew extensively—and adapted this book's title—from Forbes's own *Voyage of the Jamestown on Her Errand of Mercy* (Boston: Eastburn's Press, 1847); as I noted, an exhaustive compilation of virtually every piece of correspondence associated with the voyage, including Forbes's own summary. I also am indebted to Phyllis Forbes Kerr, Robert Bennet Forbes's great-great-granddaughter—whom I had the pleasure of meeting and talking with about Forbes and the *Jamestown*—for her outstanding compilation and editing work on *Letters from China: The Canton-Boston Correspondence of Robert Bennet Forbes, 1838–1840* (Mystic, Conn.: Mystic Seaport Museum, 1996). As I mention in the book, this collection of letters between Bennet and Rose provides the best insight into their personal and financial struggles—and a window into their characters—a decade prior to the *Jamestown* voyage.

Forbes's autobiography—about which he had been thinking for years while scribbling notes aboard ships, sojourning throughout Europe and Asia, engaging in the Chinese opium trade, or conducting business in Boston—provided rich material about Forbes and his family. He published an initial volume in 1879, but he reissued the work three years later with additional material about the opium trade, which by then was fully frowned upon by virtually all countries. Forbes titled his memoirs *Personal Reminiscences, Second Edition Revised, in Which Is Added Rambling Recollections Connected to China* (Boston: Little, Brown, and Company, 1882). Forbes initially believed that adding material about the opium trade would be interesting to readers, but afterward expressed misgivings about including it because of the country's and the world's belief that many Western businessmen had exploited China during the opium trade. "The only thing I fear is that in giving a sketch of the cause and effects of the opium traffic . . . I may say too much," he confided to a friend.

I was grateful also to refer to pages in Forbes's recently discovered Bible, which contained the birth and death dates of the four children Robert Bennet and Rose lost, as well as the birth dates of the three surviving children (more on this in the Acknowledgments).

I learned additional details (and some folklore) about the Forbes family in interviews and conversations (for which I'm grateful) with Phyllis Forbes Kerr (see above) and Robert B. Forbes, Phyllis's first cousin and Robert Bennet Forbes's great-great-grandson.

The entire congressional debate about whether the USS *Jamestown* warship should be refitted for humanitarian purposes and turned over to Forbes was riveting and can be found in the *Congressional Globe*, 29th Congress, 2nd Session, February–March 1847; the National Archives provided me with the official March 3, 1847, congressional resolution, *Food for Ireland by U.S. Vessels*, that authorized the use of the *Jamestown* and the *Macedonian* for their missions to Ireland. This can also be found in editor George Minot's *The Statutes at Large and Treaties of the United States of America from December 1, 1845 to March 3, 1851, Arranged in Chronological Order with References to the Matter of Each and to the Subsequent Acts on the Same Subject*, Vol. IX (Boston: Charles C. Little and James Brown, 1851). Information about commissioning the *Jamestown* for merchant use can be found in the *Annual Report of the Secretary of the Navy*, Navy Department, December 6, 1847 (Washington, D.C., 1847).

Among other places, I found the compelling speeches and writings by national leaders related to the *Jamestown* and *Macedonian* missions, as well as background on these individuals and the Irish crisis in general, in the following places: editor Calvin Colton's *The Works of Henry Clay: Comprising His Life, Correspondence, and Speeches* (New York: G. P. Putnam's Sons, 1904); *The Life of John J. Crittenden, with Selections from His Correspondence and Speeches*, which was edited by Crittenden's daughter, Chapman Coleman (Philadelphia: J. B. Lippincott & Co., 1873); *Orations and Speeches on Various Occasions by Edward Everett*, Vol. II (Boston: Little, Brown, and Company, 1865); *Selections from the Works of Edward Everett, with a Sketch of His Life* (Boston: Published by James Burns, 1839); editor Milo Milton Quaife's *The Diary of James K. Polk During His Presidency, 1845 to 1849 in Four Volumes* (Chicago: A. C. McClurg & Co., 1910); editors Tom Chaffin and Michael David Cohen's *Correspondence of James K. Polk*, Volume XII, *January–July 1847* (Knoxville: University of Tennessee Press, 2013); and Fletcher Webster's *The Writings and Speeches of Daniel Webster* (Boston: Little, Brown & Company, 1903).

For additional background on Robert Bennet Forbes's early life, I drew on *Gleanings from the Record of the Boston Marine Society Through Its First Century, 1742–1842*, compiled by Nathaniel Spooner (Boston: Published by the Society, 1879). Forbes joined the Society in 1827 at the age of twenty-three and was active in its hundredth-anniversary celebration in 1842. He was president at the time of the *Jamestown* voyage.

For Forbes's living situation and other general impressions of Boston, I looked at *Adams's Boston Directory: Containing the City Record, General Directory of the Citizens and a Special Directory of Trades,*

Professions, Etc., 1847–1848 (Boston: Published by James French and Charles Stimpson, 1848).

SECONDARY SOURCES

UNPUBLISHED WORKS, SYMPOSIA WORKS, AND ARTICLES

An outstanding recounting of the *Jamestown* mission and Massachusetts's contributions to Ireland during the famine is a short book entitled *Massachusetts Help to Ireland During the Great Famine*, authored by Forbes's descendant H. A. Crosby Forbes and Henry Lee and published by the Board of Trustees of the Robert Bennet Forbes House in Milton, Massachusetts, in 1967. The work, which relies almost entirely on primary sources, was published as part of a "commemorative exhibition" marking the *Jamestown*'s voyage. The authors dedicated the book to crew member John Hughes, born in Ireland and lost at sea on the *Jamestown*'s homeward voyage, and to "countless others—doctors, clergymen, government officials and private citizens—who gave their lives to help their fellow men in the famine years."

James Coleman wrote an interesting article for the *Journal of the Cork Historical and Archaeological Society* entitled "Voyage of the *Jamestown*" (Vol. 10, 1904), in which the author describes the mission in the "never-to-be-forgotten year of '47." More than eighty years later, William M. Fowler Jr. authored a similar piece, "Sloop of War/Sloop of Peace: Robert Bennet Forbes and the USS *Jamestown*," for *Proceedings of the Massachusetts Historical Society*, Third Series, Vol. 98 (1986). In 2014, Robin M. Taliaferri, then executive director of the Robert Bennet Forbes House, and Megan Birden, college intern, authored a series of six articles entitled "Forbes House Museum and Ireland's Great Famine: Who Knows the Story?" on behalf of the Forbes House Museum.

In 1891, Leverett Saltonstall offered a memorial tribute, "Memoir of Robert Bennet Forbes," published in the *Proceedings of the Massachusetts Historical Society*, Second Series, Vol. VI, 1890, 1891 (Boston: Published by the Society).

I consulted the *New York Times* obituary of Kentucky's John J. Crittenden, published on July 28, 1863, to get a feel for the contemporaneous verdict of history on the lawmaker whose 1860 compromise has been so widely criticized. The *Times* obituary writer was relatively gentle, declaring that Crittenden put forth his proposition to "avert the threatened story of secession," but to no avail; the compromise was defeated despite Crittenden advocating for its passage "with all the art of oratory of which he was master."

The *New York Times* published its obituary of Robert Bennet Forbes on November 24, 1889, referring to the *Jamestown* mission as "one of his conspicuous acts."

CONTEMPORANEOUS NEWSPAPERS

For this section and most of the others, I relied on numerous contemporaneous newspaper accounts of the *Jamestown* voyage, U.S. assistance to Ireland, and the famine in general. They are listed here and not repeated in the other sections (note that other quotes attributed to newspapers in the text were culled from magazine and journal articles or books that are listed separately; newspapers listed here were consulted independently): *Pilot* (Boston), *Boston Daily Atlas, Boston Daily Advertiser, American Quarterly Register and Magazine, Illustrated London News, Cork Reporter, Cork Examiner, Punch, Pictorial Times, Freeman's Journal, Times* (London), *Dublin University Magazine*, and *Kerry Evening Post*.

BOOKS

While *Voyage of Mercy* is the first full account of the *Jamestown* mission and the massive U.S. relief effort to Ireland during the Great Famine of 1847, I consulted numerous books in which these episodes were mentioned or summarized (some of these works are also mentioned in other sections as appropriate): John Francis Maguire's *Father Mathew: A Biography* (London: Longman, Green, Longman, Roberts & Green, 1865) devotes time to the *Jamestown*'s arrival and the interaction between Father Mathew and Robert Bennet Forbes (more on this book in the next section). Christine Kinealy does an excellent job of summarizing contributions to Ireland, including those from the *Jamestown* and the United States, in *Charity and the Great Hunger in Ireland: The Kindness of Strangers* (New York: Bloomsbury, 2013).

Other books that I found helpful for their accounts of the *James-town* were my own *A City So Grand: The Rise of an American Metropolis, Boston 1850–1900* (Boston: Beacon Press, 2010); Thomas H. O'Connor's *The Boston Irish: A Political History* (Boston: Northeastern University Press, 1995); and Cecil Woodham-Smith's classic, *The Great Hunger: Ireland, 1845–1849* (New York: Old Town Books, 1962).

Two books helped with information about trade in China, including opium: John R. Haddad's *America's First Adventure in China: Trade, Treaties, Opium, and Salvation* (Philadelphia: Temple University Press, 2013); and Dane A. Morrison's *True Yankees: The South Seas and the Discovery of American Identity* (Baltimore: Johns Hopkins University Press, 2014).

Father Theobald Mathew

PRIMARY SOURCES

By the standard definition, John F. Maguire's *Father Mathew: A Biography* (see previous section for full citation) would not be considered a true primary source, but it deserves to be included here because—thanks to the author's close relationship with his subject—the book contains virtually every letter that Father Mathew wrote, including his correspondence with Charles Trevelyan in 1846 and 1847. The book also contains numerous diary entries by Father Mathew, notes, and accounts of conversations between Mathew and Maguire. In his preface, Maguire explains that he had known Father Mathew since childhood, and from that time until Father Mathew's trip to the United States in 1849 "was more or less intimately associated with him, in private as well as public." Unsurprisingly, Maguire's biography is exceedingly favorable to Father Mathew, but any lack of critical assessment is more than offset by the book's true value—the number of rich primary sources contained within its pages. Clearly, Maguire's relationship with his subject helped him gain access to virtually all of Father Mathew's papers.

Father Mathew's riveting testimony before the House of Lords committee considering Irish emigration can be found in the *Report of the Select Committee of the House of Lords on Colonization from Ireland;*

Together with Minutes of Evidence, Session 1847 (Ordered by the House of Commons, to be Printed, 23 July 1847). Mathew's knowledge of the famine and resulting emigration are evident throughout his questioning.

The remarkable debate in the United States Senate on whether to seat Father Mathew behind the rail, which evolved into further debates on slavery, can be found in the *Congressional Globe,* 31st Congress, 1st Session, December 20, 1849.

Father Mathew's concerns about England's response to the famine are included in several official famine-related documents, including *Correspondence (from January to March 1847) Relating to the Measures Adopted for the Relief of Distress in Ireland, Board of Works Series Second Part, Presented to Both Houses of Parliament by Command of Her Majesty* (London: Printed by W. Clowes and Sons, Stamford Street, for Her Majesty's Stationery Office, 1847); and *Digest of Evidence Taken Before Her Majesty's Commissioners of Inquiry into the State of the Law and Practice in Respect to the Occupation of Land in Ireland, Part 1* (Dublin: Printed by Alexander Thom, 87 Abbey-Street, for Her Majesty's Stationery Office, 1847), and *Part 2*, 1848. I also referred to these documents for several general famine-related sections of the book.

SECONDARY SOURCES

UNPUBLISHED WORKS, SYMPOSIA WORKS, AND ARTICLES

For excellent accounts of Father Mathew's temperance work, see Moira Lysaght's "Father Theobald Mathew, Apostle of Temperance," in the *Dublin Historical Record*, Vol. 36, No. 4 (September 1983), pp. 140–152; David Beckingham's "The Press and the Pledge: Father Theobald Mathew's 1843 Temperance Tour of Britain," in *Historical Geography*, Vol. 42 (2014), pp. 93–110. I drew part of my account in the Epilogue on the unveiling of Father Mathew's statue from Antoin O'Callaghan's *The Statue: Cork's Monument to Father Mathew, The Apostle of Temperance* (Cork, Ireland: Cork City Libraries, 1997).

A colorful recounting of Frederick Douglass's meeting with Father Mathew entitled "The Great Abolitionist Douglass and Cork's Apostle of Temperance" appears in the February 28, 2014, issue of the *Irish Ex-*

aminer newspaper. A more thorough examination of Douglass's Cork visit and its ramifications was written by Lee Jenkins and entitled "Beyond the Pale: Frederick Douglass in Cork," in the *Irish Review*, No. 24 (Autumn 1999), pp. 80–95. The West Cork *Southern Star* newspaper featured a story headlined "Father Mathew Recorded the Worst Horrors of the Famine in West Cork," in its April 3, 2015, edition.

For accounts of Father Mathew's contentious battles on both sides of the Atlantic, see John F. Quinn's "The 'Vagabond Friar': Father Mathew's Difficulties with the Irish Bishops, 1840–1856," in *The Catholic Historical Review*, Vol. 78, No. 4 (October 1992), pp. 542–556; and Quinn's "The Nation's Guest? The Battle Between Catholics and Abolitionists to Manage Father Theobald Mathew's American Tour, 1849–1851," in *U.S. Catholic Historian*, Vol. 11, No. 3, "Ireland and America: Religion, Politics, and Social Movements" (Summer 2004), pp. 19–40.

For two interesting early summaries of Father Mathew's life and work, see John Augustine Hayden's "Theobald Mathew," in *The Catholic Encyclopedia*, Vol. 10 (New York: Robert Appleton Company, 1911); and M.R., "The Memory of Father Theobald Mathew," in *The Irish Monthly*, Vol. 30, No. 343 (January 1902), pp. 1–14.

BOOKS

In addition to the aforementioned, definitive, and oft-consulted *Father Mathew: A Biography* by Maguire, I also found helpful an early work by James Birmingham entitled *A Memoir of the Very Rev. Theobald Mathew with an Account of the Rise and Progress of Temperance in Ireland* (Dublin: Milliken and Son, Grafton-Street, 1840); a biography by the priest's grandnephew Frank J. Mathew, entitled *Father Mathew: His Life and Times* (London, Paris, & Melbourne: Cassell & Company, Limited, 1890); and Katharine Tynan's *Father Mathew* (New York, Cincinnati, Chicago: Benziger Brothers, Printers to the Holy Apostolic See, 1908).

For a more extensive look at Frederick Douglass's visit to Cork and his meeting with Father Mathew, see Tom Chaffin's *Giant's Causeway: Frederick Douglass's Irish Odyssey and the Making of an American Visionary* (Charlottesville and London: University of Virginia Press, 2014).

The U.S. Response in 1847 and Irish Immigration to and Settlement in America

PRIMARY SOURCES

By far the most complete compilation of primary source documents on the assistance provided by citizens and organizations in the United States can be found in the *Transactions of the Central Relief Committee of the Society of Friends During the Famine in Ireland, 1846 and 1847* (Dublin: Hodges and Smith, Grafton-Street, 1852). This is true "can't-put-down" reading upon which I built much of the narrative describing America's remarkable first full-scale charitable mission. The papers include more than 125 pages of letters from relief committees across the United States, along with responses from Ireland. Among this cache are letters from relief committees in New York; Philadelphia; Baltimore; Nashville; Detroit; New Bedford, Massachusetts; Madison, Indiana; Ottawa, Illinois; and many more, providing updates on the status of contributions, obstacles, and the overall feelings expressed by citizens on the Irish plight. These letters provide a rich narrative summary of the outpouring of American assistance from cities, farms, and the frontier, as well as the hard-dollar amounts or food quantities being delivered to Ireland. The papers also include high-level diplomatic correspondence, including letters between U.S. ambassador George Bancroft and Prime Minister John Russell on U.S. contributions, and extracts from parliamentary debates in the House of Commons on donations from the United States.

For the full congressional discussion on George C. DeKay's financial claims and overall woes about the *Macedonian*'s mission, as well as appended correspondence on the matter, I relied on the Thirtieth Congress, First Session, House of Representatives, Report No. 541, April 1848.

For a compelling look at the Massachusetts state government's concerns about Irish immigration and the increase in "foreign paupers" in Boston—a microcosm of issues that other cities wrestled with as well—see the untitled Massachusetts Senate Report No. 46 (February 1848). See also the Concerning Alien Passengers and Paupers legislation passed in June 1846 (before the bulk of Irish arrivals post-famine), which created a Superintendent of Alien Passengers with broad powers to board immigrant ships arriving in Boston, prevent ships from docking, and collect a $2 fee for each passenger to disembark.

SECONDARY SOURCES

UNPUBLISHED WORKS, SYMPOSIA WORKS, AND ARTICLES

First, a few symposia and unpublished works for this section: Malcolm Campbell delivered a paper at the Australian Historical Association Conference in Sydney in July 1998 entitled "Ireland's Furthest Shores: Irish Immigrant Settlement in Nineteenth-Century California and Eastern Australia." Versions of the paper were adapted for an article in the *Pacific Historical Review*, Vol. 71, No. 1 (2002), pp. 59–90. For background on the Charlestown Navy Yard and its history, I drew on Stephen Carlson's *Charlestown Navy Yard Historic Resource Study*, produced by the Division of Cultural Resources, Boston National Historical Park, National Park Service, U.S. Department of the Interior (Boston: 2010). As part of the University of New Hampshire Scholars' Repository, James M. Farrell wrote "Reporting the Irish Famine in America: Images of 'Suffering Ireland' in the *American Press*, 1845–1848" (2014), p. 17.

For an interesting analysis of the mass exodus of the Irish from their home country to the New World, I drew on Amira Achouri's "From Ireland to America: Emigration and the Great Famine, 1845–1852," in the *International Journal of Humanities and Cultural Studies*, Vol. 2, No. 4 (March 2016), pp. 23–38; and Peter Quinn's "The Tragedy of Bridget Such-a-One," in *American Heritage*, Vol. 48, No. 8 (December 1997), pp. 36–49.

I found several articles helpful to craft the sections on U.S. assistance to Ireland. These were Timothy J. Sarbaugh's "Charity Begins at Home: The United States Government and Irish Famine Relief, 1845–1849," in *History Ireland*, Vol. 4, No. 2 (Summer 1996), pp. 31–35; Sarbaugh's "The Spirit of Manifest Destiny: The American Government and Famine Ireland, 1845–1849," in Margaret Mulrooney, ed., *Fleeing the Famine: North America and Irish Refugees, 1845–1851* (Westport, Conn., and London: Praeger, 2003), pp. 45–68; Harvey Strum's "Pennsylvania and Irish

Famine Relief, 1846–1847," in *Pennsylvania History: A Journal of Mid-Atlantic Studies*, Vol. 81, No. 3 (Summer 2014), pp. 277–299; Strum's "To Feed the Hungry: Rochester and Irish Famine Relief," in *Rochester History*, Vol. 68, No. 3 (Summer 2006), pp. 3–22 and Strum's "Famine Relief from an Ancient Dutch City," in *The Hudson River Valley Review*, Vol. 22, No. 2 (Spring 2006), pp. 54–79.

For a description of the Odd Fellows Hall in Washington, D.C., during Daniel Webster's plea for Irish assistance, I drew on John DeFerrari's article "The Odd Fellows Hall: A Social Center on Seventh Street for 170 Years," in *Streets of Washington*, December 2016.

Phyllis DeKay Wheelock, a former art critic and literary editor at the *New York Times* and the daughter of *Macedonian* captain Charles DeKay, wrote an excellent account of her father's voyage—and the difficulties before and after—in "Commodore George DeKay and the Voyage of *Macedonian* to Ireland," which appeared in *The American Neptune: A Quarterly Journal of Maritime History*, Vol. 13, No. 4 (October 1953), pp. 252–267.

Walt Whitman paid tribute to *Macedonian* chaplain Father Edward Taylor in an essay entitled "Father Taylor (and Oratory)," in his collection of essays, *November Boughs* (Philadelphia: David McKay, 23 South Ninth Street, 1888), pp. 47–49. The August 1906 issue of *Atlantic Magazine* published a paper by Ralph Waldo Emerson on Father Taylor, drawn from two lectures the writer had given, one in 1841 and one in 1867. A double system of numbering from Emerson's lecture notes "shows that they were used in two lectures," the magazine noted. Of Taylor, Emerson noted: "He says touching things, plain things, cogent things, grand things, which all men must perforce hear." I also consulted M. R. Johnson's "Father Taylor, the Sailor Preacher," in *Canadian Methodist Magazine*, Vol. 8 (July–December 1878), pp. 448–454.

BOOKS

Several books already mentioned were helpful for this section, including my own *A City So Grand*, O'Connor's *The Boston Irish*, and Kinealy's *Charity and the Great Hunger*.

For fine books on the Irish emigration from Ireland and arrival in the United States, see Edward Laxton's *The Famine Ships: The Irish Ex-*

odus to America (New York: Henry Holt and Company, 1998); editor Arthur Gribben's *The Great Famine and the Irish Diaspora in America* (Amherst: University of Massachusetts Press, 1999); and the aforementioned Margaret M. Mulrooney, ed., *Fleeing the Famine: North American and Irish Refugees, 1845–1851.*

For works on the Irish once they arrived in the United States and North America, see Thomas Keneally's *The Great Shame and the Triumph of the Irish in the English-Speaking World* (New York: Doubleday, 1998); Michael Quinlin's *Irish Boston: A Lively Look at Boston's Colorful Irish Past* (Guilford, Conn.: Globe Pequot Press, 2013); and Carl Wittke's comprehensive *The Irish in America* (Baton Rouge: Louisiana State University Press, 1956).

For important books on the political and social situations in the United States at the time of the famine, including sectionalism, slavery, abolitionism, the Mexican War, and Manifest Destiny, I drew on (alphabetical by author): Michael F. Holt's *The Rise and Fall of the American Whig Party: Jacksonian Politics and the Onset of Civil War* (New York: Oxford University Press, 1999); Daniel Walker Howe's *What Hath God Wrought: The Transformation of America, 1815–1848* (New York: Oxford University Press, 2007); Henry Mayer's *All on Fire: William Lloyd Garrison and the Abolition of Slavery* (New York: St. Martin's Griffin, 1998); William S. McFeely's *Frederick Douglass* (New York: W. W. Norton & Co., 1991); Robert W. Merry's *A Country of Vast Designs: James K. Polk, The Mexican War, and the Conquest of the American Continent* (New York: Simon & Schuster, 2009); Allan Nevins's classic *Ordeal of the Union*, Volume 1, *Fruits of Manifest Destiny, 1847–1852* (New York: Charles Scribner's Sons, 1947); and Michael Wallis's *The Best Land Under Heaven: The Donner Party in the Age of Manifest Destiny* (New York: Liveright Publishing, 2017).

The Irish Famine in General and the Situation in Ireland

PRIMARY SOURCES

Many primary sources that I drew on for this section were already cited in full in previous sections, including:

- *Report of the Select Committee of the House of Lords on Colonization from Ireland; Together with Minutes of Evidence, Session 1847.*
- *Correspondence (from January to March 1847) Relating to the Measures Adopted for the Relief of Distress in Ireland, Board of Works Series Second Part, Presented to Both Houses of Parliament by Command of Her Majesty.*
- *Digest of Evidence Taken Before Her Majesty's Commissioners of Inquiry into the State of the Law and Practice in Respect to the Occupation of Land in Ireland, Part 1 and Part 2.*
- *Transactions of the Central Relief Committee of the Society of Friends During the Famine in Ireland, 1846 and 1847.*

Other primary sources that were important for this section included: *The Census of Ireland for the Year 1851, Part VI: General Report* (Dublin: Printed by Alexander Thom and Sons, 87 Abbey-Street, for Her Majesty's Stationery Office, 1856), which contains voluminous information on the Irish population and conclusions by census writers on the overall economic situation in Ireland.

In addition, I found valuable the Clogher Historical Society's "The Famine Archive: Distress Papers," published in the *Clogher Record*, Vol. 17, No. 2 (2001), pp. 401–656. Listed separately from the files of the Relief Commission, the Distress Papers constitute an important and substantial official archive relating to the famine period in Ireland. Within the more than 250 pages are documents that were filed between March 1846 and September 1847, the heart of the famine, and include letters from relief workers to the lord lieutenant of Ireland, records from the Office of Public Works, letters from the English Treasury sanctioning expenditures of public works, and many letters to the lord lieutenant and his senior staff at Dublin Castle from individuals and community officials throughout Ireland—letters that begged for help, issued dire warnings, or simply commented on the deteriorating state of a country and its people.

Charles E. Trevelyan's *The Irish Crisis* (London: Longman, Brown, Breen & Longmans, 1848) was published a year after the famine's most

horrible effects, and thus provides a rich firsthand, contemporaneous account from the British government official most responsible
for administering—or failing to administer—famine relief. Trevelyan's book is footnoted, and he endeavored, albeit only one year later,
to review the famine of 1847 from a historical perspective, "with the
calm temper of a future generation." He predicted that the Irish would
change their habits because of the famine, one "permanent good out
of transient evil." Trevelyan's writing, while informative, is also turgid
and—like the man himself—imperious and unsympathetic. His observations, though valuable, are imparted without remorse or responsibility for the disaster that befell Ireland. At the outset of his work he does
get one thing right when he writes, in 1848, that "the nature and the
bearings of that great event [the famine] will be inseparably associated
with the year just departed."

There are numerous firsthand accounts of the famine that offer
more powerful on-the-ground views of the famine than Trevelyan's official account. I drew on William Bennett's *Narrative of a Recent Journey
of Six Weeks in Ireland*, subtitled *In Connexion with the Subject of Sup-
plying Small Seed to Some of the Remoter Districts with Current Observations on the Depressed State of the People and the Means Presented for the
Permanent Improvement of Their Social Condition*. The book essentially
compiled letters he had written to his sister in London into book form
in late 1847 (London: Charles Gilpin; Dublin: J. Curry, 1847). Elihu
Burritt published several of his journal entries from 1847 into *A Journal
of a Visit of Three Days to Skibbereen and Its Neighbourhood* (London:
Charles Gilpin, 1847). For an interesting manuscript collection of an or-
dinary family in County Kerry, see Shelley Barber, ed., *The Prendergast
Letters: Correspondence from Famine-Era Ireland, 1840–1850* (Amherst:
University of Massachusetts Press, 2006); the Prendergast Letters Col-
lection is one of the noteworthy collections at Boston College's John J.
Burns Library.

Other important firsthand accounts include two volumes by American teacher and reformer Asenath Nicholson—the first (pre-famine)
entitled *Ireland's Welcome to the Stranger: An Excursion Through Ireland in 1844 & 1845* (New York: Baker and Scribner, 1847), and the

second (when she returned to Ireland to observe the shocking horror of the famine) entitled *Annals of the Famine in Ireland in 1847, 1848, and 1849* (New York: E. French, 1851). The Reverend S. Godolphin Osborne also offered his observations of the famine in *Gleanings in the West of Ireland* (London: T. & W. Boone, 1850).

SECONDARY SOURCES

UNPUBLISHED WORKS, SYMPOSIA WORKS, AND ARTICLES

For unpublished and symposia works, I found helpful Cormac O Grada's paper "Ireland's Great Famine: An Overview," written for the Centre for Economic Research at University College Dublin (November 2004); Nicholas Dunn's Ph.D. thesis, "The Castle, the Custom House and the Cabinet: Administration and Policy in Famine Ireland, 1845–1849" (University of Oxford, 2007); and "Local Evidence to the Devon Commission" by Brendan Clifford, part of a collection of talks entitled *Spotlights on Irish History* at the O'Keeffe Institute and published by the Aubane Historical Society in Aubane, County Cork.

Other important articles that I drew on included Tyler Anbinder's "Lord Palmerston and the Irish Famine Emigration," in *The Historical Journal*, Vol. 44, No. 2 (June 2001), pp. 441–469; William A. Dunning, "Irish Land Legislation Since 1845," in *Political Science Quarterly*, Vol. 7, No. 1 (March 1892), pp. 57–79; Joel Mokyr's and Cormac O Grada's "What Do People Die of During Famines: The Great Irish Famine in Comparative Perspective," in *European Review of Economic History*, Vol. 6, No. 3 (December 2002), pp. 339–363; Peter Gray's "National Humiliation and the Great Hunger: Fast and Famine in 1847," in *Irish Historical Studies*, Vol. 32, No. 126 (November 2000), pp. 193–216; and Stuart McLean's "With Death Looking Out of Their Eyes: The Spectropoetics of Hunger in Accounts of the Irish Famine," in *The International Journal of Social and Cultural Practice*, Vol. 43 (November 1999), pp. 40–67.

BOOKS

Numerous books that I consulted for the Irish and famine sections of the book have already been cited, most notably Christine Kinealy's

Charity and the Great Hunger in Ireland and Cecil Woodham-Smith's *The Great Hunger*.

Other important books included (alphabetical by author): Tim Pat Coogan's accusatory but nonetheless well-researched *The Famine Plot: England's Role in Ireland's Greatest Tragedy* (New York: St. Martin's Griffin, 2012); James S. Donnelly Jr.'s *The Great Irish Potato Famine* (Gloucestershire: Sutton Publishing, 2001); Thomas Gallagher's *Paddy's Lament: Ireland 1846–1847—Prelude to Hatred* (New York: Harcourt Brace & Company, 1982), which, among other things, discusses the famine's long-term implications for relations between England and Ireland; John Kelly's *The Graves Are Walking: The Great Famine and the Saga of the Irish People* (New York: Henry Holt and Company, 2012); Maureen O'Rourke Murphy's *Compassionate Stranger: Asenath Nicholson and the Great Irish Famine* (Syracuse, N.Y.: Syracuse University Press, 2015); and John Percival's *The Great Famine: Ireland's Potato Famine, 1845–1851* (New York: Viewer Books, 1995).

Beyond 1847: How America's First Charitable Mission Set the Model for the Future

PRIMARY SOURCES

The story of U.S. aid to Ireland in 1879–80, including the voyage of the *Constellation*, can be found in *Executive Documents of the Senate of the United States, Second Session of the Forty-Sixth Congress, 1879–1880* (Washington, D.C.: Government Printing Office, 1880).

Robert Withington, who served in Belgium as part of the Hoover Commission's work to deliver food behind German lines, authors a firsthand account in *In Occupied Belgium* (Boston: The Cornhill Company, 1921).

The Halifax, Nova Scotia, Municipal Archives website contains numerous primary source documents about the catastrophic explosion that led to aid from Boston and across the United States. It can be accessed at https://www.halifax.ca/about-halifax/municipal-archives/source-guides /halifax-explosion-sources.

The Harry S. Truman Presidential Library and Museum and the Central Intelligence Agency (CIA) websites both contain scores of primary source documents on the amazing Berlin Airlift. The Truman website can be accessed at https://www.trumanlibrary.org/whistlestop /study_collections/berlin_airlift/large/ and the CIA website is at https://www.cia.gov/library/center-for-the-study-of-intelligence/csi -publications/books-and-monographs/on-the-front-lines-of-the-cold -war-documents-on-the-intelligence-war-in-berlin-1946-to-1961/art-4 .html.

Irish president Michael D. Higgins delivered a speech on May 5, 2012, at Boston's Faneuil Hall entitled "Reflecting on the Gorta Mor: The Great Famine of Ireland—Some Narratives, Their Lessons, and Their Legacy," which was helpful in putting the famine in perspective. It is available here: www.president.ie/en/media-library/Speeches /reflecting-on-the-gorta-mor-the-great-famine-of-ireland.

SECONDARY SOURCES

UNPUBLISHED WORKS, SYMPOSIA WORKS, AND ARTICLES

For more on the U.S. military's use of personnel and matériel for humanitarian purposes, see David Mock's master's thesis, "The Realities of Foreign Humanitarianism and the U.S. Military: Nineteenth Century Roots," Department of History, Boise State University, 2015.

For an excellent discussion of the Hoover Commission and U.S. aid to Belgium in World War I, see Albert Winkler's "Herbert Hoover and Belgian Relief," in *All Faculty Publications* (Brigham Young University, 2013). The National Archives publication *Prologue* also has a fine story on this effort—George Nash's "An American Epic: Herbert Hoover and Belgian Relief in World War I," Vol. 21, No. 1 (Spring 1989).

For two good summaries of the conflicts that Irish neutrality presented during World War II, see Clair Wills's "The Effects of Ireland's WWII Policy of Neutrality," in the *Washington Times*, September 9, 2007; and Steve Coronella's "For Irish, a Conflicted Service in WWII," in the *Boston Globe*, May 26, 2017.

For an interesting look at how America responds to disasters, see Martin Morse Wooster's August 2006 piece "America's Response to

Disaster: The Changing Role of the American Red Cross" at https://
capitalresearch.org/article/americas-response-to-disaster-the-changing
-role-of-the-american-red-cross. And a thoughtful look at the historical
uses of the words "charity" and "philanthropy" can be found in Ben-
jamin Soskis's October 2014 article for the Hudson Institute entitled
"Both More and No More: The Historical Split Between Charity and
Philanthropy," https://www.hudson.org/research/10723-both-more
-and-no-more-the-historical-split-between-charity-and-philanthropy.

BOOKS

For this section I relied on (alphabetical by author): John U. Bacon's *The
Great Halifax Explosion: A World War I Story of Treachery, Tragedy, and
Extraordinary Heroism* (New York: William Morrow, 2017); George
H. Nash's *The Life of Herbert Hoover*, Volume II, *The Humanitarian,
1914–1917* (New York: W. W. Norton, 1988); and Andrei Cherny's *The
Candy Bombers: The Untold Story of the Berlin Airlift and America's Fin-
est Hour* (New York: Berkley Caliber, 2008).

INDEX